A CENTURY of BLACK JOURNALISM in BRITAIN

A Kaleidoscopic view of Race and the Media
[1893-2003]

LIONEL MORRISON

First published by Truebay Limited, 63 Lambeth Walk, London SE11 6DX, UK.
Email: neil@nkenlock.com.

Date: March 2007

ISBN 978-0-9555540-0-1

A Cataloguing in Publication Record for this
book is available from the British Library

Printed in Great Britain by Hastings Printing Company Limited

CONTENTS

PART I
A Century of Black Journalism in Britain

PART II
Race and Media Selected Articles

PART III
Selected Biographical Notes

Part IV
Suggestions for further reading

Part V
Commentary

ABOUT THE AUTHOR

LIONEL MORRISON OBE, campaigning journalist and media trainer for 50 years, is presently co-editor of www.diversity-online.org a website to provide European journalists, campaigners, broadcasters and media professionals with a 'non-stop shop' resource to encourage the fair reporting. He remains actively involved in the NUJ, its Black Members Council, of which he was a founder member, and is Trustee of the George Viner Memoral Trust which gives grants to aspiring black journalists. He is Vice President of Notting Hill Housing Trust, having been its Chair for a number of years.

Born in South Africa he was a lifelong opponent of apartheid, was a member of the South African Congress movement and was imprisoned several times including being the youngest detainee in the infamous Treason Trial in 1956. This was with 155 other antiapartheid activists including Nelson Mandela and Walter Sisulu. He started work as a tabloid reporter on the first black weekly newspaper, *Golden City Post* and *Drum* magazine in 1955, and founded the first non-racial media union in South Africa. He became chair of the South African National Union of Journalists, and was an organiser of the Brush and Broom Workers' and the Domestic Workers' Unions.

In 1960 after the Sharpeville massacres, he left for Britain as an exile. He worked as a reporter and helped to set up the non aligned Afro-Asian Journalists Association (AAJA) in Djarkarta and the Pan African Journalists Union in Accra. He was editor of the Afro-Asian Journalist - campaigning monthly magazine with a circulation of about 200,000 copies which were distributed in all African and Asian countries He was for a time the overseas representative of the Pan Africanist Congress of South Africa, in Indonesia and China. He became a sub-editor on the Zambia Mail.

He has lived and worked in Britain since 1969, working as a reporter, sub-editor and editor and contributed to various newspapers and magazines such as *The Indonesia Herald* and *Warta Bhakti, The Afro-Asian Journalist* monthly of the AAJA, Ghanaian *Evening News, The Zambia Mail,* and in Britain *The Sunday People, Evening Standard, Sunday Mirror* and *Sunday Telegraph.* He has also contributed to various ethnic newspapers, and journals such as *Flamingo* and was deputy editor of one of the best campaigning black newspaper in Britain -*West Indian World* and Editor of the *Asian Herald.*

As an editor and journalism lecturer and media trainer, he has helped set up and edited a number of ethnic minority newspapers and publications. He has pioneered and assisted in devising and setting up journalism courses for ethnic minority students in British colleges and universities, and journalism diversity courses for European universities.

He is a long standing member of the NUJ, was its first black President in 1987 and Member of Honour. He remains an active member and particularly of the NUJ Black Members' Council and George Viner Memorial Fund Trust of which he is chair of the Trustees and a founder member.

He is a former Principal Information and Public Relations Officer of the *Commission for Racial Equality* and Member of the Institute of Public Relations. He has been involved in and chair of various community and race relations organisations.

He has been particularly active in the housing field and for many years was chair of one of the country's biggest housing association, Notting Hill Housing Trust. He was awarded an OBE for this work in 1999.

Lionel is the author of various articles on Racism and Media and related race and community issues and is author of a book *"As They See It"* a Race Relations Study of Three Areas from a Black Viewpoint, and a contributor to *"White Media & Black Britain",* a critical look at the role of the media in race relations today.

BLACK JOURNALISM TIMELINE

A century ago black journalism was not part of the mainstream journalistic hub and existing legislation, which was implemented to combat discrimination and disadvantage over the past 40 odd years, had not rooted out the social effects of racism, homophobia and religious intolerance. Whilst many things have changed, the drivers for implementing social change have placed black journalism in the front seat. This timeline clearly demonstrates that progress towards a change in the area of race and the media has taken place and that progress towards equality and fair reporting has come about in response to the experience of the black media and journalists who faced and continue to face discrimination, racism and disadvantage on a daily basis.

1892- *Celestine Edwards* – first black editor of two magazines: ***Lux,*** a weekly Christian Evidence Newspaper from 1892 to 1895, then

1893-1897 – *Fraternity*

1905- The Indian Sociologist – edited by **Shyamji Kristnavarma.**

1907- National Union of Journalists founded in Birmingham.

1912- Duse Mohamed Ali – a penny-a-line journalist, founded and edited first black first black campaigning magazine, **The African Times and Orient Review.**

Writers of the **Review** included **Marcus Garvey,** champion of American black rights, also noted journalist and editor of various papers in America; Ghanaian philosopher, lawyer and nationalist **Kobina Seky** and **W.F. Hutchinson.**
Universal Races Congress in London (attended inter-alia by **Mahatma Ghandhi**) demonstrated the need for a "Pan-Oriental", "Pan-African" journal at the seat of the British Empire.

Sierra-Leoneon, **John Eldred Taylor –** a partner in the **Review.**

1913 John Archer elected as the first Black mayor in Battersea.

1918- Taylor became proprietor of **The African Telegraph.**

1919- Felix Eugene Michael Hercules became editor of **The African Telegraph** – general secretary of **The Society of Peoples' of African Origin** and associate secretary of the **African Progress Union.**

1919- Telegraph exposed the anti-black riots in Britain in Liverpool and Cardiff.
Hercules took to his pen against ***The Manchester Guardian*** in ***The Telegraph*** and letters to ***The Times*** when Lord Milner refused to allow any black troops in London's war victory celebrations.

1919-1921 – Claude McKay (Jamaican poet and novelist) became Britain's first black reporter. Earlier he had written for **Max Eastman's** magazine ***The Liberator*** (in America), and became widely regarded as the most blunt and outspoken black poet and journalist for his reports of the 1919 anti-black riots in Harlem, America.

McKay became a reporter for the **Workers' Dreadnought –** whose editor was **Sylvia Pankhurst.** She refused to print **McKay's** scoop on a strike of union sawmill workers where there were non-union men scabbing. Owner of the sawmill was **George Lansbury** – editor of the ***Daily Herald,*** then Britain's leading left wing daily with a circulation of 392,000. **Pankhurst** owed **Lansbury** money and newsprint and so was indebted to him. **McKay** left Britain disillusioned with the British establishment and went to the USA where he became an influential and leading light in the black literary community.

1921 – Duse Ali went to the US and in 1931 settled in Nigeria where he launched ***The Comet,*** a weekly magazine which came to play an important part in the nationalist movement.

1922 – Shapurji Saklatvala, first Black Member of Parliament for North Battersea. Also the first person in Britain to be arrested during the 1926 General Strike and charged with sedition.

1935 – George Padmore (Malcolm Ivan Meredith Nurse) worked as a reporter for ***The New York Daily Worker*** in 1928. He settled in London in 1935 as a freelance journalist and where he became ***Kwame Nkrumah's*** personal representative during the struggle for Ghanaian independence.

Second Pan African Congress attended by **Du Bois** and **Shapurji Saklatvala,** among others. It was the 'most radical' of all 1920s congresses and the most forthright in its criticism of British rule.

1941- Sir Hari Singh Gour, distinguished jurist, poet and novelist, turned away from a West London hotel on account of his colour.

1943- Learie Constantine, popular broadcaster, and one of the world's most distinguished cricketers, had the same experience.

1948- Race Riots in Liverpool – National Union of Seamen determined to keep black seamen off British ships in Liverpool.

The SS Empire Windrush docks in Tilbury in Essex. The steamship had earlier brought many of the servicemen who had been recruited in Jamaica to serve in the armed forces during the Second World War. On this voyage they brought 500 men and women from the Caribbean recruited for work.

1952- *The Caribbean News* published by the London Branch of the Caribbean Labour Congress, but folded in 1956.

1954 – Edward Scobie – working journalist in London, frequent broadcaster and scriptwriter for radio and tv, worked for Overseas Service of the ***BBC.***

1958- Race Riots in Nottingham and Notting Hill London – A white television camera operator, it was alleged by Nottingham's Chief Constable, persuaded a gang of white youths to stage a mock battle. He set off a magnesium flare which caused a lot of excitement. Twenty four people were arrested in the course of this 'white riot', five were imprisoned for three months.

West Indian Gazette and ***Afro-Asian Caribbean News*** founded and edited by **Claudia Jones,** first black female editor, with journalist and socialist activist **Abimanya Machanda.**

1959 – Notting Hill Carnival – *Claudia Jones* helped to set up Carnival.

1960 – NUJ assisted new non-racial ***National Union of South African Journalists*** – acting chair **Lionel Morrison.**

1961-1963 – Scobie edited ***Flamingo,*** monthly magazine. **Peter Abrahams,** friend of ***Scobie,*** writer for the London **Observer.**

1962 – *Pan African Journalists Union* established in Bamaka, Mali and then situated in Accra, Ghana.

1963 – *Afro-Asian Journalists Association* founded, head quarters in Djakarta, Indonesia and then in Beijing, China.

1966 – Euston Station staff 'colour bar' ends, but was an 'unofficial' policy.

1967- ***New Independent*** founded by **Aaron Haynes.**

1968- Race Relations Act, Race Relations Board set up and followed by the **Community Relations Commission.**

Sam Uba only black journalist/ sub-editor at the ***Birmingham Post.***

1969-72 – Sam Uba and **Lionel Morrison** only black reporters in **Fleet Street.**

1971- ***West Indian World*** founded by **Aubrey Baynes**-editor; deputy editor **Lionel Morrison.**

West Indian Digest founded – **Arif Ali,** editor.

1972 – Garry Gurmeet reporter with the ***Chelsea News,*** London

1973 – Asian Express founded by **Vallabh Kaviraj** and ***The Asian,*** a monthly, edited by **Tasadoog Ahmed.**

Lionel Morrison becomes first black member of the National Executive Committee of the **NUJ.**

1974 – NUJ's ***Race Relations Sub-Committee*** set up; **Union's Annual Delegate Meeting** at Wexford, Ireland unanimously passed a motion which: *'strongly condemned the practice of racism both in the employment of journalists, and in the editorial content, in the British media and instructs the National Executive Council to set up a special Race Relations Sub Committee to look into such practices and recommend positive measures to deal with them'.*

BBC's Black Londoners programme launched – **Alex Pascall** presenter.

1975 – First **Media and Race Seminar** held in London organised by the ***NUJ's Race Relations Working Party*** and *the* **Community Relations Commission.**

1976-7 – Race Relations Amendment Act – disbands **RRB** and **CRC** and sets up the **Commission for Racial Equality. Lionel Morrison** beomes the first black Press and PR Principal Officer of the CRE.

1979 – Root – first national black lifestyle magazine – co-publisher **Neil Kenlock.** Editor – **Hal Austin.**

1981 – Brixton Disorders – Lord Scarman's Report.

Caribbean Times founded and edited by **Arif Ali.**

Black Media Workers' Association (BMWA) established – one of the most important pressure groups in the media scene.

1982 – ***The Voice*** founded and edited by **Val Mc Calla.**

Sue Woodford, Commissioning Editor at ***Channel Four*** for Multi-Cultural Programmes.

1983 – Beverley Anderson presenter of ***'Sixty Minutes'*** on ***BBC1.***

1984 – First **Journalism Course for ethnic minorities** with the help of the **CRE'S Information and Public Relations Department,** at the **Polytechnic of Central London,** now **University of Westminster.**

Bandung Production, makers of ***Bandung File,*** a magazine programme for Asian and Afro-West Indian communities, broadcast by **Channel 4 TV,** co-founder **Darcus Howe.**

1987 – Lionel Morrison – first black President of the NUJ.

RRWP pushed for the creation of a NUJ Trust Fund – ***The George Viner Memorial Trust Fund*** – to financially help aspiring black journalism students with their college and university fees.

1990 – Black Members' Council succeeds ***RRWP – BMC*** aims were to scrutinize and comment on the ethnic monitoring of ***NUJ*** members undertaken by the Union; to act as a formal liaison between the union and the black communities.

Choice FM, first Black radio station, founded by **Neil Kenlock.**

1991 – *Black Britain* launched and edited by **Joseph Harker,** former ***Voice*** journalist. **Isobel Appiah** and **Richard Adeshayo**, editor and deputy editor of the **Weekly Journal**

Weekly Journal launched by ***Voice*** as a 'spoiler' to ***Black Britain.***

1996 – *New Nation* launched and edited by **Richard Adeshayo.**

1997 – Ethnic Media Group – managing director **Garry Gurmeet** – buys ***New Nation, Caribbean Times, African Times*** and ***Asian Times.*** Becomes part of Group with ***Eastern Eye.***

1999 – Stephen Lawrence – Sir William Macpherson's report into the police handling of the murder of Stephen Lawrence is published. It introduces the expression 'institutional racism' and sparks the most profound reappraisal of race relations and justice system since the Brixton disturbances in 1981.

2000 – *The BMC* reported that there were nearly 800 black members of the NUJ.

2001 – First *Claudia Jones Memorial Annual Lecture* set up by the ***BMC*** – in memory of **Claudia Jones.**

2001-3 – Aftermath of 9/11. An increase in sensational and racist reports in British media and attacks on Muslims and multiculturalism.

Acknowledgements

Thanks to Neil Kenlock for making this book possible and for his enthusiastic support and advice throughout. Liz Morrison, my wife, has fully earned the usual clichéd thanks, and as friend, her contribution has been singular. Thanks to all my journalism students, colleagues, and my trade and professional union, the National Union of Journalists, who gave succour and inspiration. Thanks to all friends, who have usually inconspicuously, but knowledgeably, contributed to the production of this book. But mostly thanks and my indebtedness to the readers who act upon it.

I have, where possible tried to crosscheck and correct any errors. Indeed many stories and events still remain to be told and recorded. Covering as much as it does, I am perfectly sure that readers will find inaccuracies and lacunae in these pages. Such gaps, however, do suggest areas for future study by journalism students and scholars who are seriously interested in documenting the role of the media as they have related to racial minority groups. *'Knowledge is like the baobab tree; one cannot encompass it'* a West African saying describes it all.

Given the drama and emotion of the times there will be – there must be – different and equally important interpretations of individual events and situations mentioned here.

What is essential is not that everyone shall speak, but that everything worth saying shall be heard — Alexander Meiklejohn

" Every house has its foundation and every community its history. This is a contribution to the history of black Britain. By looking at the last hundred years of black journalism in Britain, we can perceive what and what not to aim for in the 21st Century. Black consciousness is good if it allows more light and understanding of the complex struggles of of the past and of those still looming ahead.....".

Introduction

A hundred years is a long time – a great slice in the life of a nation, but that is how long the black media and black journalists have been in Britain. There were small black publications, large ones, struggling ones and successful ones. But now, as then, all faced a constant struggle to keep going. For all of them there was and still is a life-struggle. Most publications and the journalists they employed held their campaigning banners high. There were political and social publications and then there were also a few commercial ones. However, there was and is still a common anchor-line. All of them were born, immersed and inspired in the struggle for equality and belief that black people were like others also creatures and children of God.

The Black press emerged as a response to the free market of ideas in the white press. In this marketplace of their own making, black people fought against racism, prejudice and discrimination and the right to be full citizens with full citizenship rights. Their publications, which began as reactions to the denial of access by the white press, grew to be independent forums that met the changing needs of their constituencies by providing information, education, and inspiration.

Many black editors saw themselves as educators as well as journalists and the black press served a vital political function. Whether they were and are still fighting for integration into the political system or equal economic opportunity, black journalists informed, inspired, unified and mobilised their readers. They not only offered information, they exhorted their readers to act on this information and told them how to do it. Originating both because and in spite of adversity, the black press has had a rich, varied volatile history. It gave blacks and Asians a voice of their own and an opportunity not only to answer the attacks printed in the mainstream (white) press but to read articles on black accomplishments, marriages and deaths that the white press of the day ignored. It is the story of the persistent struggle against widespread prejudice, racism and discrimination, mirrored by stereotyping and rejection in the conventional white media.

In summing up this campaign the legendary authoritative Black American paper, ***Freedom's Journal,*** says it all in a polite but impassioned statement of editorial purpose in its inaugural edition in 1827: 'We wish to plead our cause. Too long have others spoken for us. Too long has the public been deceived by misrepresentations in the things that concerns us dearly'.

This is a story covering the years from 1893 to 2003 of the forgotten chronicle of the ideas, goals, and actions of those at odds with the norms of their day. It is, an albeit, short saga of powerless, often penniless men and women who devoted their energies, and sometimes risked their lives, in the hope of bettering the condition of not only their black sisters and brothers but also of those understanding white colleagues. The journalistic effort of blacks and Asians in this country is one part, one very important part, of the political and economic struggle for equality that continues today.

At the risk of seeming to offer an abridged: "Who's Who in Black Journalism in Britain," a volume that indeed would be useful, this brief 100 odd year journey tells the stories of a few black journalists and their media. Some have gained public attention, others national awards, for their work. And at a further risk, that of offending those omitted, it should be noted that this account makes no pretence of being a definitive directory or catalogue. For the same reason persons and publications have gone unmentioned, but this narrative does not pretend to be an encyclopaedic record. It seeks, to explore the nature of a hereto neglected and subordinated press, depicting it today against its background. It seeks, also, to relate the media to the social movements now attracting the attention of many black people in this country. Its objective is neither to put the black press in a necessarily positive light nor, on the other hand, to emphasise shortcomings, but simply to report on that press with a grasp of how it came to be and why it is what it is. What we want is all our black experience, the good, the bitter, the grapetime and the in-between time. As we stand today in the throes of cataclysmic social change, our young people seem to be seething in a boiling cauldron of discontent. Like the youth of every generation they want to know, read and they demand to be heard. I see it as if we are taking a walk around ourselves. Some of the things we see, we like. Some of the things we see, we mean to change. I have also not always capitalised the word 'black' because black is a state of mind which we accept. It does not have to call attention every time to itself. It, simply, is.

College and university educators responsible for the training and ethical development of young media professionals have been slow to meet the challenge of integration for an increasingly diverse British society. The record shows little and there is a small rank-and-file support across the spectrum of journalism educators. The academic professionals in journalism and mass communication remain virtually all white, and course offerings, for the most part, remain void of contextual recognition of the minority experience, Much work, therefore, looms ahead for those who would actively pursue the challenge of integrating the mass media in Britain.

Some of the men and women accounted here have worked only for the black media; these are emphasised and there are the professional activities of those associated mainly with white publications and broadcasting. Both are here, as well as others who helped to open the communications industry and made visible the invisible minorities. There are several who are no longer alive; they should not be passed over. They and their media have played their part, and no small part... and it is to be hoped, not without some usefulness. The black press has demonstrated, in large measure, the mental and literary possibilities of people of colour and there should be meaningful synthesis of the best that our struggles have taught us. As in all living things there must be a certain unity, a principle of vitality and growth. It is this growth, understanding and involvement of these men and women and their industry that this piece is chronicling and profiling. And although this account as a whole is a thoroughly eclectic one, a kind of order does emerge.

It seeks to give the reader, especially the young and potential black media workers unfamiliar with these journalists and their media, an idea of their work, of the accomplishments and the hurdles they had to surmount. Therefore, hopefully, this is a history of the past and present with projections for the future. Yet, the past is not forsaken; a true sense of black community and black identity hopefully flows throughout. I have had my share in all this for nearly 50 years and have myself been part of it and entered into its inner courts. That is a reason why, on this occasion, I write in my own name of my involvement and in a way also as a critic, spectator or voyeur.

There are Five Parts. Part I is a protean 100 years journey of black journalism in this country. Part II contains, a limited selected number of articles, talks and reports about race and media which I have written over the past 30 odd years and Part III features a selection of biographical notes about myself by other media peers. Suggestions for Further Reading includes books and articles on race and media and Ethical Media Codes are in Part IV. In Part V I have included a Commentary, which encompass some hurdles, hopes and direction for the future, but in its final assumption it is not to provide definitive answers but to pose vexatious and unpalatable but essential questions.

PART I

A Century of Black Journalism in Britain

A newspaper is of necessity something of a monopoly, and its first duty is to shun the temptations of monopoly. Its primary office is the gathering of news. At the peril of Its soul it must see that the supply is not tainted. Neither in what it gives, nor in what it does not give, nor in the mode of representation must the unclouded face of truth suffer wrong. Comment is free, but facts are sacred. – C.P. Scott [1846-1932], in the Manchester Guardian -1921.

The bigger the information media, the less courage and and freedom they allow. Bigness means weakness – Eric Sevareid,1959

CHAPTER 1

The Emergence of Black Journalism in the first half of the 20th Century

The birthplace and hub of Black journalism and its most intense centre of activity was London. Britain's first black editor, **Celestine Edwards,** a seaman and a staunch upholder of human rights and brotherhood, was born in Dominica in 1858 and settled in Britain. In a lecture in Hackney, London, on September 16th,1886, he had this to say of racism: *'It is sad and terrible thing to see nigh a whole generation of men and women comparing those whose skins are black to baboons and the like'.*

He took a theological degree in London in 1891, embarked on the study of medicine and became the editor of two magazines. The first was ***Lux,*** *'a weekly Christian Evidence Newspaper'* from 1892-1895, and then ***Fraternity,*** published from 1893-1897 which was the monthly organ of the *Society for the Recognition of the Brotherhood of Man,* of which **Celestine Edwards** was executive secretary and which numbered Quaker humanitarians among its members.

In 1905, ***The Indian Sociologist,*** a well documented monthly journal, was published and edited by **Shyamaji Krishnavarma. Krishnavarma** travelled and lived in both London and Paris and the journal had much influence on Indian opinion. It had a short life.

Duse Mohamed Ali, a penny-a-line journalist and ill-paid touring actor, founded in July 1912 and edited the first Black magazine, the ***African Times and Orient Review.*** This was the first campaigning journal produced by and for black people ever published in London, in partnership with Sierra-Leonean businessman and journalist **John Eldred Taylor** – who later became proprietor of the **African Telegraph** in 1918. **Ali** kept the magazine alive, despite financial uncertainties and with certain gaps, until the end of 1920. The ***African Times and Orient Review*** was a by-product of the *Universal Races Congress* that had been held in London in 1911. This Congress was attended by **Dr W.E.B. DuBois,** American champion of black rights who was a noted writer and journalist and editor of various papers in America, **Mahatma Ghandhi,** then leader of the Indian minority in South Africa, who later in India sealed the fate of the British Empire, and other African representatives.

According to **Ali,** writing in the first issue of the magazine, the Congress had clearly demonstrated the need for a *'Pan-Oriental, Pan-African journal at the seat of the British Empire which would lay the aims, desires and intentions of the Black, Brown and Yellow Races within and without the Empire-at the throne of Caesar'.* For *'the voices of millions of Britain's enlightened dark races are never heard. And their capacity was underrated and they were victims of systematic injustice,'* the paper enjoined.

The first issue gave a shameful example of this injustice when it movingly described the humiliating public flogging at Zaria in Northern Nigeria the previous February, 1912, of the two African railway clerks named **Hall** and **Taylor,** who refused to prostrate themselves before a third-class British Resident named **Laing.**

The quality of the ***African Times and Orient Review*** was consistently high and built an international circulation. It was read by black intellectuals in Africa, north

America and the West Indies and expounded Afro-Asian solidarity and still better it was disliked and rather feared by the Colonial Office, Foreign Office and the India Office. It was a treasure trove of information, which consistently unearthed abuses of colonial rule in British colonies and passed on information to Labour MPs who asked embarrassing questions in the House of Commons.

One of the contributors to the ***African Times and Orient Review*** was then young Jamaican **Marcus Garvey,** the first black leader to inspire millions of African Americans with pride in their race. Others were Ghanaian philosopher, lawyer and nationalist **Kobina Seky,** then a 20 year-old student who was called to the bar in 1919; and Ghanaian **W. F. Hutchinson.**

They met with many black visitors to London, who made **Duse Mohamed Ali's** tiny Fleet Street newspaper office their general meeting place and informal headquarters, a hub of activity where new friends were introduced and old friendships were cemented.

In 1921 **Ali** went to the United States and in 1931 settled in Nigeria where he launched the ***Comet,*** a weekly magazine which came to play an important part in the nationalist movement. He died in Lagos in 1945.

Ali's personal and business friend, **John Eldred Taylor,** offered **Felix Eugene Michael Hercules** the editorship of the ***African Telegraph*** in 1919. **Hercules** was born in Venezuela in l888 and grew up in Trinidad. During the First World War he came to London and took a BA degree at London University. He also became general secretary of the *Society of People's of African Origin* and associate secretary of the *African Progress Union.*

Hercules' editorials were scrutinized by the authorities, who accused him of *"inciting the negroes to take matters into their own hands."* He exposed the anti-black riots in Britain – in Liverpool and Cardiff in 1919. During the hot summer of 1919 black people in Britain were not only being attacked physically, in their homes and in the streets, they were also attacked with the pen by those who excused the aggressors by blaming their victims. ***The Manchester Guardian,*** for instance, blamed black people for daring to defend themselves against lynch mobs.

But **Hercules** took to his pen against ***The Manchester Guardian*** in editorials in his paper, and in articles and letters in ***The Times.*** When **Lord Milner** refused to allow any black troops to take part in London's victory celebrations, the much trumpeted Peace March on 19 July 1919, **Hercules** lambasted the government in his editorial on the eve of his departure for the West Indies.

Hercules put into words what every black person in the country was feeling about British ingratitude, injury and insult and went on to draw the necessary political conclusion:

> *"Every ounce of strength was put into the struggle by the black man. He fought with the white man to save the white man's home ... and the War was won. Black men all the world over are asking today, "What have we got?" Residences of black men were demolished; black men were pounded on the streets... No black troops were allowed to take part in the Peace March... The supineness of the Imperial government during the race riots drove home the fact they approve of them, that they are in line with Imperial policy."*

Hercules' journalistic tradition of radicalism is so aptly summed up in **James Russell Lowell's** words:

'We will speak out, we will be heard,
Though all the earth's systems crack;
We will not bate a single word,
Nor take a letter back.'

They did speak. While the white, conventional press of the early 20th Century offered colourful human interest stories of white British life, Blacks spread their separate messages in newspapers and journals of their own making.

Another contemporary of **Hercules** was **Malcolm Ivan Meredith Nurse,** later known as **George Padmore,** who was born in Arouca, Trinidad in 1902. After working as a *reporter,* **Nurse** went to the United States in 1924 and wrote for the ***New York Daily Worker*** under the cover name **George Padmore,** which he had adopted by 1928. He became editor of the **Negro Worker** and resigned later. In 1935 **Padmore** settled in London, making a living by private teaching and journalism. He died in 1959 in Ghana. He had been **Kwame Nkrumah's** personal representative in London during the struggle for Ghanaian independence. **Nkrumah** led Ghana to become the first British colony in Africa to wrest its independence, and his philosophy was based on Pan Africanism, a system of thought developed not least by Africans in the diaspora. **Padmore** was the originator of the Pan African movement.

Britain's first black reporter was young Jamaican poet and novelist **Claude McKay,** the youngest son of hard-working and relatively poor peasants. He was born in l890 and lived in London from the end of 1919 to the beginning of 1921.

Two years in the United States had taught him *"how completely his race was being exploited"*. He won sudden fame for his sonnet ***"If We Must Die"*** written for **Max Eastman's** magazine ***The Liberator*** under the impact of the 1919 anti-black riots in Harlem, United States. He came to be widely regarded as perhaps the most blunt and outspoken black poet and journalist of that period. Commenting on the race riots, **McKay** wrote:

'If we must die, let it not be like hogs,
Haunted and penned in an inglorious spot
While round us bark the mad and hungry dogs,
Making their mock at our accursed lot.
If we must die, O let us nobly die..."

Here, obviously, is an act of quintessential homage.

Sylvia Pankhurst, English suffragette and editor of the small but influential circulation of the left, ***Workers' Dreadnought,*** offered **McKay** a job as a reporter. But his articles were spiked by **Pankhurst** when he wrote a scathing report about non-union men scabbing in a sawmill owned by **George Lansbury,** then leader of the *Labour Party.*

McKay left disillusioned with the British liberal establishment and went to the United States where he became an influential and leading light in the black literary community. His fourth volume of Verse, ***"Harlem Shadows"*** (1922) was a powerful stimulus and he wrote his first novel ***Home to Harlem*** in 1928. He died in Chicago in 1948 and was posthumously honoured by his native Jamaica.

It is clear that during the first half of the 20th century, governments and almost everybody else in the country, viewed the plight of the black settlers with utter complacency. The racism that poisoned the every day lives of black people in Britain between the end of the First World War and the end of the Second characteristically did so in the form of what was called "colour bar".

In many industries white trade unionists resisted the employment of black workers, as in Wolverhampton in 1955. The immediate background to the anti-black riots of 1948 in Liverpool was a determined effort by the *National Union of Seamen,* since the end of the war, to keep black seamen off British ships.

Before 1944 it was common for London's West-end hotels to refuse accommodation to black people. In 1941 **Sir Hari Singh Gour,** a distinguished jurist, poet and novelist, vice President of Delhi and Nagpur universities and deputy president of the Indian Legislature, was turned away from a west London hotel on account of his colour. Two years later in 1943, Trinidadian **Learie Constantine,** one of the world's most distinguished cricketers, had the same experience. **Constantine** became a popular broadcaster, served as high commissioner for Trinidad and Tobago, was knighted in 1962 and created a life peer – **Baron Constantine of Marvel and Nelson** – in 1969.

Black people were portrayed in the media, if at all, as troublesome versions of 'the white man's burden' and corporate announcements of senior appointments scarcely ever showed a black. Discrimination was and still is pervasive. Yet, because of its subtle collusive nature, attempts to redress merely brought choruses of, *"If they don't like it here, they can go back to where they came from".*

The various riots and disturbances in Liverpool, Cardiff, Nottingham, Camden Town and Notting Hill, through the 1920's, 30's, 40's, and 50's show the black media or its black journalists in the forefront in reporting and exposing the harassment, brutality and racist attacks.

The rising racism in Britain spawned more black magazines and newspapers; but conversely the anti-black riots were also encouraged, to some extent by sensational journalism in the white press.

CHAPTER 2

The 1950s...

In 1952, the ***Caribbean News*** appeared, published by the London Branch of the Caribbean Labour Congress. It ceased publication in 1956. ***The Gleaner*** was established in 1951, but it was a Jamaican paper and focussed on Jamaican news and reports and it was only in the 1980's that it really started to involve itself in British black issues.

1958 was the year of race riots. In Nottingham thousands of white people were in the street, shouting, *"Let's get the blacks"* or others were shouting *"Let's lynch them",* but black people stayed off the streets.

In the absence of black victims, a white television camera operator, so it was alleged by Nottingham's Chief Constable, persuaded a gang of white youth to stage a mock battle. He set off a magnesium flare which caused a lot of excitement. Twenty four people were arrested in the course of this all white "race riot", five were imprisoned for three months.

Edward Scobie reported that Nottingham's black community felt that the police were *"biased and not fair in their dealings with coloured people."* His reports on the riots were carefully crafted, accurate and passionate.

Dr Edward Vivian Scobie was born in 1918 in Dominica, a former British Colony. As a working journalist in London from 1954, **Scobie** became a correspondent for the ***Chicago Defender, Ebony*** and ***Jet Magazines.*** He teamed up and worked with a black bandleader called **Ross.**

Scobie was a mentor for many young black students who flocked to his small office. He was always a far-sighted media professional, contributing to many London newspapers, magazines and the wire services. He became a frequent broadcaster and scriptwriter for radio and television and worked for the Overseas Service of the **BBC.** A rare black face in Fleet Street.

From 1961 to 1963 he edited ***Flamingo,*** a hard hitting campaigning monthly magazine published in London for black people in Britain, Africa and the Caribbean. I met him in 1961 and was a contributor to ***Flamingo.*** He was passionate about the black cause and believed that black people were the equals of any white person. He mercilessly defended the existence of the black media. When I interviewed him in 1963, I posed this question to him: *"What is the validity of the entire concept of a black press?"* His answer was crisp and to the point: *"Nearly always, whites ask about the future of* ***Flamingo*** *or the* ***West Indian Gazette*** *or the black press in an integrated society, but they don't ask about the future of the* ***Times*** *or* ***Guardian*** *or the white press".*

To paraphrase him: if we really get rid of racism we will concede the fact that the black press has just as much right to exist as the white press. Nobody ever raises the question of what is the future of the white press, and they have been discriminating more than the black press all through the years. But when you ask about the black press you want to know what's going to happen to it. This is a kind of discrimination which is abominable.

The black press is needed mainly because all the old battles have not yet been won and because there are so many new ones. Without the black press, the black men and women would not know who they are nor what is happening to their struggle for the freedom of citizenship. Perhaps less important now than in the past, though still vital, is the need for facts about themselves; such as coverage of black society, still neglected in the main by the white press which deals mostly in racial conflict, crime, and news of blacks known to whites from the sports and entertainment worlds.

Scobie was no victim and I remembered what he told me more than once that it was not what happens to you, but it was how you let it affect you. He allocated space to established writers and to younger talent like **Syd Burke,** who became a well respected broadcaster and **Bill Patterson,** a well known photographer. He was one of the few editors who were prepared to give publicity to one of the most commanding South African revolutionaries, **Robert Sobukwe,** whose role in the 1960 and 1970's apartheid era is a vital part of the history of South Africa. **Sobukwe's** leadership and percipience, was as influential as **Nelson Mandela**, but **Sobukwe,** as leader of the *Pan Africanist Congress of South Africa,* was demonised and marginalized by the liberal white British media.

When my profile of **Sobukwe** was published in ***Flamingo*** (1962), **Scobie** was pilloried and disparaged by the 'left' in Britain and others in South Africa. **Scobie** at that time told me that there were many heroes in the struggle, and he was glad to open his pages to all South African liberation and antiapartheid groups, organisations and leaders and whose struggle in South Africa could not be obliterated from the pages of history in the media.

After leaving Britain, **Scobie** was twice Mayor of Rouseau, capital of Dominica and Vice-President of the Dominica Freedom Party. A major authority on the African presence in early Western Europe, he was the author of numerous scholarly articles and historical essays on the subject, including a series of five articles for the ***Journal of African Civilisations.***

One of these articles ***"African Popes"*** discussed the lives of the three African pontiffs: **St Victor I** (189-199), **St Miltiades** (311-314) and **St. Gelasius I** (492-496). A second contribution was called, ***"The Black in Western Europe".*** In ***"The Chavalier de Saint George",*** **Scobie** documented the life of the remarkable black composer, conductor, violinist, swordsman, equestrian and soldier of eighteenth century France.

At the time of his death of acute myocardial infarction, on 14 November 1966, **Edward Scobie** was Professor Emeritus of History, Black Studies Department, City College of New York. Previously he had taught at Princeton and Rutgers Universities.

He was a champion of black rights and had a belief in the history of black people. He wrote in his well researched and seminal book ***Black Britannia,*** the passage which is a worthy epitaph to his own meteoric journalist life: *"There is substantial evidence in the pages of European history (ironically enough) of Africans in that area of the globe who gained positions of respect and a kind of glory on their merits."*

A close friend of **Scobie** was the gifted black South African exiled writer and broadcaster **Peter Abrahams** whose book – ***Mine Boy*** was published in 1946 in Britain. It was a description of the urban Black reality in South Africa and presented a class analysis of South African society and challenged a whole white-dominated genre within South African fiction. His other books such as ***Tell Freedom, The Path***

of Thunder and ***Wreath of Udumo*** fling the gauntlet in the face of the keeper of the mighty fortress of inevitability, of black inferiority, of the white man's 'civilised' mission, of the blacks inability to withstand the traumas of social change, that guards the white self-image in its fictive enactment of the saga of the migrant labourer.

Abrahams travelled to African countries and left for Jamaica where he wrote for ***The London Observer.*** There was gifted travel journalism, political writing in the Jamaican press, radio work, intense and politicised involvement in Jamaican cultural life.

In 1985, he wrote his longest, most complex and powerful work on fiction – ***The View from Coyaba.*** Here he reviewed the entire history of the relationship between whites and blacks in the old and new worlds from the beginnings of black slavery and set out to create a black historic identity. His journalism and his writings are a summation- a consistent final movement to the symphony of a longtime's thought and writing.

A contemporary and friend of his was **Claudia Jones,** the first black woman editor in Britain. Feminist, black nationalist, political activist, community leader, communist and journalist. Born in Belmont, Port-of-Spain, Trinidad in 1915, at the age of eight she moved to Harlem, New York with her parents and three sisters.

For over 30 years she lived in New York and during this time became an active member of the American Communist Party, an organisation in which her journalistic and community leadership skills were maximised. By 1948 she had become the editor of ***Negro Affairs*** for the party's paper the ***Daily Worker*** and had evolved into an accomplished speaker on human and civil rights. In 1955 she was tried, convicted and imprisoned for 'un-American' activities, for one year and one day.

She was deported from the US and given asylum in England, where she spent the remaining years working with London's African-Caribbean community. In 1958 she founded and edited ***The West Indian Gazette*** and ***Afro-Asian Caribbean News*** together with fellow socialist activist **Abimanyu Machanda** who had a wealth of journalistic background, accumulated both in Britain and his native India, and who became managing editor.

The paper was, according to her, a major effort designed to stimulate political and social thinking. This paper, she said, *'has served as a catalyst, quickening the awareness, socially and politically, of West Indies, political equality and respect for human dignity for West Indians and Afro-Asians in Britain, for peace and friendship between all Commonwealth and world peoples'.*

For eight years the ***Gazette*** existed on a shoestring, kept alive by the determination of **Claudia** and her staff. Members of the black community made donations to keep it going. Famous artists such as **Paul Robeson, James Phillips,** one of the first black South African exiles – **Nadia Catouse, Corine Skinner, Carmen England** and **Pearl Presod** performed at fund raising events for the paper and helped in different ways. Claudia was able to involve the writers of the day, including **Donald Hinds,** the paper's principal reporter whose articles have appeared in anthologies, newspapers and journals, and **George Lamming,** a prolific writer and poet.

1958 was a year of one of terrible racist attacks, particularly the attack on black people in the Notting Hill area of London. By bringing reliable information to the black community the ***Gazette*** gave invaluable support to the victims of abuse. **Claudia**

Jones and **Amy Ashwood Garvey,** widow of **Marcus Garvey**, were active participants on the committee which was set up to assist those who were arrested while defending themselves against racist onslaughts.

Her courageous anti-imperialist stand gained her an international reputation and resulted in many invitations to visits overseas. Her last visit abroad before her death was to China in 1964 where she had a meeting with **Mao Zedong.** It was during that time that I met **Claudia Jones** who was also a guest of the 40 strong Afro-Asian journalists union of the *Afro-Asian Journalists' Association* ***(AAJA)*** of which I was a bureau member and editor of the ***Afro-Asian Journalist,*** a monthly, with a circulation of about 200,000 and distributed in most Asian and African countries. It was combative and informed, and I edited it for two years. **Claudia Jones'** independent thinking and internationalist perspective highlighted the immediate struggles as part of a larger movement to create the conditions for the development of truly democratic states and was warmly welcomed by the ***AAJA*** who gave financial support to ***The Gazette.***

Her lasting legacy is undoubtedly the Notting Hill carnival, which she helped launch in 1959 as an annual showcase for Caribbean talent, and which is now an annual prestigious European-wide event. She was described as the mother of the Notting Hill carnival. These early celebrations were held in halls and were epitomised by the slogan, *"A people's art is the genesis of their freedom."*

The diversity of her political affiliations clearly illustrate her multifaceted approach to the struggle for equal rights in the 20th century, and her contribution to campaigning journalism.

The demise of ***Flamingo*** and ***The West Indian Gazette*** in 1966, resulted in a lull in black journalism in Britain. Various small publications appeared but had no staying power.

A contributor to the ***Gazette*** had been **Aaron Haynes,** a former teacher, Director of the black orientated Community Roots College and Community Relations Officer for Wolverhampton.

With the folding of the ***Gazette,*** **Haynes** had become involved for a short period with the publication ***Magnet.*** He then helped found the weekly ***New Independent,*** both small black weeklies. It was a difficult time for any small campaigning black paper. When the ***New Independent*** ran a front page story headlined *"Will the Home Secretary turn a blind eye to this",* with a picture of a brutalised black man, exposing police brutality during the arrest and detention of the man, who had earlier attended a black society wedding, it suddenly faced a situation of advertisers mysteriously withdrawing their advertisements overnight, and newsagents refusing to stock and sell the ***New Independent.*** The paper's offices were also burgled and vandalised. It was forced to close down and in the words of controversial, provocative and no-nonsense pragmatist **Haynes** *'and so died a beautiful effort'.*

Later **Haynes** and I both worked at the ***CRE;*** **Haynes** as a Principal Community Relations Officer and then as Chief Executive, and I as Principal Information and Public Relations Officer until 1990. **Haynes** then said he *'believed and still does that what is vital for the black community is the need for the facts about themselves, i.e. coverage of the black society, still neglected by the white press which unfortunately still mainly deal in racial conflicts, crime, and news of blacks known to whites from the sports and entertainment worlds'.*

CHAPTER 3

Can black journalists get into the mainstream press?

In 1969 I returned to London from Asia and Africa, after working as a sub-editor on the ***Zambia Mail,*** a weekly paper. There my job was to help change the broadsheet paper into a tabloid. Earlier I had been editing and regularly contributing to newspapers and magazines such as ***Warta Bhakti, Indonesian Herald*** and the ***Evening News*** in Ghana, and as a journalism trainer in various African and Asian countries where I had helped to set up journalism unions from 1963. In 1962/3 I helped to set up the ***Pan African Union of Journalists (PAUJ)*** with **Kofi Batja, President Kwame Nkrumah's** press officer, from Ghana where the headquarters were situated after it had been transferred to Accra from Bamako, Mali. The ***PAUJ*** assisted in the formation of the ***Afro-Asian Journalists Association (AAJA),*** in the wake of the Bandung non-aligned conference. I headed an ***AAJA*** delegation to various African countries and got especially welcoming support from Ghanaian **President Kwame Nkrumah,** Mali President **Modiba Keita** and Tanzanian **President Julius Nyerere**. After the October 4th 1964 savage military coup against **President Sukarno** by **General Suharto**, who was later ousted, the **AAJA** left Indonesia and was offered offices in China.

It is in the late 1960's when the intermittent struggle began to push a foot through the pearly gates of the lily-white Fleet Street news-rooms. This was part of a wider campaign as there were then no black journalist faces in news-rooms in national or regional newspapers and broadcasting.

The media, which then, and still now generally mirrors the way minorities are perceived, was plagued by stereotypes. Even worse perhaps than the racial and ethnic stereotyping of ethnic minorities was the almost total lack of any images which might serve to reinforce positive attitudes-or any attitudes about black people in Britain. In 1970, a black colleague put it succinctly to me in our discussion: *"Mirror, mirror on the wall tell me do I exist at all".*

The mirror of course, was the media, polished and held up by the image-makers, whether they were advertisers, radio station owners, commercial and public television executives, producers, editors, writers or artistic directors. As a collective body, they helped to reinforce the artist's concept of Britainwhite on white. No flies in the butter-milk.

And it was then in 1970 that black journalism, like a latent germinating seed, was, astoundingly sprouting again, and it was during the forthcoming years that black journalism would take huge and salient strides in helping to change the concept of community journalism and the entry of black journalists in the 'mainstream' media.

For the continued growth of any community group, effective communication is essential to maintaining social awareness and social action. It must be able to communicate with both its members and with the larger society. In most groups the community newspaper serves this purpose. The paper reflects the group's aspirations, concerns, and maturity and is both its voice and its critic. And black publications, inevitably, have a dual role. Their close ties to the black community and their responsibility to that community mean that they must walk a fine line between advocacy and balanced journalism if they are to protect their credibility.

The biblical adage is that three scores and ten years usually affirm the journey's life span of a person. But, alas, contrary to this predication, the soldiery journey of black journalism in this country has instead injected new life, resilience, determination and forethought, showing that there was an obvious confidence which had been sown in the past 70 years.

With the increased social awareness of the 1960's, Britain's black community in the 70's saw the need for black journalists and publications that accurately reflected their place in Britain's society . . . something the mainstream press and employers seemed incapable of doing then and still seem incapable now, to a great extent.

In 1970, one of the biggest challenges facing black journalism in Britain, was and still is, the entry of black journalists into the 'mainstream' media. In the 1970's it was just as difficult for black journalists to get into lily-white newsrooms as it was for a camel to pass through the eye of that biblical needle. For myself, and for many other black journalists, it was a phenomenal struggle. I was one of the few who managed as a freelance and writer in the early 1970's to get into Fleet Street's lily-white newsrooms like the ***Sunday Telegraph, Sunday People,*** and the ***Evening Standard*** and for the first time some positive features and articles on black individuals and events appeared in these papers regularly under my by-line.

In 1970, I was asked by **Bob Edwards,** Editor of ***The Sunday People,*** to investigate police-black relations in Notting Hill, London after the Portnall Road clashes which had led to the famous *Mangrove Nine* trial. Together with two other seasoned, hard-nosed, white, journalist colleagues from the national paper – **Mervyn Pamment** and **Sidney Foxcroft** – we interviewed over a hundred Notting Hill residents, both black and white. Despite its history of race riots, Notting Hill was an area where relations between white and black were reasonably good. However, as our interviews showed there was a serious breakdown in relations between the police and the black community, and the one name which frequently cropped up was that of PC Pulley. **Edwards** opined : 'It seemed to us that the troubles all centred around the behaviour of one policeman who, deservedly or not, had become a hate figure and symbol of persecution.' The article – *The Good Policeman Pulley – Why we say he should be moved from Notting Hill* appeared in ***The Sunday People*** on Sunday 16 August.

PC Pulley sued ***The Sunday People*** for libel, claiming that he had been 'pilloried'. He was awarded damages by a jury in a ten day trial two years later. If ever there was a case which demonstrated the opposing viewpoints held by the police and the media about race relations this was a classic.

A disturbing feature of the case, commented on by **Mr. James Comyn, QC** for ***The Sunday People,*** was that the police had made intensive investigations into the political and professional past of the reporters. They especially tried to make me appear a "man of violence" because of articles I had written in the ***Afro Asian Journalist*** while working in South East Asia, my links with **Michael X,** as his right hand lieutenant, and my politics in South Africa. This line of questioning provoked the judge, **Mr Justice Bean,** in a remarkable summing up, to say that one of the features of the case was possibly the innuendo *'that **Morrison** (who was born in South Africa) had been prejudiced, not least because of an article he had written six years ago when secretary of **The Afro-Asian Journalists' Association**'. "I doubt* *whether you will get much help from that", he was driven to say.*

He added: *"**Mr. Morrison** has never sought to hide that he was naturally biased by reason of his colour and by his experiences in South Africa, where he had had the distinction and misfortune to be one of the defendants in the infamous treason trial in which l56 defendants were happily acquitted after a tremendous ordeal." (See full Articles and comments in Part II)*

In August, 1973 a white teacher, in a letter to the ***Evening Standard,*** congratulated the paper *"on the very creative series it has been publishing on the black presence in England..."* Ordinary black men and women and personalities, many of the 'firsts' in Britain were highlighted, and their stories gave the white readers a clear peephole into the creatively eidetic and vibrantly kaleidoscopic black world of multi-racial Britain.

Here are a few of the many who were profiled, by me, in these newspapers: There was **Althea McNish,** one of the few black designers of printed dress fabrics and furnishing fabrics in Britain, **Len Woodley,** a barrister-who became one of the few black High Court Judges in Britain, **George Berry,** first black publican of the 'Coach and Horses', **Sam Springer,** the first black Mayor of Hackney, **Edgar Rennie,** the first black local councillor of Tory blue Kensington and Chelsea Borough Council, **Len Dyke,** one of the most notable black businessman, **Carmen England,** the first black woman in Britain to establish a hairdressing salon in 1948, and one of the handful of top hairdressers in the fashionable West End of London, **Earl Cameron** a well known actor, **Wilfred Wood,** later Bishop of Croydon in the Diocese of Southwark, **Frank Cousins,** the first black artistic director of the Guildhall School of Music and Drama, **Beryl Gilroy,** one of the first black headmistress of one of the most cosmopolitan primary schools in London, **Petronella Breinburg,** the outdoor story teller for the Lambeth Libraries, who is now a Professor at a Dutch university, **Ian Hall,** the first black music graduate from Oxford University and the first black person to present a major television series in the UK in 1972 -*'Songs that Matter,* and **Oscar Abrahams,** who set up the *Keskidee Centre,* a black self-help centre.

There were many reasons for the difficulty in opening the white news pages to black people and black events. Firstly, the news media, like the British white population, was unable to accept that Britain was a multi-racial society. Many of the problematic aspects presented by the media are shared by all black people. Fundamental problem areas are inter-related, and include a lack of minority-group members in positions of responsibility in the media employment structure, and insufficient minority ownership of print and broadcast media operations. Another contribution was the biased reporting of events concerning minorities, specifically the presentation of negative, inaccurate stereotypes, the biased selection of events which often depict minorities in a negative light, and the lack of comprehensive ongoing coverage of all facets of community life.

One point seems of utmost importance with respect to reporting minorities, namely that *"that old definition of news as something that happens is too narrow. They are going to have to unlearn their knee-jerk reaction that when something doesn't happen, it's not news".* This approach would vastly improve the quality of news reporting not just for black people, but for society as a whole.

I highlighted these reasons in a paper I presented to a *Media and the Race Seminar* in London, October 1975, held by the then Community Relations

Commission and the National Union of Journalists' Race Relations Working Party- of which I was then chair. This was the first of its kind. The arguments are still germane and seminal and this is what the paper said:

> *"What it means is that newspaper staffs ought to contain the variety of views, life-styles and groupings within the changing society they seek to reflect and of course, they don't and for various reasons.*
>
> *There is no doubt that the majority of newspapers that are praised for their attitude to race relations still operate in a framework of liberal paternalism; for example, they are careful not to employ black writers or reporters, except as freelances – and then usually insist they work with white reporters or check every fact they write*
>
> *Many editors, when explaining the absence of ethnic minority journalists in the staffrooms of their papers, make points like: few, if any, black youngsters with the right 'O' and 'A' levels approach them for jobs; they are not prepared to lower educational standards just to employ ethnic minorities; those ethnic minorities with the right qualifications who have arrived in this country as journalists need years to get to know the nuances of white Britain, and would therefore not make good journalists on British papers.*
>
> *But I know of a few Black and Asian youngsters who have the necessary qualifications and who have disappointingly made the rounds to local papers. I also personally know of one or two local editors who have actually told me that they have never been approached by suitably qualified black youngsters, and who when approached by such suitably qualified youngsters, when there was a vacancy on their paper's conveniently found excuses not to employ them.*
>
> *No-one expects editors to lower their educational requirements – not even black people. What black people do want is to be employed because they are capable and have the correct qualifications. They don't want concessions, what they want is just a fair chance.*
>
> *There is yet another obstacle facing black people who want to enter the world of British Journalism. That is the white "black expert" journalist – the race relations experts. These "experts" are the ones who have fashioned to a great extent the stand of their various papers on race relations. They are "the experts" on Black issues. They jealously guard their position and resist any newcomers and intruders in the field. They react even more vehemently when the intruder is black. No doubt this is a consequence of the old paternalistic doctrine which was and still is so strong among some liberals. They know the black person, his desires and shortcomings better than black people themselves. So that whatever the British media has to say, the media image we- both black and white – have of ourselves is written or broadcast by a pure lily-white hand with all its dire consequences.*
>
> *It is this desire, this temptation for the media to make race a "topic" that even normally responsible journalists find it difficult to resist. Just as race unfortunately ranks with sex, drugs and "permissiveness", as sure-fire sensational material, racism and journalists are bound together with the stickiest of verbal glue.*

In words that are as applicable and as pertinent to Britain as to the USA, and to reporting of foreign as well as domestic conflicts, the National Advisory Commission on Civil Disorders (popularly known as the Kerner Commission) which was appointed by President Johnson following the race riots which took place in the summer of 1967, said it all:

"Along with the country as a whole, the press has too long basked in a white world, looked out of it, if at all, with white men's eyes and white perspective. that is no longer good enough."

Let me suggest that the white media on the whole believes that the necessary ingredients for the total life of the black community are reggae, soul and jazzed up social radio commentary once a month.

Indeed it isn't, especially if the media as a whole accepts, which I am sure it does, that Britain is a multi-racial and multi-cultural society. If here, too, it should take the terrible and unforgivable nature of race riots to change things, the British communications media industry will indeed be deeply culpable. And unless we all in this marvellous profession of ours, do something positively now and stop pretending that there is no problem in our indefatigable British way of determinedly denying its existence by constant verbal expression of British tolerance and refusal to acknowledge discrimination in our own journalistic backyard when it occurs.

By obscuring the reality beneath a consensus acceptance of British tolerance, a screen is provided for the practice of discriminating behaviour, which by popular judgement and official utterance is unacceptable in a tolerant society. The steps that we in the media must take on this issue are nothing but clear "

One of the few black journalist participants at the Conference, was Nigerian-born **Sam Uba,** Home Sub-Editor of ***The Times.*** **Uba** was at that time the only black sub-editor at ***The Times.***

Earlier he had managed to get a job at the ***Birmingham Post*** as a sub-editor in August 1968 but he told the Conference that :

"In spite of my success in achieving my ambition, before I was told to take a job with the Post Office, or with British Rail or London Transport, and continue writing as a freelance, I must report that the journey was hard, frustrating and painful. Many times I came close to tears and nearly gave up. Today, after seven years in British journalism, I cannot, in good conscience, say that merit, or potential ability, has been the overriding consideration in the non-employment of black journalist...

" What I can say is that experiences from the inside have convinced me that the failure to employ black journalists and the failure to give more responsible positions to the few who have managed to make it, cannot be divorced from discrimination based on race and colour. The discrimination is subtle, and it exists at all levels of the British newspaper industry. The British newspaper industry is the one corner of Britain where the wind of change, in terms of race relations, had been blowing too slowly for comfort, and far too slowly for the good of this country.

Uba was never given a front line reporter's job, which he had asked for. ***The Times*** management despite his reporting skill and ability did not want him as one of the paper's frontline reporters. His black face it seems was not a good match for the lily-white reporting desk. *'Racial discrimination',* as **Martin Luther King Jnr,** told his followers when he launched the direct action phase of the contemporary Civil Rights Movement in America, *'scars the soul and degrades the personal'.*

CHAPTER 4

Into the 1970s and then the 1980s influence of West Indian World

By the beginning of the 1970's a number of newspapers and magazines appeared including, ***West Indian World, Grass Roots, The Black Star, The Hustler, The Gleaner, The Nation, Cinnamon, West Indian Digest, Black Dimension, Flambeau, Black Liberator, Scope, Focus, The Link, Chequers, Sepia, Caribe, Caribbean Times*** and ***Magnet News.*** Another was ***The Asian,*** an informative, thoughtful and provoking monthly, edited by **Tasadooq Ahmed** who owned a restaurant called The Ganges,(first in Soho and later in Paddington-London) which became a lively meeting place for many black activists and journalists. Not many of the newspapers and magazines survived, but ***West Indian World*** and ***Caribbean Times*** had the most endurable influence for the 1970s and early 1980s.

The ***West Indian World's*** mandate, according to it's editor **Aubrey Baynes,** at its inaugural reception at the Commonwealth Institute in June, 1971, was to promote multi-culturalism and racial harmony by making the black community feel they belong in and can be successful in Britain. His business partners, **Reynold Francis, Zeina Mason** and **Conrad Gome** supported him for the time when he was editor.

Aubrey Baynes, born in St Vincent, published ***Daylight*** – an entertainment and sport paper, ***Magnot News*** and ***Cinnamon*** in mid 1960s. Contributors included, **Jan Carew** – who was the editor for the initial editions of ***Magnet News,*** **Rudolph Dunbar**, one of the most distinguished black international conductors, **Andrew Salkey,** one of the best black novelists and poet, **Ernest Eytle, Barbara Blake,** who later became a Jamaican Senator and writer **Sheila Brown.** These papers were short-lived.

Baynes gathered around him for the first editions of the ***WIW*** an unprecedented number of seasoned black professional media specialists: **Conrad Gomes** as Development Manager, **Len Renwick** in charge of Advertising, photographer **Bill Paterson, Wayne Wilson** – one of the best creative and innovative art designers, **Roger Norman,** a practised hand and astute sub-editor. He later became editor of the ***South East London Mercury,*** and employed **Iva Davies –** sharp and talented- as the first black reporter on the ***SELM.*** I became Deputy Editor and leader writer of the ***WIW.*** After four editions of the weekly paper it again expounded its philosophy in its editorial: *"This is a glorious challenge and opportunity which faces us all, irrespective of race..... Our concern is not so much with the narrow view of one's colour, but rather of justice; with which is right; with objectivity and with the unique philosophy of what constitutes a West Indian or a black person in Britain".*

The paper caught the imagination of the black community, which liked and enjoyed the irreverent strident views, editorials, typography and contents. Vigorous in writing tone, appearance, and in policy, the ***West Indian World*** encouraged, trained and invited young people and others with potential who wanted to become contributors to the columns of the paper. After six months the paper charted its progress in its editorial:

> *"When, on June 11th of this year* **West Indian World** *was launched there were any number of sceptics of all shades who maintained it could not be done. No such has ever succeeded in Britain before, they maintained. 'It won't work"? Well it has completed its 27th issue of unbroken production. Our paper is selling near 25,000 copies weekly; and each week, it digs deeper and wider within the totality of our community in Britain.*
>
> *After six months, copies go as far as Edinburgh; the north of England, the midlands, the south east and back to London. Naturally, and while we cannot afford in any way to be complacent, we are somewhat pleased with the limited progress which we have made to date. And this staying power has, to a large extent, depended upon the support which you, the readers, have given us. It is, after all, your paper.*
>
> *Our success so far has depended too on the brilliant support given by our printers. This has resulted visually. in a paper that is far superior to the* **Mirror** *and the* **Sun.** *And we believe, too, that* **WIW** *is also superior in tone and quality when compared with these two Fleet Street tabloids.*
>
> *The basic principles which have been the moving force behind our paper still stand. We believe that* **WIW** *is both vital and necessary for the following reasons. Until* **West Indian World,** *and – in spite of the basic changes in the structure of British years, no paper in England has had the guts enough to reflect an opinion of the Black Community.* **WIW** *does. The ever growing hostility in human relations which seems a part of today's world makes the voice of* **WIW** *a necessity. Our responsibility, we feel, is one which will create a paper though ostensibly for the blacks should, if anything, be a paper that will lend itself to better human understanding.*
>
> *For the coming year the scope of* **WIW** *will be widened in sport, in entertainment, personalities in the news wider news coverage. Our paper too, will begin its penetration of the Caribbean and Canada".*

And the paper did. By the end of the year the number of regular contributors to the paper increased. There were new faces, some well known personalities in the community, young enterprising talent and well-wishers. There was an impressive array of writers and contributors. Not all of them were journalists, but they had the potential which was utilised. **Sheila Brown,** had a regular column – *Wonderful World of Woman,* a provocative writer on fashion and fads, **Louis Chase** – a freelance writer and part time lecturer at Morley College, London and now a Baptist minister in the USA; **Caudley George** a photo-journalist; **Rosemary Stone, Judi Oshowole; Tony Douglas** who had a *Youth Today* column. **D. Sinclair Da Breo** – a freelance writer and broadcaster; **Roger St Pierre,** the paper's music reviewer, **Henderson Dalrymple; Cathy Castillo,** a freelance writer; **Chris Buyon and Rudolph Dunbar,** a talented musician and noted conductor, were all regular contributors.

1972 was a year of consolidation and expansion of the paper. Columns like *Leisure and Art, Inside the Caribbean, Out of Africa, Daylight on America, Business World Sounding Off*, an astrology column – *Stars* by **Teri** (a pseudonym). A column on black history – *Genesis,* opened the paper to a bigger and eager readership, and the column *Scales of Justice* – a legal advice column of all aspects of the rights of the individual, became one of the most popular under red-blooded human rights campaigner and dauntless controversial barrister **Rudi Nayaran.**

It's letters' page was, indeed, a most vibrant one – the nerve of the paper – and so it ought to be in any paper worth its ink. No other black paper before, in this country, had such a wide and interesting one. Readers were supportive, sometimes abusive and angry. They wanted more information, wanted help and support. They believed the paper voiced their fears, hopes and successes and felt that it empathised with them. They encouraged columnists and writers and sent in interesting and sometimes useless bits of information. They argued, took the paper to task discussed and encouraged. The pages were open to all of them, subject only to liberal libel constraints.

More writers and contributors, mostly young, were attracted to the columns of the paper. They included journalist **Barbara Blake** and **Pat Lewis. Hal Austin** – versatile, capable and professional-a probation officer, who started writing regular stories in the paper, and later moved to Fleet Street ***(The Daily Mail*** and ***Financial Times)*** and edited **Roots** a classy monthly magazine. **Noel Coombes** was the paper's Northern Correspondent and he had a keen insight into Britain's northern black areas. There was **Hazel Dan, Robert Govender –** a seasoned South African journalist, **L. Foster-Davis,** who had wide experience in sales, distribution and circulation, **Hugh V. Lynch,** a freelance contributor, **Stephen Bulgin** – who for a short period founded and edited a paper and **Betty Page. Clive Meadows** (a pseudonym for myself). I also wrote at that time for various Fleet Street papers like the ***Sunday People, Sunday Telegraph*** and ***Evening Standard.*** There was **Dorothy Kuya**, a leading community worker, who wrote a series of articles on the troubles in Liverpool, **Leo Pamment** – who joined the staff as a designer, **Robert Sye** – who was one of the most entertaining entertainment editors. Two years later **Sye** founded and edited a feature-based magazine ***Focus*** which was a menu of a mix of music, entertainment and political profiles and for which I was a founder contributor.

Neil Kenlock – was a young keen and enterprising professional photographer who later became a founder of ***Choice Fm*** – one of the most successful black community radio stations- and joint owner of ***Roots,*** a stylish monthly magazine. **Christopher Boyle** wrote features, together with **Carmen Sloan, John Hughes, Premindra Vaniak** and **Roy Sawh –** a community activist who was as bold as brass as his articles were incisive. Saturday mornings in the small cramped North West London office of the ***WIW*** was usually thick as hops with contributors and supporters.

There were only a small handful of staff members – some with dismally lowly wages, others like myself who worked for nothing – the rest were freelance and community activists. What they all had in common was a proud involvement in the paper. Its editorials were incisive but moderately phrased and broached many subjects; on some news stories it had more penetrating coverage than some of the daily national newspapers. The paper gave the impression of being newsy with its punchy headlines; now and again it presented the treatment of some topics in depth, such as a several – part article on *'The Race Relations Industry'.* Many of its stories, like the archetypical tabloid story, was a piece of high precision engineering. They were factual, and its many news stories and features were a treasures' trove and yet made reading enjoyable.

West Indian World at its first year celebration of publication was able to categorically say what it stood for.

> ***"WIW** is a black paper" it said. "Owned by black people and staffed by black people. It is an independent paper which exists only on its circulation and advertisements. It receives no gifts of grants of any kind ".*

And then it particularised its belief:

> *'A good newspaper, we believe should not only be a good purveyor of news, but should also be a medium of expression which has to capture the mood of its readers correctly and truthfully. Such a paper would naturally become a standard bearer....We have not been afraid to expose the high, the mighty; the powerful and the low whenever and wherever they have deserved such exposure. Some people have not liked some of the things we have been saying for the past year. We have continuously stood for what we believe to be in the best interest of both black and white community. Ours is to use our columns to help build a better society; free of racial discrimination and all its attendant evils......'*

A senior white Fleet Street journalist once described ***WIW*** as a *'handsome tabloid weekly'.*

A year later I left the paper because of my other Fleet Street journalistic and ***National of Union Journalists'*** commitments. And **Baynes,** whose financial acumen and sagacity was gaseous unlike his perceptive editorial abilities, became disillusioned with the paper's financial viability, and hurriedly left the paper in May 1973 returning to St Vincent. Despite its popularity and its wide circulation the paper could not attract big enough white corporate advertisers.

WIW was dependent on an advertising base made up of small retail and service businesses with scarce advertising sterling. In general, these businesses do not consider advertising a priority, cannot afford to treat it as such and public services at that time were not interested in using ***WIW*** since it was a pioneering risk. Just like all other black papers, before and presently in Britain, it was subject to market conditions which inhibited its growth.

As a result it operated at a level where it barely managed to stay out of the red. This is part of a cycle...businesses need to advertise to be successful but cannot afford it. It tried to seek advertising from the larger business sector, but this was and still is a solution that is difficult because of the way the ethnic market is perceived by many large white advertisers.

Arif Ali – editor of the monthly magazine ***West Indian Digest,*** was persuaded by the paper's directors and with the assistance of various community activists and leaders like **Aston Gibson, William Trant, Cliff Lynch, Ralph Straker, Roy Sawh** and **Irwin Adams,** to assume editorship of ***WIW.***

Ali left the paper in 1976. ***The Times*** Diary reported a 'dramatic coup', organised by members of the ***WIW*** staff and the chairman of the newspaper's printers who ousted him from his position as editor whilst he was away working in the Caribbean. It became clear that **Ali's** anti- racist campaigning and strident views did not sit well with the printers and some of the staff.

WIW continued until 1984 and under the control of **Tony Douglas** and **Caudley**

George who were the leaders of the 'coup'. By then it was limping and a ghost of what it was before. During this period it's edge and its authoritative approach was enervating; its unhealthy internecine battles with rival black papers was professionally damaging; typographically it became somewhat uneven and its articles tedious, rambling and as dull as ditchwater. It had various editors, reporters and contributors – **Flip Fraser, Claire Shepherd, Mike Phillips** a very notable journalist who became a journalism lecturer and writer, **Alfred Chow, Marc Wadsworth –** later a reporter for ***Thames TV,*** **Isabel Appio** – who years on became editor of the ***Journal*** – and **Rosalind Yarde** later joined the ***BBC's*** World Service News as a senior broadcast journalist. A sad and doddering demise for ***WIW.***

In Oct 1979, **Godfrey Hope,** a wealthy young Guyanese, the financial backer, **Neil Kenlock, Patrick Berry, Wayne Wilson** and **Hal Austin** founded ***Roots,*** a stylish monthly magazine. The idea was to produce a British ***Ebony,*** only more connected to the reality of how people live in Britain. **Austin** – as editor – and **Wilson** were the editorial and production team. I was one of the many contributors together with **Yvonne Thompson, Paul Greene, Marc Wandsworth, Martine Dennis, Mike Phillips** and **Brian Moyo** who became editor in 1982. There is no doubt that for its first three years it was the most interesting launch in Britain's periodical production. ***Roots*** was sold in 1987 to ***Hansib Publications.***

There is no doubt that ***West Indian World*** was a first, a trail-finder and a mentoring guide which echoed the hopes, frustration and progress of the black world in Britain. It made an indelible mark on campaigning journalism and opened the white-coated bolted media oyster – albeit slowly and unwillingly. It gave many young black men and women, for the first time for many years, a taste for journalism. Many of those who wrote and worked for ***WIW*** travelled further, some into Fleet Street, others into commercial and community radio and television and others worked as journalists or editors on new oncoming black newspapers, magazines and broadcasting.

Without its encouragement and foresight there would have been no discerning glittering beacon. Other black papers now would not have to invent the black journalism wheel again, but only improve on it.

CHAPTER 5

New Publishing Ventures

Arif Ali was born in Guyana in 1935, came to live in Britain in 1957 where he worked for London Transport and was an active trades unionist. His first excursion into the publishing field took the form of a duplicated news sheet featuring local news as well as information culled from Caribbean newspapers and circulated amongst the immediate community in North London.

In 1971, **Ali** with **John Chapman,** published ***Westindian Digest*** – a 48-64 page monthly magazine. **George Griffiths** was the paper's photographer. It's first editorial expounded it's credo:

> *'**The West Indian Digest** is not a Pro Anyone, or Anti Anyone Magazine. It's only aim is to improve Community Relations....We will endeavour to keep it a simple straightforward magazine so that the ordinary person will find it easy to read...we hope to inform, enlighten and explain subjects that pertain to a better relationship among different people of different background.'*

Ten years later its editorial team included **Ken Campbell** and **John St Lewis** – both unflagging, professional and complaisant. Its contributors included **Al Hamilton,** a versatile sports writer, **N. D. Patel, Stephen Bulgin** an expeditious reporter, **Dan Harriot** and **Patrick Friday,** also photographers **Salim Karim** and **Ivan Corea.** It had widened its content and featured well written African, Asian and Caribbean issues and had offices in Barbados and Jamaica and Finsbury Park, London. By 1989 it was the longest running black publication.

In 1973 **Ali,** launched the year book, ***Westindians in Britain*** (forerunner to ***Third World Impact***). Then, together with **Ashton Gibson,** in 1977 he launched the ***Westindian Voice.*** In 1980 he set-up ***Hansib Publishing*** which produced the first ***Visible Minority Survey Report* –** which is still cited as an authoritative text – and in 1981 started ***Caribbean Times.*** Two years later the ***Asian Digest*** was launched and replaced two years after that by ***Asian Times.*** In just over one year it had grown into the biggest English language Asian weekly. Also in 1973 **Vallabh Kaviraj,** founded and edited the ***Asian Express,*** an irregular and sparsely filled paper and ***The Asian,*** a monthly political educative magazine, edited by **Tasadooq Ahmed.**

The ***Asian Times*** – its managing editor **Prakash Singh** and reporters **Nisa Ali** and **Kamscilla Naidoo –** was an easy reading paper. It made dramatic use of photos-despite its emotional, often strident voice-created by use of large headlines as well as simply understood words. The paper succeeded in selling advertising space to some corporate companies. Policies appeared in the news columns through selection of events which were stressed and for many years it made a speciality of running interpretative stories on racial issues.

In a Dec 1983 editorial the paper has this to say :

> *"Not for the first time, the gutter press has gone from the gutter to the drains, and seems to have reached a permanent state of the pits of*

> *journalism. How could any responsible newspaper allow its columns to be used for such racially inflammatory material like describing the Chinese people as the "little yellow inscrutables",with 'funny eyes'. Perhaps for the author it is a funny joke, but for us it is not funny at all, given the nature of the British society and race relations. About* ***The Sun*** *newspaper, there is not much to say because the newspaper's history speaks for itself, nowhere has it said anything commendable about people who are not white.."*

African Times was launched on April, 1984 with the aim of filling a void in the African community and what **Ali** described 'as a growing community that needed positive representation'

In its first edition ***African Times*** proclaimed its birth and echoed the credenda of ***Hansib Publications*** in its article *'Why African Times?"* written by myself:

> *"***African Times*** *will be both a creature of the developed black sense of solidarity and an index of the developing consciousness and an unwillingness on the part of blacks to remain in a subordinate position, a helot in a society in which many of their children have been born and in which they are fully and responsibly participating.*
>
> ***African Times*** *will bring news and views from Africa. It will articulate the dreams and fears, the problems and successes of the African community in Britain. It will, in no uncertain terms, expose what needs to be exposed, but it will do with a dignity and sensitivity which will do justice to its birth. It will always remember and assert* ***Martin Luther King's*** *injunction that as blacks....and whites 'we must learn to live together as brothers or we will all perish as fools'. As such* ***African Times*** *can only be a harbinger of hope, unity and truth"*

The ***African Times,*** with **Ken Campbell** as its Executive Editor, and associate editors **Wiseman Khuzwayo, Kamscilla Naidoo** and **Brian Moyo** – who years later also became editor of ***Roots*** – from its inception was a newsy-looking paper with an orderly and attractive editorial page. It contained a lot of news, some written in a lively style, and its editorials were punchy. An outspoken paper, it was militant short of extremism, exciting in tone and treatment of the news, but making room for other columnists to provide other view-points. It's regular weekly column *Where Lies the Truth* by **Mfana Tshabalala,** was pithy, provocative, home-thrusting, albeit evidential and had one of the biggest letter postbags. Another columnist was **Poon Yick Hoh. Russel K.Pierre** became managing editor four years later, **Ruth Ansah Ayisi** as assistant editor and **Keith Bennett** its political editor.

The Caribbean Times after the journalistic demise of ***West Indian World*** followed in the steps that ***WIW*** had pioneered. It became the hub, cynosure and stamping ground of the community. It became a campaigning community newspaper with a national vocalic flair and content. And its centre was **Arif Ali** who managed to attract a number of journalists and community leaders around the papers.

Community leaders like **Navnit Dholakia** – a former principal officer of the ***Commission for Racial Equality (CRE)*** **–** and who was created life peer **Lord Dholakia of Waltham Brooks** in 1998, **Sam Springer,** first black mayor of Hackney and one of the founders of ***Black Rights UK,*** **Rudi Nayaran,** one of the best known black barristers, **Gulam Meeran** and **Kuttan Menon** both from the ***CRE*** and both of whom now hold high public positions in the judiciary, and **Roy Sawh,** director of ***Black Rights UK*** became an advisory group which gave editorial advice and assistance to the newspaper. I joined this group. **Hansib's** publications pages were opened to the community which made it one of the most popular and influential.

Well designed, ***Caribbean Times*** was at that time typographically much in advance of other black papers. It emphasised background stories on urban problems, race relations and education, rather than spot news. Much space was devoted to human interest features. Some of the feature writers and reporters were **Russell Pierre** – a proficient journalist, **Dan Harriott** and **Henderson Dalrymple** (all three of whom edited the paper), **Mark Kamba, Kizzi Knwocha, Al Hamilton, Tricia Reid, Victor Ndovi, Claire Hynes –** who later went to the ***Voice*** and then the ***BBC***, **Paul Coleman, George Alagiah –** who later became a well known ***BBC*** reporter, **John Doe, Nisa Ali, Kamscilla Naidoo, Robert Govender, Wiseman Khuzuwayo, Janet Tappin** and **Philip Straker.**

Better written than many a purely commercial paper, the story topics were at times of broader than minority interest. Its columns were '*From Where I Stand*' – caustic and topical – by *The Limer* (a pseudonym for **Roy Sawh**), '*Acquired Taste – Food and Fashion*' by versatile writer **Devinia Sookia,** and '*The Man with the Walking Stick*' (a pseudonym for myself). The latter was described as 'astringent, gossipy, cannily, knowledgeable and entertainingly' by **Clifford (Robbie) Robinson,** the then Deputy Chairman of the ***CRE*** who helped to underpin and cement its news and features

Hansib Publications dominated the black media scene for the latter part of the 1970's and the first part of the 1980's. Apart from its newspapers – ***Caribbean Times, Asian Times*** and ***African Times –*** in 1983 it also acquired ***Roots,*** and promoted and published a growing list of book titles.

Hansib became one of the longest established Third World-oriented publishing houses in Britain and by that time was becoming the largest publishing house in Europe run by and for the visible minority communities. It was proudly self financing and established its own distribution outlets because the conventional (white) distributors were constantly discriminating. It was only when it succeeded that the conventional distributors started to handle ***Hansib Publications'*** papers and as a result of its campaign other black newspapers and magazines were given more sympathetic support by the conventional distributors. It's book titles ranged over a wide variety of disciplines from literature, history, tourism, law, the arts, sports, children's books and political writings to reference works.

Hansib's bustling and eventful head office in north London, over the years hosted numerous distinguished political visitors from Britain and overseas. It's *Community Awards,* established in 1983, became a landmark in the social calendar of the visible minority communities and a valuable and indispensable support to the black community's striving for real equality justice, achievement and excellence. By the end of the 1980's there were over 150 Community Awards recipients.

Recipients of the Awards included journalists, broadcasters and writers – **Syd Burke** – an indefatigable broadcaster who hosted the popular *Rice 'N' PEAS* **LBC** radio programme, **Russell Pierre, John Lewis, John La Rose –** a well-known play-writer, **Flip Fraser, Nisa Khan, Moira Stuart –** a leading newscaster on ***BBC TV***,

Trevor McDonald (now knighted as **Sir Trevor McDonald**) was then the main black presence on *ITV's News at Ten,* having covered every aspect of current affairs. **Stephen Bulgin, Darcus Howe** – a broadcaster and writer with a strong flavoured and mordant bite in his reports and broadcasts, although sometimes over-subtle. **Howe** became editor of the political and cultural journal ***Race Today*** in 1974 and ten years later he co-founded *Bandung Productions,* the makers of *Bandung File*, a magazine programme for the Asian and Afro-West Indian communities, broadcast by ***Channel 4 TV.***

There was also **Tariq Ali, Diane Abbott,** press officer for Lambeth Council and a prominent member of the ***Black Media Workers Association,*** who became the first black woman Member of Parliament, **Roy Sawh, Zeinab Badawi** – presenter of ***Channel 4 News,*** a keen linguist and the first woman from the visible minorities to become an ***ITN*** newscaster, **Sam Selvon,** a writer who wrote a number of books and made frequent radio and television appearances, **Ian Moo-Young,** artist, playwright and animator and **Alex Pascall**, who in 1974 hosted and presented a lively well documented five days per week *Black Londoners* programme together with a colleague **Vince Herbert, Hal Austin** and **Anne Marie Grey –** who later hosted the ***BBC Radio London's*** breakfast time show '*Rush*'. **Pascall l**ater became a chairman of the *Notting Hill Carnival and Arts Committee*. I was one of the Community Awards recipients in 1984.

In 1997 **Ali** sold the titles to ***Ethnic Media Group,*** a profitable national newspaper company, whose Managing Director was **Garry Gurmeet,** forward-looking and professional. **Gurmeet** was one of the journalist participants in the 1975 seminal *Media and Race Seminar* in London which looked at media and racism issues.

He had come to Britain in 1968 from Kenya. The first careers officer positively discouraged him when he mentioned his interest in newspapers. *'I informed him of my journalistic experience in Kenya and of my educational qualifications....he told me that I would be wasting my time...and instead sent me off for a craft apprenticeship with an engineering firm'.* **Gurmeet's** entry into journalism had to be unconventional – he joined the editorial staff of ***Workers Press,*** the left-wing daily and two years later was appointed editor of its weekly off-shoot. In 1972 he managed to get a reporter's position with the *London Newspaper Group* **(Chelsea News** etc), and in 1974 he joined the ***Middlesex County Times.***

'I was surprised to learn that I was the first black reporter to be employed by the newspaper, which circulates in an area with one of the country's highest concentrations of black community', he said. **Gurmeet** later became Managing Director of ***Middlesex County Newspapers*** and is now Chairman of the ***Ethnic Media Group.***

Another prolific writer and political editor, **A Sivandandan,** came to Britain from Sri Lanka in the wake of the race riots of 1958 – and walked straight into the riots of Notting Hill. He is one of the most brilliant, unnerving, and one of today's seminal thinkers on Marxism, imperialism and racism. His books, collection of short stories and penetrative articles in ***Race & Class,*** a journal on racism, empire and globalization, is one of the few scholarly quarterlies that 'bridges the gap between the academic and the ghetto', according to ***The Guardian***. As founder editor of ***Race & Class*** he has drawn in some of the most significant political, journalists, novelists, politicians and Third World activists and intellectual thinkers of the post-war period.

The journal is undoubtedly the foremost English language journal on racism and imperialism in the world today, and for about three decades, it has established a reputation for breadth of its analysis and global outlook. **Siva,** as we know him, is also the Director of the ***Institute of Race Relations (IRR),*** and it was his unflinchingly struggle in the early 70's which changed the ***IRR*** from a theoretical organisation into a campaigning research body. **Sivandandan** remains today a key figure in the black movement, an often trenchant critic of the Left and an award winning novelist.

CHAPTER 6

Broadcasting industry and Vernacular press

Broadcasting:

Although the ***BBC*** in the 1970s and 1980s had made attempts to reflect the variety of ethnic cultures in British society, the overall picture was and still is far from adequate. In those hard times of recession and cuts the first programmes that were affected were, and still are, ethnic programmes. This was a tragedy in broadcasting terms and above all it seriously harmed the entire process of good race relations.

But despite this a number of Black and Asian broadcasters, many of them unsung heroes, played an important part within the broadcasting network.

The idea of a Radio Programme for the black community was conceived in the mid-seventies by **Sam Morris, Ray Cruikshank, David Shackman** and **Barry Claylon.** They approached the manager of ***Local Radio BBC Radio London,*** **Peter Redhouse** with the proposition to do a monthly programme entitled ***Black Londoners*** for the station's access slot. The concept for a monthly magazine programme was accepted and broadcast commenced on Friday November 22, 1974, jointly produced by **Keith Yoemans** for the ***BBC*** and **Barry Claylon** for ***Black Londoners*** and presented by **Alex Pascall.**

This was the first programme of its kind in Britain- a broadcast voice for the black community which proved to be the forerunner for black radio and, subsequently, television.

Black Londoners set out not merely to report current affairs within the community and reflect the views of black people of all walks of life, but also black opinion on world events, particularly those in the Caribbean and Africa. The growth and strength of the programme's output resulted it in becoming a weekly in 1976 and in May 1978 it occupied a daily slot in the station's output. **Juliet Alexander-**who had earlier worked as a reporter on the ***Hackney Gazettte,*** joined ***Black Londoners,*** and later worked in TV in the Midlands.

It's strident viewpoint did not fit in too well with some of the ***BBC's*** senior management, and the station was peremptorily closed down in August 1988 and reopened as ***GLR.*** **Pascall** and the black presenters were pushed out and he accused the ***BBC*** of racism. In later years, after the ***Macpherson Report,*** the 'beeb's' Director General, **Greg Dyke**, openly admitted that the Corporation was 'whiter than white'.

Ivan Corea, a seasoned broadcaster and writer, was ***BBC*** Local Radio's Asian Programmes Officer, who at the beginning of the 1980s embarked on an ambitious course to train Asian and Black broadcasters for the ***BBC.*** There were then only two TV programmes for Asians: ***Nai Zindagi Naya Jeevan*** (New Life) presented by **Mahendra Kaul** and ***Gharbar,*** a magazine for women produced by **Ashok Rampal** and directed by **Bish Mehay.**

On ***London Weekend Television (LWT)*** an occasional series *Skin,* presented by **Trevor Philips** (who in 2003 became Chair of the *CRE* and before that was Chair of the *London Assembly),* **Vera Gilbert, Lincoln Brown, Simi Bedford** and **Beverley**

Anderson, who made her first television appearance as presenter of '*Black on Black*', a ***LWT*** production of ***Channel 4.*** From 1983 she was one of the presenters of '*Sixty Minutes*' on ***BBC1.*** **Sue Woodford,** formerly a Producer/Director for ***World in Action,*** became Commissioning Editor at ***Channel Four*** for Multi-Cultural Programmes. **Woodward,** who later became **Lady Hollick,** was one the best and supportive Commissioning Editors and was insightful. When she was asked in an interview what she thought was wrong with the media in relationship to black people, she answered that *'basically the problem is that the media is almost exclusively controlled by white people, and the television programmes are made by white middle class men on the whole. Therefore there is no opportunity for any different perspective to come through, because all the people who are making decisions are part of nothing but a very narrow group...television doesn't reflect the black community in any sense – there is no outlet, for their views, opinions or perspective. Television doesn't even employ black people in any numbers and certainly there are almost no black people in decision-making positions in television. The end result of that has to be that you get a racist broadcasting perspective".*

On the ***BBC Derby*** we had **Yvonne Guy** and **Glenton Wright,** presenting the *Blackroot* programme and on the ***BBC Leeds Calypso*** was represented by **Glen English,** whilst the *Herdle White Show* packed a powerful musical punch on ***BBC Radio Leicester*** and *Meeting Place* on Merseyside was well presented by **Linda Loy. Steve Barnard,** a veteran black disc-jockey was the founder of *Reggae Time* on ***BBC Radio London,*** whilst his commercial counterpart, **Greg Edwards** hosted a soul music programme on ***Capital Radio.***

There was **Samir Shah,** producer of ***Eastern Eye,*** moving further into the top hierarchy of the ***BBC.*** **Anita Bhalla,** presented ***Eastern Eye,*** before joining the ***BBC*** in 1987 as full time producer at *Radio WM,* **Shyama Perera, Aziz Kurtha, KaraThapa** – who worked before in the features department of ***The Times*** as *West Africa* correspondent – and **Dippy Chaudhary** who worked before with the ***Gazette Newspaper*** group in West London, were presenters of the forth-nightly news programme. **Pauline Black** was a presenter of *Black on Black* ***Channel 4.***

Other presenters and producers on ***BBC Local Radio*** were: **Leroy Wallace** with *Back-a-Yard* (Nottingham), **Michael Keith** and **Marie Bennett** on *Back-a Yard* (Sheffield), *Sound System* presented by **Maxime Shervington** (Midlands). *I'N'I Rule OK* was presented by **Paul Williams** in Manchester.

Vernacular press

By the late 1970's there were five main Bengali papers. ***Janamot*** – edited by **A. T. M. Walie Ashraf,** ***Jagoran*** – edited by **Dr Talukdar,** ***Bangla Dak*** – edited by **A. G. Chowhury,** ***Bangladesh Weekly*** and ***Sagar,*** a bi-monthly edited by **H. Bahattacharya.**

The two Gujarati weeklies were divided on class basis, and were fierce rivals. ***Gujarat Samachar*** was a well organised weekly by **C. B. Patel,** a veteran and supportive editor as well as a sharp businessman. He also edited ***New Life,*** a weekly English language paper which started in 1976. **Ramniklal Solankilike Patel,** an astute businessman-owned and edited ***Garavi Gujarat.***

The Punjabi press had three weeklies – ***Punjab Times*** – serious in tone – editor – **G. S. Sahni,** ***Sikh Courier*** – a monthly journal of the Sikh Cultural Society, catering for a more specialised interest and informative articles about the Sikh community, and ***Des Perdes*** a lively paper, editor – **T. Purawel.**

Three Hindi papers – ***Amar Deep*** a weekly edited by **Jagdish Kaushal;** ***Navin Weekly*** edited by **Ramesh Kumar** and ***Madahosh*** a monthly.

There were nine Urdu papers. ***Daily Jang*** (1971) edited by **Asaf Jilani,** ***Mashriq,*** the oldest Urdu weekly, started by **Mahmood Hashmi** in 1961 and now edited by **A. T. Bungish,** ***Miilap,*** a weekly edited by **Ramesh Soni,** ***Daily Milap*** an international weekly edited by **Mr Yudhvir,** ***Akhbar-e-Watan,*** a weekly edited by **S. M. Sathananthan,** ***Daily Millat*** edited by **Inam Aziz,** ***Ravi*** a fortnightly, edited by **Mrs Farida Sheikh,** ***Masawat*** (now ceased), and ***Inqilib.***

Many of the Asian and Chinese vernacular papers like ***Sing Tao,*** a daily, edited by **S. T. Wan** and other black papers, were and are still being dogged by financial resources. Most of the papers are run by members of the family and the majority of their revenue comes from the ethnic minority businesses, through grocery stores, video shops, restaurants and other small business establishments became an established pattern of distribution. This was complemented by mailings and household distribution in areas of heavy black concentration.

CHAPTER 7

NUJ and Anti-racism

In April 1974, the Annual Delegate Meeting (ADM) of the NUJ in Wexford, Ireland, unanimously passed a motion which *'strongly condemned the practice of racism both in the employment of journalists, and in the editorial content, in the British media and instructs the National Executive Council to set up a special Race Relations sub-committee to look into such practices and recommend positive measures to deal with them'.*

As chair of the Committee, I had moved the motion and it was the first time that the NUJ had discussed or grappled with racism and equal opportunities issues in its delegate meeting forums. I was the only black delegate to this 400 – strong delegate ADM. The *NUJ* embraced the issue and, **Ken Morgan,** one the best general secretaries of the Union, ensured that top officials including **Eric Blott,** the deputy secretary general and his successor **Charlie Harkness** became the serving officers for the Race *Relations sub-committee,* which later became the *Race Relations Working Party (RRWP).* This helped to 'legitimise' the Sub-Committee. Its aim was to better race relations in journalism and to improve journalistic standards in coverage of race issues in the media in general. The other black member of the *Race Relations sub-committee* was **Garry Singh (Gurmeet)** who later became a successful media proprietor.

Although the issue of racism, discrimination and equal opportunities had not reached the NUJs' Annual Delegate Meetings until this ADM at Wexford, one union branch in late 1959 and 1960, the London Central Branch, had been in touch with the recently formed non-racial *National Union of South African Journalists (NUSAJ).* The established SA Society of Journalists, a member of the IFJ, was a white union and only allowed black journalists as non voting members and disbarred them from becoming Board members. To combat this exclusion, black journalists and some liberal white journalists had decided to form their own Union, *NUSAJ*. At that time I was working on the weekly ***Golden City Post*** and ***Drum,*** the most influential and popular black newspapers. I became the NUSAJ's first Chair.

We contacted the *NUJ,* through the London Central Branch and petitioned them to expel the exclusive and white controlled *SASJ* from being a member of the *IFJ.* I had to leave South Africa and came to London in 1960 as a political refugee. This was after spending some time in prison because of my anti apartheid activities and writings. I had been put on trial for High Treason with 155 other South African anti apartheid leaders, including **Nelson Mandela,** who after 27 years in prison became South Africa's first black President in the New South Africa. On my arrival I contacted the *NUJ.* I found the Central London Branch were taking a lead in expelling the *SASJ* and I was able to persuade **Jim Bradley,** the general secretary, to get the *IFJ* to discuss the matter.

Leading London Central Branch members, **Robin Corbett** – who was a NEC member and a subeditor on the ***Farmers Weekly,*** and later became a peer, **Leolin MacClean** – Central Branch Committee member and the Press Association's racing correspondent, and **Marie Buchanan** branch clerk – one of the most thorough and knowledgeable on the union's affairs – not only lobbied to ensure that the issue would be discussed at the NEC meetings, but they raised money to help the *NUSAJ,* train the new Union's secretary, **Ronnie Fisher,** in Trade Union administrative issues, and smuggle banned anti-apartheid material into South Africa. To a question at that time from me, **Buchanan,** remarked that in all her knowledge of the union she had never heard about or had met any black *NUJ* member, since the *NUJ's* founding in 1907.

The 1961 ADM carried the following motion *"that this Annual Delegate Meeting welcomes the formation of the multi-racial National union of South African Journalists and extends the hand of friendship to the chairman Mr Lionel Morrison, and the secretary, Mr Ronald Fisher, and all the members.*

Recognising that the abhorent policy of apartheid has produced special difficulties for trade unions in South Africa, the ADM expresses the hope and belief that the new union together with the South African Society of Journalists, will co-operate to further the freedom of the press and democracy generally in South Africa."

When **P. W. Jarrett,** NUJ organiser conveyed this ADM resolution to me, I thanked him for the welcoming of the NUSAJ, but told him how disappointed we were that sections of the NUJ still believed in the racist and segregated white SASJ.

The *London Evening News* on 4 April 1973 led their front page with the scaring headline *School Mobs in London Race Riot*. The story said that a mob of black youths had attacked mainly white pupils and that passers by cowered in shop doorways as the white and black groups clashed. It mentioned one gang of more than 100 coloured teenagers armed with weapons including a shot gun, stiletto, iron bar and milk bottles and quoted the Headmaster of Kingsdale School, one of the schools involved as saying, *'I have never seen anything like it'*. The other school was Tulse Hill.

The Headmaster denies saying that. Indeed he was so disturbed that he immediately issued a statement emphasising that no white pupils had been involved. This was an undisputed fact which all other papers accepted. Accounts of the numbers of children and police involved, of the number and nature of the weapons, of the damages, varied widely. What was commonly accepted by all except the *Evening News* was that the fight was between black pupils from both schools.

The *Daily Mail's* headline blamed *'The Outsiders bussed in to keep a racial balance'*. The headmaster of both Tulse Hill and Kingsdale supported by the Inner London Education Authority, deny that any of their pupils are bussed in. *'Nor is there any policy regarding racial balance'*, the Headmaster of Tulse Hill said.

The Mail also said the children involved were *all truants from their respective schools*, an allegation both Headmasters vehemently denied.

The Evening News the next days ignored all the new facts and authoritative denials and claimed: *Hundreds of parents decided not to send their children to Kingsdale School today*. It added that the school bore the signs of the violence: *More than 20 windows are smashed. Locked doors can be seen to have been broken and blinds wrenched off.*

The headmaster immediately replied that attendance that day was, *absolutely normal* and that *no damage at all* had been done to school property; there had been no fighting on school premises.

The chief Information officer of ILEA complained to the *Evening News* about both stories, but with particular reference to the headline *"Race Riots"*. *The News* replied that it stood by its story and undertook to reply to the accusations of misreporting which it has not done satisfactorily up to now. A week later ILEA referred the *Evening News* to the Press Council.

On the April 4, 1974 the Press Council which is not known for its radicalism, upheld the complaint by the ILEA that the *Evening News* published an inaccurate story under an unjustified headline. It also ruled that although the editor invited the complainants to write a letter for publication he declined to publish a correction and apology.

The Press Council in the adjudication said the story was inaccurate in a number of details and incomplete in so far as it did not include the headmaster's denial that a fight took place on the school premises: *'The words "race riot" in the headline were unjustified and in the conditions existing in the area they were irresponsible. The newspaper should have published a retraction and the complaint is upheld'*.

The Press Council's decision was immediately welcomed by the Black community which was as surprised as was the *Evening News* at the outcome.

The two *Evening News* reporters immediately complained to the NEC of the National Union of Journalists (NUJ) that they were unfairly criticised in the Press Council's adjudication. The National Executive Committee's (NEC's) sub committee reported to the July NEC that the Press Council's finding was based on the headline, its accusation that the story was inaccurate was not justified.

According to a report in *The Journalist:*

Deputy General Secretary Eric Blott said there was nothing in the story that was not repeated in stories published in the following day's Fleet Street papers. The reason a complaint was laid against the Evening News was that an editorial executive 'dressed up' the copy and put an irresponsible headline on it. The sub committee went on to recommend the NEC to accept that the criticism of ***O'Kill*** *and* ***Joseph*** *was unwarranted. It was agreed that the NEC decision should be conveyed to the Press Council.*

How the NEC reached such a decision, especially since only the *Evening News* described the fracas between black pupils of the two schools as a Race Riot only becomes possible if one is aware of the hostile attitude the NEC and the NUJ as a whole took to a motion submitted by the London Freelance Branch of the NUJ to the Wexford Annual Delegates Meeting of the NUJ in 1974. Moved by myself.

The motion was partly rejected by the NEC which argued that it should be referred back to it for action. Arguments against the motion at he ADM ranged from those who felt it was the wrong way to go about it. Many journalists actually argued that racism just did not exist in the media and among the ranks of the NUJ. The attitude to the London Freelance Branch motion was not the first time the NUJ had taken such a stand. In 1966 the Central London Branch passed a similar resolution calling for a code of conduct covering race relations. It was rejected by the annual conference.

However, all does not seem to be lost with the NUJ. Immediately after the Wexford ADM a London Liaison NUJ Committee of various London branches was set up to look at the whole question of racism in the media. Members were: **Elaine Cox; Peter Strick,** reporter on the ***South London Press*** - London SW Branch; **Gary Gurmeet; Geoff Sheridan,** London Freelance Branch; **Dave Clark,** Deputy Editor of ***Race Today*** - Magazine Branch; **Caudley George,** reporter on ***West Indian World*** - London North Branch; and I was chair of the committee - Freelance Branch. Although unofficially it geared various people into action, as a Sub Committee. The black community itself took up the whole matter by holding various seminars and meetings to discuss the issues involved.

The Sub-committee and the *RRWP* spearheaded the anti-discrimination and anti-racist policies of the Union. It organized Race and the Media discussions and meetings in various parts of the country, which went a long way in sensitizing white journalists and newspapers on race issues, and brought media players and the black community together. Editors were exposed to equal opportunities, anti racism and the black presence in this country. I was by then chair of the *RRWP,* and the first and only black member of the National Executive Council of the NUJ for a decade.

When in 1977 I campaigned for the post of President of the Union, racism and bigotry pointedly showed its face at the elections at its Annual Delegate Meeting. There were two other candidates – one from the 'right' of the Union's faction and the other from the 'left'. After the first voting count, when the 'right' candidate (**Ted Simpson,** senior sub at the ***Evening Standard*** and an editor of the Union's journal, ***The Journalist)*** had been eliminated, the 'left' candidate (**Dennis MacShane,** a BBC reporter who was then the left's darling and tub-thumper. tergiversated and effortlessly slid into the Labour Blairite camp to become – for a short tenure – a government junior foreign affairs minister) and I had the same votes. In distributing the remaining voting preferences of the 'right' candidate's, the votes went to **McShane,** despite the fact that the 'right' and 'left' voters were at each other's throats, were traditionally politically apart and hated each other's views of the Union and themselves. The 'right' voters were happier to let the 'left' candidate win, than to let a black candidate become President of the Union. Prejudice and racism was still rampart and unchallenged in some of the ranks and leadership of the Union. It took me a decade to become the first black President of the Union, in 1987 and Member of Honour of the Union in 1995, although the Union still has no black full-time official organisers.

In 1976 and 1977, together with other black and Asian community leaders, I campaigned for a change in the Race Relations Act which would empower a better and more powerful race body. *The Race Relations Board* and the *Community Relations Commission* were merged into the *Commission for Racial Equality,* which I had helped to set up.

I became its Principal Press and Public Relations Officer and not only handled all the Press information, but also trained key staff and Commissioners on press issues. But my most important brief was to sensitive my journalist colleagues and the media generally to race and discriminatory issues. Fourteen years later I left the *CRE* disillusioned with its progress, its inability to win the black community over, and its ineffectual leadership with a chair – **Michael Day** – who seemed not to know or understand what discrimination and racism was really about. (See article in Part II)

However, some progress was being made in the Union. It was the *RRWP's* campaigning, which in 1978 resulted in the inclusion of Clause 10 in the *NUJ's* Code of Conduct and Rule on Working Practices. This stated that:

> *'He/She shall not originate material which encourages discrimination designed to encourage discrimination on grounds of race, colour, creed, gender or sexual orientation. Furthermore, no journalist shall discriminate in*

the course of his/her job – whether in employing other journalists on in his/her editorial capacity – against members of ethnic, religious or national groups or against individuals of one sex or sexual orientation, on the grounds of that person's membership of such a group'.

And the next year in 1979, the Union at its Annual Delegate Meeting *'recognized the urgent need to secure training and jobs for black people in the media industry.'* The Unions' chapels were urged to ensure that black job applicants were fairly considered, and where possible were to visit schools and in other ways positively to encourage black teenagers to take up journalism. It also pressed for the inclusion of the NUJ's Race Guidelines in the National Council of Training Journalism (NCTJ) Council's training curriculum. The RRWP was responsible for devising the Union's Guidelines for Reporting on Race and Guidelines on Reporting Racist Organisations, which among others stated that Union members should *'press for equal opportunities for employment of black staff, particularly in area of extensive minority group settlement'.*

In 1982 the *NUJ's* ADM urged the Unions' Industrial Councils *'to ensure that all claims include demands for positive action to be taken to encourage the employment of journalists belonging to ethnic minorities'.*

The *Working Party* periodically held meetings around the country, normally in cities where complaints had been made about race coverage. *NUJ* chapels were visited and the *Working Party* helped with race related issues. Meetings involved newspaper editors and management from local radio. Public meetings were also held to which journalists and black community groups were invited. In the last three years meetings were convened in Liverpool, Bristol, Leicester, Dundee and Glasgow. In Leicester representatives of the Asian community reported that their activities were not covered by the local paper, ***The Mercury,*** which had no black reporters or anyone covering race issues.

The public meeting in Liverpool was packed and discussion was animated. ***The Liverpool Post*** editor had to defend the paper's coverage of muggings in Liverpool 8, where a majority of the city's black community live, against allegations of racism.

The RRWP assisted with a conference for black media workers in Birmingham at which there were 140 black people. The conference played a vital role in shoring up the confidence of black media workers who had previously been isolated in their own newspapers, magazines and broadcasting stations.

When the five commissioners of the CRE were sacked by the Home Secretary, **William Whitelaw,** the Working Party protested. The sackings were seen as a deliberate political move against the five who were pressing for more radical action against discrimination, and **Charlie Harkness**, deputy general secretary of the NUJ and the RRWP'S servicing officer, told the home secretary that *"Events in Bristol and elsewhere have shown, we feel, a need for dynamic action of the problems of our inner cities and the question of race relations generally. In this respect the announcement on reappointment is a severe blow".*

The Working Party also worked closely with the **Black Media Workers Association**, and gave it financial support.

The number of black journalists as *NUJ* members were still negligible, but as a result of the campaigning of the *RRWP,* more black journalists started to join the

Union and to get involved in the Working Party. These included **Shiv Ayer, Gary Gurmeet, J.Thackara, Nisa Ali, Linda Syed, Beulah Ainley, Linda Mitchell** (the former Head of Diversity, ***BBC***), **Yasmine Khan,** a young, energetic talented journalist and the first black reporter on the ***Liverpool Post,*** she is now a qualified psychologist, **Rudi Singh, H. O. Nazareth, Rafiq Mughal, Nahdra Iqbal Singh, Marc Wadsworth** and **Jim Boumelha.** One or two white journalists colleagues were empathetic with and supported the work of the Working Party and became active members. This was welcoming for the Working Party. One such a colleague was **Phil Cohen** and the other **John Brophy,** an Irish journalist. Both of them felt very strongly about issues of discrimination and had been tireless in their support of the Working Party.

The *Working Party* continued for many years fighting a rearguard action against the most blatant cases of race reporting where members of the Union showed no regard for the Code of Conduct. For the next 15 years the *Working Party* was instrumental in ensuring that the Union recognised the challenge of racism and adopted, at least on paper, a programme dealing with race reporting and the grievances of black and ethnic minority journalists.

In the early nineties, black members started questioning the Union's track record and its ability to create a space for black journalists despite the mountains of policies adopted over many years. There was therefore a belief that the *RRWP* had outlived its usefulness, and that the time was ripe for replacing the ad-hoc advisory status of the *Working Party* with a more permanent constitutional body.

These aspirations were further reinforced by important shifts taking place in other trade unions and were looked upon favourably by the *TUC.* This quest for change created conditions for the establishment of Black workers groups which mushroomed in several trade unions.

A similar message, emerging from several trade union race surveys, pointed to the need for the trade unions to create autonomous structures within the overall constitutional arrangements to guarantee that issues concerning race equality were top of the agenda of the decision-making structures of the unions.

This debate lasted for several years and as a result the *NUJ* changed its rules and replaced the *RRWP* with the current *Black Members' Council (BMC)* in 1990.

Its aims are to scrutinize and comment on the ethnic monitoring of *NUJ* members undertaken by the union and advise officials on how and where to recruit black members and retain them in membership. It is also involved in the elaboration of the Union's equal opportunities policy and the selection of staff. It engages media institutions and watchdogs on the issue of portrayal and advises on training and education. One of its campaigns has been to question the record of the Press Complaints Commission. It revealed that the Commission did not uphold a single one of the 112 complaints of representations to editors on issues of portrayals and employment.

It continues, as it predecessor body, to monitor the discrimination that is still rampart in the employment practices of many media organisations, and brings journalists together in workshops, conferences, roundtables and training seminars on race issues. One of its most recent successes had been the Media after Lawrence Conference – *Fresh start or the same old story?* – held in London in October 2000.

It leads campaigns inside the Union and the broader trade union movement and the media industry and represents the Union at seminars and congresses, such as the TUC annual Black Members' Conference.

It also acts as a formal liaison between the Union and the black communities and builds a critical relationship with the small but diverse black and ethnic minority media and the way in which it services their communities as well as addressing wider questions of ethnicity from a black perspective.

The *BMC* now plays a central role in the work of the ***International Media Working Group against Racism and Xenophobia (IMRAX)*** – founded and steered by the *IFJ.* This includes setting up networks with European journalists, campaigners, broadcasters and media professionals in a programme helping journalists deal with racism and xenophobia. Its website, ***IMRAX*** **www.diversity-online.org** is supported by the *BMC,* I am its co-editor, and it aims to provide journalists and other media workers with a 'one-stop shop' resource to encourage the fair reporting and writing of stories concerning ethnicity, racism, tolerance, xenophobia. anti-Semitism, minority rights and refugee and asylum matters, which do not always get fair treatment.

Here are some of the journalists who were and are still involved in the *BMC.* So far six have become members of the almost lily-white *NUJ* NEC and two of us have become President. **Alex Pascall, Marc Wadsworth, Rotimi Sankore** – a seasoned, provocative and un-awed human rights journalist from Nigeria who is also involved in fighting for a free democratic press in Africa; **Adli Hawwari –** a campaigning broadcast journalist; have all been *NEC* members. **Jim Boumelha,** a tireless and productive intrepid journalist, who spearheaded the changes from the *RRWP* to the *BMC,* had been NEC member and was the second black President of the NUJ in 1993. He was a sub-editor in magazines, press officer in Haringey (London) Council and is currently Honorary Treasurer of the *IJF.* He compellingly lobbies for quality journalism and better training. Others have played or are playing their part. **Beulah Ainley, Hal Austin, Simon Hinds, Sarah Olowe, Sohair Soliman, Arjum Wajid, James Jukwey** and **Themon Djaksam.** The cartoonist **Tayo Fatunla,** who has exhibited his work internationally and produced cartoons and illustrations for newspapers, **Barbara Campbell** (who was an editor of ***New Journal*** and now edits an informative and lively monthly ***Live Listings Magazine)*** and **Chinedu Onyejelem,** who runs a paper in Ireland. I have been treasurer of the **BMC** for the past 7 years. The *BMC* has its own newsletter, ***The Black Journalist* –** edited by **Jim Boumelha** – which is a popular voice for black journalists and highlights race and media issues.

The ***BMC*** founded the *Claudia Jones Annual Memorial Lecture* in honour of **Claudia Jones** in 2002 and two distinguished black colleagues have so far been invited to speak on relevant present day issues as they affected Black and Asian communities and journalists. The Inaugural Annual Lecture was delivered by **Professor Harry Golbourne** of South Bank University, London, who set the record straight in telling the story of **Claudia Jones** and her legacy to all journalists, and the second Annual Lecture by **Professor Manning Marable** of Columbia University. **Marable** has written a political commentary series, *'Along the Color Line,'* that appears in over four hundred newspapers and journals worldwide and he is regularly featured in national and international media. His incisive, consummating, fully explorative and eye-opening lecture *'Structural Racism in the United States Today: A Rendezvous with Race and History',* sets it in the context of the struggle in America and makes it possible for black media workers to contextualise the Black struggle and presence in this country.

CHAPTER 8

Training and Employment

An illuminating survey on employment of black journalists carried out in 1974 by the ***NUJ's*** Birmingham Branch, after prodding from the Freelance Branch, where I had initiated discussions on race and media issues in the Branch, showed that Birmingham had no black journalists despite a large black population.

As one of its first practical step, the *Race Relations Sub Committee* sent a questionnaire to all NUJ branches seeking information about the discrimination on grounds of race and colour.

The questionnaire covered the number of black journalists employed; sizes of immigrant communities; possible reasons why few black people apply to be journalists and whether concern was felt about this; coverage of ethnic minority group stories; attitudes about positive discrimination against black people in employment or news coverage; how chapels and branches were contributing and promoting racial harmony; unfair reporting or unnecessary mention of race or colour; and omission of relevant information, unfair selection of material, or omitting to publish at all.

The response was interesting and enlightening. About 72 per cent of the branches replied. A preliminary analysis of the replies confirmed our fears on the question of employment, that only a handful of black journalists were employed.

The Black Media Workers' Association (BWMA) was one of the most important pressure groups to have emerged in the 1983 media scene. It vigorously pushed for an equal deal in training and employment opportunities for black workers in the mainstream press and broadcasting. And also pressed for better training, pay and working conditions for workers in the independent black controlled press and energetically campaigned against racist contents. Founded in 1981, with an inaugural meeting attended by over 100 people working full-time and freelances in the mainstream British press and broadcasting as well as the black press, the ***BMWA's*** research report – *Black Workers' in the Media* – provided definitive evidence of exactly how few people there were working in all areas of media work.

The 1982 research, which was carried out by **Marina Salandy-Brown,** a resolute professional broadcaster, identified 684 people working in all mainstream newspapers and broadcasting, representing dismally 0.07 per cent of the total British media workforce of approximately 40,000. At that time it could be established only 35 black people were found working in British television It also highlighted that in all sectors of the media industry, apart from radio, the proportion of black employment was below 1.5 per cent and some sectors such as the mainstream journalism the proportion was 0.17 per cent of the 3,400 people employed as freelances. The black and Asian media, including regional community publications, employed about 370 people. This was more than any other sector of the media.

The career structure in the black media was dogged by the lack of financial resources. And according to the research, there was very little sideways mobility for journalists and no possibility of moving into the main stream local papers which could enhance career opportunities. Unlike mainstream newspapers, work in ethnic minority newspapers were not clearly demarcated – the journalist worked as a reporter, news-editor, sub-editor, advertising executive, circulation manager and editor, all rolled into one.

Some of the people actively involved in the ***BMWA*** were **Sadhana Ghose** – full-time national organiser and co-ordinator; **Diane Abbott** – secretary, **Shiv Ayer** – an industrious, and able writer, **Glen Noble, Lynda Syed, Lynn Campbell, Shehina Fazal, Naqi Ali, Beulah Ainley** – and as training officers were **Mike Phillips** and myself.

The ***BMWA*** decided to help in training black people in journalism skills and with a grant from the *Greater London Council (GLC).* The journalism training course, a short-term training project and news-pool, was situated at the then *Polytechnic of Central London, now University of Westminster.* It was the first 'taster' part-time journalism training course in Britain for black and Asian students. I ran the Print Course and **Mike Phillips** the Radio Course. It was popular and oversubscribed.

The major media employers consistently advanced the excuse that not many black people apply for jobs in the media, and also that not many trained black professionals were available for work.

In 1984, as the Chief Public Relations and Press Officer of the **CRE,** I challenged this absurd theory and managed to persuade the *Manpower Services Commission* to finance the first full-time one-year course in journalism for black and Asian men and women. When the London College of Printing was given the opportunity – with a generous grant – to set-up an ethnic minority journalism course they refused. They argued that having an ethnic minority journalism course was reverse racism – their journalism courses should be open to ALL. I called their reasons '*recidivist*' racism.

The journalism course at the college was overwhelmingly white and there were no incentives by the college to recruit black journalists or lecturers, or include diversity issues-like anti-racism/sexism issues – in their journalism syllabuses. *The Polytechnic of Central London* (now the *University of Westminster)* was more open to change, jumped at the offer, and welcomed help in devising the syllabus. The *Polytechnic* recruited **Mike Phillips** as its first black radio journalism lecturer, after we lobbied for this position. Some of the first graduates from this course managed to get into mainstream papers and broadcasting and the course continued at the *Westminster University* for a number of years. Later I became an External Examiner of the MA (International) Journalism Course at the University.

A few years later, using what we had learned, I teamed up with **Tony Goldman.** He was an experienced Jewish local journalist and an incisive sub-editor who is also one of the best journalism lecturers and now co-editor, with me, of **www.diversity-online.org.** We set up a series of successful ground-breaking journalism courses for ethnic minority journalism students at Lambeth College, London. For the first time. diversity issues, which included black history, ethical, race and gender issues, were included and integrated into the syllabuses, and some were later used in some journalism colleges and universities, both in this country and Europe.

Over 5 years we trained over 200 black journalism students, who graduated from the National Council of Training Journalism (NCTJ) and NVQ Level 4 courses. Some of them are now working for local and national newspapers and broadcasting. But most of them did not get jobs in the newspaper industry and broadcasting, not because they were not successful graduates, but because the goal posts were again changed by editors. The circular excuse – first that there were no black journalists, then that they were not trained, and when they were trained, their faces did not match their lily-white newsrooms.

The Illusive Number of Black Journalists

The actual number of black journalists in the mainstream newspapers and broadcasting was always a slippery guesstimate number.

How many black and Asian journalists are there now in the media industry? In 1975 we knew the number of journalists generally. There were only 22000 journalists in the UK and there were less than a dozen black and Asian journalists.

Eight years later the *Black Media Workers Association (BMWA)* in 1983 were able to publish a survey *Black Workers in the Media Industries.* The 684 black people identified working in all media, apart from the black press, represented 0.07 per cent of the total media force.

In the early 1990s, the number of black members in the *NUJ* had increased to about 1.9% from the 0.8% of 1975., and the national minority population is now 5.27% compared to 3% in 1975. On the face of it there are more black faces – more visible yes – but then there are also measurably more white faces.

And then in 1999 :

- London-based national papers (13 in number) employed only ten ethnic minority editors, 13 writer/reporters and one columnist.
- Throughout the entire ITV network, there were fewer than 160 ethnic minority staff in programme departments.
- The proportion, out of a total of 8100 staff employed by ITV and Channel 4, just 300 (3.7 per cent) came from ethnic minorities.
- The proportion of people from ethnic minorities employed by the BBC in London, where most of the staff is based, actually fell from 7.5 per cent in 1996-97 to 7.4 per cent in 1997-98.
- The situation in magazines and local and regional newspapers was even worse, and we could not get a number.

By mid 2002, the august *Journalism Training Forum,* an advisory body, funded by two national training organisations, conducted a new survey across the whole landscape of UK journalism. Some of the key facts were that there are roughly 70,000 journalists in Britain and by 2010, research suggests there will be a further 20,000. Of the 70,000 – 60,000 are in publishing and 10,000 in broadcasting. Journalists are mostly white (96 per cent) indicating that they do not come close to reflecting, in ethnic terms, the populations among which they work. About 4 percent of journalists came from ethnic backgrounds-and the rest from white middle-class families.

The *Forum* pointedly reported that it was clear that it needed to get its act together about ethnic diversity. The figures in this survey came as no surprise. We have been saying this for over 30 years, but what this survey now also indicates that there is now no hiding place. British journalism is an occupation which is in danger of drifting in the direction of an 'unintended apartheid'.

Without strong measures to address recruitment and career development of people from the black communities, British journalism has no chance of representing the communities it seeks to serve, and the communities from where the industry seeks to draw its advertising.

By the end of 2002, the *BMC* was able to report that there were nearly 800 black members of the NUJ and we were also able to identify some who were not in the Union. Most were freelance journalists, some in periodicals, regional papers and about two dozen in the national newspapers such as **Garry Younge**, a forceful, incisive provocative columnist, **Joseph Harker**, Assistant Comment Editor of ***The Guardian***, **Karmal Ahmad**, ***Observer*** reporter, **Wale Azeez**, Broadcast Editor of ***Press Gazette***, **Anita Singh** – ***Press Association***, **Navaz Batliwalia**, Fashion Editor of CosmoGIR and **Maya Jaggi**, writer of ***The Guardian*** and a distinguished author. The number in broadcasting is twice as big. They include **Sir Trevor MacDonald**, **Moira Stuart**, **Lisa Aziz**, main anchor on ***Sky News***, **Dippy Chaudhary** – ***BBC*** London, **George Alagiah** – anchor man at the ***BBC***, **Fatima Salaria**, ***BBC 2***, **Krishnan Guru-Murthy**, *Channel 4* News presenter, **Nadene Ghouri**, a journalist on ***Radio 5*** Live, BBC, **Clive Myrie** at the ***BBC***, **Konnie Huq**-Blue Peter presenter, and **Ragesh Omaar**, who was a trainee at ***The Voice*** and ***City Limits***. He is, the African Correspondent of the ***BBC***. According to many media colleagues, **Omaar** and **Clive Myrie**, are 'proving an inspirational figure for young black reporters'. **Omaar** is one of the most unassuming, unaffected journalist who is committed to his job.

We were able to report these figures because of our continuous insistence and pressure, for nearly 30 years, from the Union's Race Relations sub-committee, Race Relations Working Party, Black Members' Council and black members, for a comprehensive ethnic monitoring policy.

The BBC is committed to achieving overall ethnic minority employment levels of 10 per cent in 2003. **Channel 4** is currently employing nine per cent of staff from ethnic minority groups and this will be increased to more than 11 per cent by 2003, and will be revisited for 2005. There is also ethnic minority representation of the board of **Channel 4**, and three of the editorial heads of department/commissioning editors are from ethnic minority backgrounds (15 per cent)

Channel 5 currently employs 11.9 per cent of its staff from ethnic minority groups, and it has set a target of more than 13 per cent by 2003. Currently the company employs 8.12 per cent of its senior staff from ethnic minority background.

In 1987, the RRWP pushed for the creation of a *NUJ* Trust Fund – **The George Viner Memorial Fund Trust (GVMFT)** – which would financially help aspiring black journalism students with their college and university fees. *The Fund,* sponsoring black students to become journalists, is maintained by voluntary contributions and its main source of revenue is from the annual allocation of a percentage of *NUJ* members contributions. One of the main proponents of the Trust was **Beulah Ainley,** then a member of the RRWP and the BMC, and a freelance journalist. **Dr Ainley's** thesis looked at African-Caribbean and Asian people employed in the British media. She has been a Trustee of the Fund since its inception. Other Trustees are **Jim Boumelha, Jeremy Dear,** General Secretary of the NUJ, and **Carole Plaster,** the daughter of **George Viner,** the former Training Officer of the *NUJ,* after whom the Trust was named. I was actively involved in the founding of the Fund and has been Chair of the Trustees since its inception.

The *GVMFT* is the only such Fund in Britain. It has helped over 100 black journalism students with their course fees, books and accommodation, and has made it possible for them to get into a range of journalism learning centres, often unavailable to them before. Many of them now work in Black and mainstream Broadcasting and newspapers. Sponsors, such as **Lord Dholakia** and **Sir Bill Morris**, assisted the Fund Trust.

CHAPTER 9

Into the 1980's and the 1990

During this period various newspapers and magazines were launched like ***The Voice,*** **Weekly Journal,** ***The Nation, Pride, Westindian Post, Eastern Eye, Afro-Caribbean Post, Focus, Asianews, Community Roots Digest, Muslim News, RISINGSUN, Westindian Voice*** and ***Scope*** – a well documented feature bi-monthly life-magazine edited by **E. P. Rodriques.** The high mortality rate of some of these titles were sometimes Pickwickian, but it was The ***Voice Group*** and ***Ethnic Media Group*** which dominated the scene.

In 1982 ***The Voice*** newspaper was founded and published by **Val McCalla.** Born in Jamaica in 1943, **McCalla** arrived in Britain in 1959 and worked for the Royal Air Force (RAF) as a book keeper for 5 years. He worked as a reporter for the ***East End News,*** where he became editor of the paper's "Black Voice" pages. When the paper reached a funding crisis in 1982, **McCalla** left with some staff and set up ***The Voice*** in Bow, East London.

McCalla's ambition was to become one of the wealthiest black newspaper owners and one of his fellow shareholder said that **McCalla** was insistent that he was going to be the 'Murdoch' of the black media. He was resourceful, astute and believed that the financial problems of black papers lay in their difficulty to attract large white corporations and he was not shy to ask for government grants. In 1982 he approached the *CRE* with a business plan and made a request for a grant. This was unprecedented. The paper was little different from other black papers, except for the intention of making it available to a wider readership, and the *CRE* did not wish to favour one over others. A subsequent approach to the *Greater London Council (GLC)* was, surprisingly, successful and demonstrated **McCalla's** powers of persuasion with the assistance of **Alex Pascall,** who had joined him as a shareholder and who became responsible for the marketing and media relations of the new paper. It was the first time that the *GLC* or other government or local authority had given such a substantial grant to a black paper, although others had earlier demonstrated that they had a good record track.

McCalla and **Pascall** managed to persuade **Robert Govender,** who became editor, **Flip Fraser** and **Sharon Ali,** a young journalist, to leave ***Caribbean Times*** and join the paper.

There were promises of reliable pay cheques and better salaries than their competitors. Poaching from other newspapers was part of the history of the tabloids on which **McCalla** was modelling his paper. An aim was that the paper would become commercially viable. It was a professional product, well written, with modern typography in tabloid style.

However, controversy was immediate because of the emphasis on economic rather than ethical and political considerations. Up until then black papers had existed with assistance from the community and black businesses and had been unable to get a foot into the corporate advertising world because of their outward anti-discriminatory editorial philosophy. Early on the paper faced accusations of supporting companies which were upholding apartheid by trading with South Africa.

In addition he managed to get an attractive low interest loan from Barclays, the bank which was being boycotted by the anti-apartheid movement in Britain and South Africa. As a result some staff left.

Shareholders felt they were being short changed, as the profits were not forthcoming or they were being invested somewhere without their knowledge or approval. One of the dissatisfied shareholders was **Pascall,** who parted from **McCalla** with severe financial losses.

Nevertheless, circulation of ***The Voice*** increased and the paper was becoming one of the biggest black papers. Technologically the paper was modern and young writers joined. Good campaigns were run such as encouraging voters to register. A newsy, generously illustrated tabloid, with much space devoted to human interests as well, with profiles well crafted and story topics were sometimes of broader than minority interests.

Work conditions were, however, unacceptable. There was also inadequate training, an anti-union position was taken and staff were discouraged from joining the *NUJ.* Payment has always been a problem for reporters on black papers and, unfortunately, the promises made by ***The Voice,*** at the outset were not fulfilled. As one writer said of **McCalla:** *'Legend has it that in the earliest days,* **McCalla** *would bring in fewer salary cheques than there were employees, to be dished out on a first come, first-served basis'.* To some of the employees it was anything but a legend.

There were serious blind spots such as expressions of homophobia which was rife for many years in reporting and in editorials. Also at the time of discussion of the hated stop and search powers of the police which so adversely affected the black community, ***The Voice*** was alone among black papers in supporting the police in these issues. **McCalla** could also be ruthless with anyone who crossed him, and no one was immune from sudden sacking. As a result ***The Voice*** had more Industrial Tribunal complaints against it for unfair dismissals than any black or mainstream newspaper.

However, as a result of doing so well with advertising, **McCalla** decided to extend the company and purchased and relaunched a magazine, ***Pride,*** which was a classy magazine aiming for the up and coming young black reader, and edited by **Annie Steward.**

If the black newspaper in particular is to climb out of the position of being the second paper in the reader's fare it will more easily to do so if it attains a personality of its own. And such a personality is based heavily on a publication's physical appearance, quality and most important is its tone and affinity with the progression of the community, and not wallow in its lowest denomination. There is also the question of the relationship to advertisers and the scepticism of their readers from their papers' independence.

According to various staff the managerial atmosphere was not congenial and attempts were made by a number of staff to break away and start their own papers.

Joseph Harker assistant editor of the paper, in 1991 launched ***Black Britain,*** a weekly tabloid. He aimed at reporting the positive aspects of the black community and targeted a more upmarket audience. The response was good for a range of reasons including its positivity.

However, **McCalla** had never wanted competition and on this occasion responded by starting a "spoiler" paper, ***The Weekly Journal,*** a broadsheet. This was a regular ploy by Fleet Street papers when a new interloper appeared. Using the facilities of its sister paper it enabled its viability. Unable to compete, ***Black Britain*** folded a year later and **Harker** now has a senior editorial post in the ***Guardian.***

The Weekly Journal was unlike the tabloid ***The Voice.*** It was a serious, thoughtful, readable paper edited by **Isabel Appio** and **Richard Adeshayo,** a well respected and professional journalist, and was welcomed.

It was at this time when the Apartheid regime was on its way out and it became possible for all political exiles to return to the country of their birth, that **McCalla** approached me to help him in introducing his two papers, ***The Voice*** and ***The Weekly Journal,*** and ***Pride*** magazine into South Africa. We would first concentrate on ***Pride*** and ***The Weekly Journal*** and would also share black South African and British black experiences, problems, struggle against racism and inequalities and the issue of media and race. It was an experimental but viable proposal which was welcomed by black South African media workers. I set up an office in central Johannesburg and recruited a black South African reporter, contacted printing press companies, and set up a Board of Directors. Proceeds of profits would go substantially to the South African ***Voice*** group which would develop the SA subsidiary company and train and employ more black journalists. When everything had been set up, **McCalla,** with no call or consultation, a few months later whimsically reneged on all financial and employment agreements. It seemed that he urgently needed money to keep his personal horse racing commitments. As a result of his action I had to terminate the employment of the local journalist and close the spaciously newly opened office. His precipitated and cavalier action resulted in legal labour action in South Africa and antagonised disappointed black journalists. I battled bitterly, but successfully, with **McCalla** to ensure that the reporter would get a decent severance pay package, after **McCalla** had tried to pay the journalist only one month's salary.

The Weekly Journal was 'sold' to its editor, **Isabel Appia,** and became ***The New Journal,*** under the editorship of **Barbara Campbell,** a competent and eager journalist. It was reorganised and began to make money.

After ***The Weekly Journal*** was "sold", **Richard Adeshayo** attracted money from the son-in-law of **Rupert Murdoch** to set up ***The New Nation,*** a tabloid weekly, in competition with ***The Voice*** and attracted a number of experienced journalists, many from ***The Voice,*** who were disgruntled with the paper.

McCalla apparently still had the majority share in ***The Weekly Journal*** that he had "sold". He therefore clawed it back a year later in 1997 and again took over ***The New Journal.*** **Barbara Campbell,** one of the many successful graduates of the pioneer all-black Lambeth College's Journalism Training Course, left the paper and launched her own monthly magazine ***Live Listing,*** a magazine aimed at young black people, which now has a circulation of 50,000. The monthly has a number of young journalists such as **Domin Harewood, Lorna Campbell, Aysha Igba, Claudette Althea-Douglas, Rani Singh, Ama Badu** and **Kemi Lewis.**

Some of the editors and journalists of ***The Voice Group*** included **Winsome Cornish,** who became Head of Programming at ***Spectrum Radio,*** **Steve Pope, Mike Best, Isabel Appia, Richard Adeshayo** and **Claire Hines,** who later worked at the **BBC, Annie Steward, Deidre Forbes,** who is now Group Editor of the paper, **Vic Motune, Shirin Agular** and **Jesse Quinones.**

When **McCalla** died in 2002 he left a seemingly financially stable company. His family took over the reins and **Linda McCalla,** his wife, became managing director of the company. But even a few days before his death, the instant scalp was again in action when the incumbent editor **Mike Best** was unfairly dismissed. This was dealt with by an Employment Industrial Tribunal.

There is no doubt that **McCalla's** papers did as earlier black papers, especially ***West Indian World,*** did before him. At a time of limited opportunities, doors opened for black people to the alabaster newsrooms of mainstream papers and broadcasting. A number of the journalists who worked for him went further ahead to mainstream newspapers, broadcasting and other professions.

The New Nation's proprietor ran into difficulty and could not continue to support the paper and it was sold to ***Ethnic Media Group*** whose managing director was **Garry Gurmeet. Gurmeet** added ***The New Nation*** to ***Eastern Eye.*** Later, in 1997, he bought ***Caribbean Times, African Times*** and ***Asian Times*** from ***Hansib Publications.*** There are now two big publishing companies, ***The Voice Group,*** and the ***Ethnic Media Group,*** the latter of which is the bigger and has interests in Europe.

The position a black paper or a chain or group of such papers should take in the racial turmoil of today is one of the major problems facing the owners and publishers. Here it is enough to note that the large black newspapers that support the ideal of justice for black citizens in all matters are impatient with the issues of discrimination, exclusion from the citadels of power making and institutional racism. Those that are cautious, non-committal, or mostly silent are experiencing circulation problems. The highest circulations of all are held by those papers that take strong stands on issues.

Eastern Eye is a professionally edited weekly paper, aimed at the Asian community. It is sensational in the presentation of news and views, but does not make an apology for that. It's former editor and founder, **Sarwar Ahmad,** indefatigable and businesslike, became chief-editor of ***The New Nation*** when it joined its stable. He told me at that time that *'we shall go on being sensational to the best of our ability. Sensationalism does not mean distorting the truth. It means vivid and dramatic presentation of events so as to give them a lasting impact on the mind of the reader'.* In summing up this view I interpret that it means big headlines, vigorous writing, simplification into everyday language, and the use of illustration by photograph. This is really a credo of all tabloid craftsmen. There are so many problems facing us and they will only be understood by others who are busy with their daily tasks in fighting racism and discriminations, if they are hit hard and often with the facts and truths. As a tabloid journalist colleague used to tell me: *'readers prefer the vigorous to the timid and the vivid to the dull'.*

On the ***Eastern Eye,*** its editor is now **Amar Singh,** and there are others as **Burthan Ahmad, Maria Ahmed, Sarah Gill, Asjad Nazir, Herpeet Grewal** and **Saleem Usmani.**

Sarwar Ahmad, left ***Eastern Eye*** and founded and became editor of ***Asian Xpress,*** where he used the same successful production and editorial methods. Its managing editor is **Sanjay Gohil,** and staff such as **Aysha Igbal, Virchand Pindoria, Poorna Shetty, Fuad Omar, Reena Bagga** and **Zulika Bibi.** The ***Asian Xpress*** is now competing with the ***Eastern Eye*** for young Asian readers.

As the ***The New Nation*** joined the ***Ethnic Media Group*** it had a good track as its dowry, but it still had to join its 'sensational' credo. The weekly, under the editorship of **Michael Eboda,** flamboyant, professional former Fleet Street reporter, became a forceful, sombre paper, which mixes vigorous writing, campaigning editorials with quality photos and large headlines. Staff on ***The New Nation*** include **Janise Elie,** as chief sub-editor, **Justin Onyeka,** as its ***Pulse Editor,*** **Adenike Adenitire, Akosua Annobil-Dodoo, Lianne Dillsworth,** its junior news reporter, **Jerome Defreitas,** and sports reporters **Ronnie Ruff** and **Raymond Enisuoh.**

Many of ***The New Nation's*** stories are fact laden and enjoyable. It is stimulating to go through the paper because of the large amount of original news coverage, especially written features and orderly plan of content. Refreshingly, it is in the mould of earlier campaigning papers like ***West Indian World*** and ***Caribbean Times*** in its near earlier days, those of ***Flamingo*** and ***West Indian Gazette*** in the 1960s, and ***African Times and Orient Review*** and the ***African Telegraph*** in the early years of the 20th Century.

The Ethnic Media Group titles have the same format, similar typography and layout and the editorial strategy of the newsgroup eloquently illustrates the different audiences that are commercially and politically identifiable within the black community. And here again it learned from the editorial and political strategy of ***Hansib Publications.***

Many of the journalists on these papers, magazines and broadcasting stations are young and aspiring. This is a positive trend and will be an effervescent push to help change the face of black journalism and assist in mainstreaming the British media.

Presently there are a number of other smaller and also newer papers and magazines, ethnic TV stations and ethnic radio stations.

There are about 90 black newspapers, including Asian and Arabic language newspapers and magazines, 11 Radio Stations and 10-TV stations. About 2600 mainstream newspapers: 10 daily national newspapers, 9 Sunday national newspapers, 1,269 regional and local newspapers, 25 mornings, 74 evenings, 21 Sundays, 509 paid-for weeklies and 640 free weekly papers.

The 2003 updated and constant changing list of the black media, although a small percentage to the mainstream media, is testament to the mix and diversity of the black media in present multi-cultural and multi-racial Britain. Here, in 2003, the make-up and identity of communities can be seen to be reflected in the rich flora of the British minority ethnic press.

Newspapers and periodicals:

Asian Xpress (weekly) – Editor : **Sanjay Gohil**
AD-DIPLOMASI NEWS REPORT (weekly) – Editor: **Raymond Ataliah**
AL-ALAAM (weekly) – Editor: **Dr. Sead Mahamed Shehabi**
AL-AHRAM INTERNATIONAL (weekly) – Editor: **Abdalla Attia**
AL ARAB (daily) – Editor: **A. S. Elhluni**
AL HAYAT (daily) – Editor: **Jihad El Khazen**
AL MUHAJIR (fortnightly) – Editor: **Mr Mohammed Assou**
ASHARQ AL AWSAT (daily) – Editor: **Abdul Rathman Al-Rashid**
ANANDA BAZAR PATRIKA (Daily and Sunday weekly magazine, Bengali/English) – Editor **Shrabani Basu**
JANOMOT (weekly) – Editor: **Mr N. Uddin**
NOTUN DIN (weekly) – Editor: **M. Chowdhury**

PROBASHI SAMACHAR (quarterly) – Editor: **S. Mazumdar**
SURMA (weekly) – Editor: **Mohammed Choudhury**
WEEKLY POTRIKA **–** Editor: **A. U. S. Chowdhury**
SHANG YE XIAN FENG (bi-monthly) – Editor: **Emile Bekheit**
SING TAO DAILY (European edition, daily) – Editor: **Mr S. T. Wan**
THE AFRICAN (monthly) – Managing Editor: **Zaya Yeebo**
THE ASIAN AGE (daily) – Editor: **Abhik Sen**
ASIAN ENTERTAINMENT GUIDE (weekly) – Editor: **N. Gosai**
ASIAN EXPRESS (fortnightly) – Editor: **Vallabh Kaviraj**
THE ASIAN (fortnightly)
THE ASIAN NEWS (English) – Editor: **Mr M Shafique**
ASIAN TELEGRAPH (Telegraph On Line) – Editor: **Jafar Raza**
ASIAN TIMES (weekly) – Editor: **Ishara Da Silva**
CHINESE BUSINESS IMPACT – Editor: **Juliet Zhou and Jamie Kenny**
CHINATOWN MAGAZINE (bi-monthly) Editor: William Ong
CHUP MAGZINE (bi-monthly) – Editor: **Moni Ali**
ECHO ME (bi-monthly) – Editor: **Kemi Adebayo**
OPINION (monthly) – Editor: **Vipul Kalyani Kutir**
ASIAN VOICE SCOTLAND (weekly) – Editor: **Ian Stewart**
AWAAZ ASIAN VOICE (daily)
BLACK PERSPECTIVE (quarterly) – Editor: **Victor Amokeodo**
CARIBBEAN TIMES (weekly) – Editor: **Ron Shillingford**
CINEBLITZ (monthly) – Editor: **Dr Arvind Sikand**
CIPHER (bi-monthly) – Editor: **Joan Smith**
EASTERN EYE (weekly) – Editor: **Amar Singh**
THE FILIPINO (bi-monthly) – Editor: **Mr Bong**
THE GLEANER (weekly) – Editor: **Colette Hibbert**
IMPACT INTERNATIONAL (monthly) – Editor: **Ahmed Irfan**
INDIA ABROAD NEWSPAPER **–** Editor: **Sanjay Suri**
INDIA – HOME AND ABROAD (quarterly) – Editor: **K. Singh**
INDIA LINK INTERNATIONAL (bi-monthly) – Managing Editor: **D. Krishanna**
INDIA TIMES **–** Editor: **Ravinder Hanspal**
INDIA WEEKLY – Editor: **Regina Motalib**
INDIAN EXPRESS **–** Editor: **Shekar Gupta**
MAURITIAN INTERNATIONAL (quarterly) – Editor: **Jacques K. Lee**
MAURITIUS NEWS (monthly) – Editor: **Peter Chellen**
THE MUSLIM NEWS (monthly) – Editor: **Ahmed Versi**
THE NATION (English/Urdu) – Managing Editor: **Mr M. Sarwar**
NEW NATION (weekly) – Editor: **Michael Eboda**
NEW HORIZON (monthly) – Editor: **Mr Ghazanfar Ali**
NEW IMPACT JOURNAL (bi-monthly) – Editor: **Elaine Sihera**
NEW WORLD (weekly) – Editor: **Dhiren Basu**
THE NEWS **–** Editor: **Zahoor Niazi/Shahid Ullah**
NIGERIAN NEWS (fortnightly) – Editor: **Olubiyi Ayodeji**
NORTH WEST ASIAN NEWS (monthly) – Editor: **Steve Hammond**
PAHAYAGAN (Filipino bi-monthly) – Editor: **Mrs C. Pedrosa**

PRIDE MAGAZINE (monthly) – Editor: **Amina Taylor**
Q NEWS INTERNATIONAL – Editor: **Shagufta Yakub**
SALAAM! (monthly) – Publisher: **Khan Iqbal Khan**
SCOTLAND'S ORACLE **–** Editor: **Ahsan ul haq**
2ND GENERATION (bi-monthly) – Editor: **Imran Kahn**
SHANTI COMMUNICATIONS (news agency) – Editor: **Parveez Syed**
THE SIKH COURIER INTERNATIONAL (quarterly) – Editor: **A. S. Chatwal**
THE SIKH MESSENGER (quarterly) – Editor: **Indarjit Singh**
SPICE MAGAZINE (monthly) – Editor: **Parminder Singh**
TEAMWORK (bi-monthly) – Editor: **E. Francis**
TOUCH MAGAZINE (monthly) – Editor: **Vincent Jackson**
THE VOICE (weekly) – Editor: **Diedre Forbes**
GARAVI GUJARAT (weekly)
ASIAN ***TRADER*** (fortnightly) – Editor: **Ranniklal C Solan**
GUJARAT SAMACHAR (weekly)
ASIAN VOICE/ASIAN CONVENIENCE RETAILER – Editor: **C. B. Patel**
AMAR DEEP HINDI (weekly) – Editor: **J. M. Kaushal**
NAVIN WEEKLY – Editor: **Ramesh Kumar**
AWAZE QUAM INTERNATIONAL (weekly) – Editor: **Raghbir Singh**
PARDESI PUNJAB **–** Editor: **Pritam Singh Rahi**
PERDESAN MONTHLY – Editor: **Mrs G. K. Bedi**
THE PUNJABI GUARDIAN (fortnightly) – Editor: **Inder Jit Singh Sandhu**
PUNJAB MAIL INTERNATIONAL (monthly) – Editor: **Gurdip Singh Sandhu**
PUNJAB TIMES INTERNATIONAL (weekly) – Editor: **Harjinder Singh Mandair**
WEEKLY DES PARDES – Editor: **Mr Virk**
THE DAILY JANG – Editor: **Zahoor Niazi**
MILAP WEEKLY **–** Editor: **Ramesh Soni**
RAVI NEWS WEEKLY – Editor: **Shappir Moughal**
SADA URDU MONTHLY – Editor: **Iqbal Mirz**

Radio Stations
ASIAN SOUND RADIO – Head of Programmes: **Paul Shah**
CHOICE FM (South London Radio) – Programme Director: **Patrick Berry**
GALAXY 102.2 – Programme Director: **Alex Carruthers**
GALAXY 105 – News Editor: **Pete Wilson**
KISS 100 FM – ***Programme Controller:*** **Andy Roberts**
RADIO CEREDIGION – Head of Programmes: **Sharar Shahwan**
RADIO ASIA – Contact: **Shanta Saluja**
RADIO XL – Prog Director: **Barry Curtis**
SABRAS SOUND LTD – Contact: **Don Kotak**
SPECTRUM RADIO – Head of Programmes: **Winsome Cornish**
SUNRISE RADIO – Chief Executive: **Dr Avtar Lit**

TV Stations
APNA – TV Editor: **Daxa Joshi**
ASIA 1 TV – Contact: **Sam Thaper**

ASIA NET LTD – Chief Executive: **Dr Barnard Viswanath**
ASIAN TELEVISION – Station Controller: **Mr Shafaat Choudhry**
CHINESE NEWS & ENTERTAINMENT – News Editor: **Poon Sui Mui**
MIDDLE EAST BROADCASTING (MBC) – Chief Executive: **Ali Al-Hadaithi**
NAMASTE ASIAN TELEVISION NETWORK EAST– Head of Asian Programming: **Paresh Solanki**
SONY ENTERTAINMENT T.V. ASIA – Contact: **Rajan Singh**
ZEE TV – News Editor: **Anita Anand**

CHAPTER 10

The Black Press and its Future.

As shown before there is a very considerable infrastructure of black media and this rich reservoir of a Century of black newspapers and magazines is an indication that the internal mix found within the black community is to some extent reflected in the diversity of print media available to serve them.

Some of the black press was, and is, unequivocally and unashamedly partisan; seeing itself as *'the voice of the community'*. In taking this position they are acknowledging the distinct processes of social exclusion that defines the situation of *'their community'* in relation to the majority population. They are also indicating, sometimes vehemently, the failure of the majority 'mainstream' – white press – to accurately and appropriately reflect this reality.

The black media undoubtedly helped the *'invisible'* community understand, and then realise, their political potential. In fact, some Black and Asians, used journalism as a springboard into politics. Many of those have been profiled in these pages. For some such political positioning, campaigning journalism, is passé and sometimes not relevant to the interests of their younger readers, whom they define as British and young as well as having minority ethnic identity.

There are clearly papers that in their editorial position and identified target audience seek to address the informational needs of first generation migrants and older members of minority ethnic communities. This divergence is apparent in the house style of particular papers and its implications for the future development of black media is interesting.

Future researchers will find a mélange of formats, styles of writing and viewpoints when they examine the 100 year-old black weeklies and monthlies that exist in the shadows of the white mainstream newspapers and magazines. There existed, as chronicled earlier, for instance, in the 1960s a group of vigorous if not always well produced papers, some energetic in aims, others clumsily written and edited, and still others sedate and substantial in their news coverage. Here is also a real choice to be had amongst papers offering a choice of language, a choice of editorial commitment to social, religion and politics reflected in the rich flora of the British ethnic media.

Then there were also some who in their business operations experienced the uncertainties and obstacles like many of the latter 'new technology' produced tabloids, and appeared for a year or two and then departed. This haemorrhage was unnerving. They have the same tentativeness, the same insecurity, same shrillness of tone. Both are deeply concerned with the right to raise the black people to first class citizenship, along with other goals and all the major activities that were directed towards the question of equality and fairness springs from an ethos-a group spirit. Both types are essentially opinion papers, voices of protest.

Protest papers, as has been shown, are nothing new in black journalism. The successful and influential black local and national voices are those that seek not only to arouse their readers to do something about the injustices of the day, but also are service papers that give readers a substantial budget of news and facts that support opinions. Clustered in other conurbations, weeklies and monthlies will turn up, some commercial, some mere political tracts.

The rationale for many a black newspaper was described by one of the editors of such a paper when he said that his paper was *'to bring out the positive things',* and the mainstream white media, he said, print only such black news as crime rates and immigration figures in the black community. *'Financially',* he said further, the paper *'has been a disaster, but it has been a gratifying experience to see how the black people in this country have responded to our efforts.'*

Many black journalists want meaningful work which contributes to the solution of social problems facing the nation or humanity as a whole. The pursuit of personal affluence may be the goal of many journalists or would be journalists but by no means all. Some uncounted number is standing off critical of the status quo, seeking ways to have its part in eliminating or correcting what is wrong.

It is also true that in various fields, a measurable percentage of the black people have moved up the ladder in the last decades. Their achievements can be measured from two points of view-the comparatively and the proportional. When one compares the present status of blacks with what went before, an optimistic picture emerges-more black faces on TV screens, more by-lines of black journalists in mainstream newspapers, lawyers, doctors, businessmen and women, MP's and local councillors-but when one compares achievement in statistical terms as a proportion of the population, the picture is rather dismal. These are some of the inferences to be drawn from what we know and see.

Idealistic black journalists are also torn between the opportunities offered in the white and the black worlds of journalism. They see on the one hand, the higher salaries in white mainstream papers, the prestige connected with certain publications, and the chances for future accomplishments, especially in these days when blackness alone offers an entry to some positions.

Another point of view exists, however. The black press in the opinion of many black people themselves, is 'beautiful', and deserves the loyalty of the people it is published to serve. Because it is not getting such fealty, publishers of newspapers are confronted with numerous problems. There are staffing, the philosophical and political battles going on in the black society, the broader interests of the enlarging black population or market, as the businessmen call it, the methods of reaching a receptive black community, the temptation to pander for the sake of advertising, the threat of new competition, and the antagonism towards unionisation.

The beckoning finger of opportunity, part of a holding for higher salary cheques than most of the black press can afford, comes not only from the offices of the relatively few affluent black publishers. A look at the biographies of the black journalists chronicled in these pages, shows that a large number went either from small black and pioneering publications to the larger ones or left black journalism for white ones entirely.

The *'come join us'* invitations now arrive more often and strongly than ever before from broadcasting companies, public relations agencies and other divisions of white industries and professional groups.

This staff raiding undercuts the possibilities of building reasonably permanent staffs on the black publications. Also irritating black owners is the fact that although financial conditions are improving for a few of them, enabling them to do somewhat better with salaries than before, they have not yet become competitive, by any means.

If the large black papers and magazines survive it must win white as well as black readers to be of influence in the white world as well as the black. This effort can be motivated by both the desire for commercial success as well as the hope of bringing about greater understanding between the people of each race. It is dubious, however, that it can offset the economic hazards of mass circulation. Black journalists must, constantly and attentively, keep their ears to the ground for the big story that affects the black community one way or the other and the black press for the sake of its own survival has an opportunity now to play an important part by providing leadership to its readers by its editorial, commentary and news emphasis. It is a responsibility and challenge which involves not only black journalists and the black media but as in the words of that great black American civil rights leader **Whitney Young** *'The Open Society will come about when ALL decent people, both blacks and whites, are galvanised to change the present society'.*

Every house has its foundation and every community its history. This is a contribution to the history of black Britain. By looking at the last hundred years of black journalism in Britain, we can perceive what to and what not to aim for in the 21st Century. Black consciousness is good if it allow more light and understanding of the complex struggles still looming ahead.

What we have to understand, is that somewhere the soul of this ethos which continuously and sharpening manifest itself, are the techniques and means of our elevation. The question remains, what has changed? When shall we reach beneath the surface, beneath the concrete of the practical hour and its headlines and deadlines? How do we learn to touch those things which we are real, which are ours? How do we get to that dirt path....? It is likely, therefore, that a black press will always be available in the United Kingdom, unless *fully integrated* means the complete eradication of the black experience, culture, temperament, and personality. Whether it will be an important and influential press depends upon, among others, its acceptance or rejection by its natural audience, the course of the black revolution now under way and the social changes occurring without respect to race. Always in danger, the black press has survived for more than a century, despite great losses, and as an institution has continued. *'We need a press of our own',* wrote editor **Duse Mohamed Ali** in 1912 in London. It is no less true in the 21st Century.

ADDENDUM

In this section of Part I my contribution derives from my own particular personal experience in working in British news media and reporting race relations and dovetails into the preceding Chapters. It provides a powerful indictment of the British Press, and what it does indicate how various are the pressures, from outright job discrimination, racism in the media and newsrooms, lack of training, colour blindness and financial leverage to the everyday routines of journalism which make responsible reporting of race relations so difficult to achieve. In the final analysis the growth of minority people in Britain has forced the 'white' media to re-examine the ways they have traditionally dealt with minority groups.

*A BLACK JOURNALIST'S EXPERIENCE OF BRITISH JOURNALISM

One autumn morning in early November 1969, I had an appointment at the editorial offices of a liberal daily morning paper. The appointment had been arranged a few days earlier, after I had made enquiries about a possible subbing vacancy on the paper. I had been asked by the then night editor either to contact him or the chief sub.

I announced my presence that morning to the receptionist who then duly informed the night editor. He said he would come to see me.

After about ten minutes, a gentleman emerged from one of the sections on the floor, came down the foyer, passed me and the receptionist at her desk and peered around looking for someone. Not finding who he was looking for, he then approached the receptionist and asked her where *Mr Morrison* was, as he could not see him. The receptionist had the grace to blush and pointed at me. The gentleman did not blush, introduced himself as the night editor and invited me to an office for a talk where the chief sub would join us.

As I got up to follow him, I pondered the problems of having a Scottish surname and an 'non-black' accent, and of not having informed him before that I was a black journalist.

The interview, especially with the chief sub who put me through a thorough interview, was, however, fruitful. Another sub was leaving in two weeks and could I then start? They were happy with my qualifications and experience and wished me to start on the usual three months' probation. They would inform me when exactly to come in. Handshakes all round as I left, and I was prepared to forget the whole foyer incident. Had I not, after all, got the job?

A black journalist, I graciously argued, was the last person the night editor had expected to meet, especially since I had informed him in my letter that I had had newspaper experience in South Africa, Asia, Europe and other parts of Africa, had been to university and had travelled extensively. Experiences expected more from white journalist than black ones.

After two or three weeks there was no communication from the paper, and it was than that I saw an advertisement in the *UK Press Gazette* for a sub-editor for the same paper, requesting the same qualifications and experience as previously for the same job.

Needless to say, I did not apply for the post and have not heard since from either the night editor or the chief sub.

There was and still is no doubt in my mind that I did not get the job precisely because I was black. When I started applying for jobs in Fleet Street in 1968, after returning to this country from Africa and Asia where I had held senior journalistic posts, I did not for one minute think it would be easy. I knew there was race prejudice in Fleet Street and in the British news media as a whole. But I had hopes of exceptions, like the liberal paper of my memorable experience.

Blacks have been brought up to believe that the British 'liberal' press is the most enlightened, the most concerned and the most sympathetic. But my own experience and that of other black journalists tends to place a doubt on these general attributes.

Their news reports speak up strongly against racism, discrimination and prejudice, but unfortunately that is far as their liberalism goes. It does not extend inwards into the holy sanctum of the reporters' rooms where the media image we have of ourselves, whether black or white, is written or broadcast by a pure white hand.

It is this hypocrisy and dichotomy of standpoints on race, which is the hallmark of our liberal press in this country. So that the biblical injunction that it would be easier for a camel to squeeze through the eye of a needle than for a rich man to get into the kingdom of God, can aptly be applied to the heavenly world of British journalism, if one interchanged the rich man for a black journalist. Indeed it is so rare to meet a black journalist on British newspapers, TV and radio that the few who are there are real curiosities.

Of the 28,000 journalist working on British newspapers and magazines, less than two dozen (or 0.09per cent) are black. (Compare this to the country's black population percentage of about 3 per cent.) Most work on the various West Indian and Asian language papers and magazines and the overwhelming majority are unfortunately not trained nor professional in the journalistic sense. The rest, who are professional and experience number less than a dozen and work on the hundreds of daily, weekly and monthly British magazines which play such an enormous and vital role in shaping people's community and race relations ideas and actions.

There are two black journalists in training on two newspapers in the country at the moment. One in Bradford and the other on the *SouthEast London Mercury,* whose editor, *Roger Norman,* is one of the few local newspaper editors who does not hide behind a plethora of excuses like, 'if blacks would only apply', or, 'they don't have the right qualifications'.

In the subbing field there are more at Thomsons and the Westminster Press papers, where they are hidden behind desks away from the public that accompanies actual reporting.

The number of actual frontline black reporters is indeed rare and in Fleet Street I know of only two others beside myself.

It is quite true that journalistic standards for ordinary entry to the NCTJ (National Council for the Training of Journalists) proficiency certificate scheme have risen and candidates need at least five 'O' levels. And the tendency to go for graduates or 'A' level applicants has also increased. With the educational system as it is presently for black children, the problem becomes understandable. But an obsessive acceptance of this argument was quite rightly slammed by someone very well placed to know what he is talking about.

In a letter to the race relations journal, *Race Today* (September, 1973), *Mr J.*

Clement Jones, CBE, past Editor of the *Wolverhampton Express and Star* had this to say:

'There are now a number of alert young West Indians and Asians who would make every bit as good a showing as some of the white youngsters who offer themselves for selection and subsequent training as journalists. Much of the trouble is that dissuasion for blacks starts well before the selection stage – in fact by school careers masters and youth employment officers.

That the majority of editors who are in the market for trainees certainly are not racist is happily true. But the majority are content to take a passive line and to duck out from underneath, with the familiar formula 'of course, if the right black boy or girl came along etc....' and in this way they are aided by the career advisory system to preserve the status quo ante immigration (author's emphasis).

The position on the journalistic side of the communications industry is, however, in advance over the attitude on the printing and associated sides. I have watched black stone-hands and lino-operators working with considerable skill and expertise in their own countries, but there is overt colour prejudice in the print shops of Britain. Moreover, on the commercial side of the communications industry black advertisement representatives are regarded as a grave embarrassment when there has to be face-to-face confrontation a point of sale.

Sadly the race relations industry as a whole has chosen to look the other way when It comes to dealing with the communications industry, out of a sense of fear that if it embarrasses the industry on the equality of employment front, it will itself get inequality of treatment on the publicity front.

And commenting on *Race Today's* hope that the injunction of the Kerner Commission into Civil Disorders set up by *President Johnson* to inquire into the race riots in America in 1967, that 'The communications media (in the US), ironically, have failed to communicate and that they have not communicated to the majority of their audience – which is white – a sense of the degradation, misery and helplessness of living in the ghetto', should not come true in Britain, Mr Clement Jones says it is already too late. *'Of course we have failed, because we of the communications industry have never ever really wanted to succeed and consequently never tried'* (author's emphasis).

This serious indictment of the British press, by a respectable former editor of one of the leading provincial papers illustrates the hypocrisy, which governs the press's attitude to racism in theory and fact. It is so much easier to condemn racism in columns of print, but it is a different matter to do something positive about it, like training and employing black journalists.

My own experience in this field aptly illustrates this point. Between late 1968 and early 1969, after my interview with that liberal Fleet Street paper, I applied for *over ninety* jobs. Ninety per cent of these were advertised vacancies and the remaining a cross section of Fleet Street papers, which I thought or had heard might have a vacancy. Between the two sorts, I virtually covered the whole of Fleet Street except for about three or four papers.

The papers covered North, East, West and South England, the Midlands and most of Greater London papers.

I informed all but ten that I was a black journalist. I got replies from these ten. Three in the provinces offering me a job, the rest had already filled them. Because of the very low salary offered, I did not take any of the three offered jobs.

Of the eighty whom I had informed that I was a black journalist, 45 per cent had the courtesy to reply. Some of those who did not reply went on advertising for the vacancies weeks afterwards.

The standard reply from the 45 per cent (or forty replies) were:

(a) The Posts were filled and they thanked me for applying. (Fifteen replies)

(b) The post were unfortunately filled, but they were grateful for my interest and would retain my application in their files should a review of the position or another vacancy arise in the future.(Twelve replies)

(c) They were seeking professionals from UK papers only. This was not to say they would necessarily exclude journalists from overseas under different circumstances. (Eight replies.)

(d) The vacancies were filled, or they had no vacancies presently, but they would like to meet me. (Five replies.)

In relation to:

(a) Advertisements for the same post in at least half the papers appeared two or three weeks after their replies to me.

(b) None ever contacted me again, in spite of the fact that numerous vacancies appeared in their respective newspapers during the past three years.

(c) White South African, Rhodesian, Australian and New Zealand journalists who had never actually worked on UK papers before got jobs from these paper with no difficulty.

(d) When I went to see those in this category, it was clear that 80 per cent wanted to see me out of sheer curiosity. As one editor remarked to me: *'it is the first time I've had the pleasure of speaking to a coloured journalist who was resident in this country'.* The remaining 20 per cent were genuine in their attempts to help me on a freelance basis, as they had no staff jobs available. They included the then editor of *The People,* Mr Bob Edwards (now editor of the *Sunday Mirror)* to whom I owe a lot.

In my quest for a job, the papers I had not approached in Fleet Street included the *Telegraph* and the Beaverbrook Press groups. The reasons were obvious. These papers I had been told and believed were so right-wing, especially as far as race relations reportage was concerned, that for a black journalist even to harbour the thought of contributing to them was a gross sacrilege. As my efforts to get a decent job on any British paper failed one after the other.

I decided to go freelance. I took a pot shot at the *Sunday Telegraph* for freelance assignments. To my surprise I found this paper had none of the hypocrisy which so many Fleet Street papers so vociferously suffer from when it comes to accepting contributions from a black freelance. *George Evans,* assistant editor of the *Sunday Telegraph* and in charge of the famous in-depth and investigative 'Close-up' section of the paper, asked me after a long discussion to help the Close-up team in some of their investigations. This was the beginning of a fruitful journalistic liaison between me and the *Sunday Telegraph.*

Although I must categorically state that I do not share the paper's general stand on race relations, I would not and have never been asked to write anything on race relations, which was against my beliefs.

I also started freelancing, with long contracts, with *The People* at about the same time, where I found a similar non-hypocritical atmosphere.

Because of the political and racial atmosphere which then prevailed – Powellism was at its height – and the competitive journalistic market, there was no alternative but to specialise in race and community relations even though one resented the Fleet Street assumption that black journalists were only good and expert on reporting exclusively about blacks.

It might be asked why do black journalists accept this situation? The answer can be nothing but a purely pragmatic and non-altruistic one.

Fleet Street is saturated and it is the vogue, whether one likes it or not, for specialization.

To make a living it is best for a black journalist, especially where and when there is no encouragement for him to report on general matters, and where in any case he would be trampling on someone else's toes, to capitalize on his position of being black. One can also argue that it is better for a capable and involved black journalist, knowledgeable of the black scene, that a white 'black expert', to report first-hand on blacks in this country.

I think, however, there is a line which black journalists must draw in this argument. If it means being given race relations stories, especially when they are treated on a crisis scale, then no self-respecting black journalist worth his salt should accept such a commission. It is the duty of all journalists, both black and white, as well as editors and broadcasting authorities to make every effort to portray ethnic groups in other than conflict situations. Jamaican-born *Barbara Blake,* who worked for both Thames and ATV, left and returned to her native country precisely because she felt she was being given race relations stories when they were handled as 'the wogs are making trouble again'.

In deciding to specialize as a black 'black expert', I found no difficulties on certain papers where my special knowledge was welcomed. The problem arose on the so-called liberal papers who had their own white 'black experts', their own race relations experts.

These experts are the ones who have fashioned to a great extent the stand of their various papers on race relations. They are the 'experts' on blacks. They jealously guard their position and resist any newcomers and intruders in the field. They react even more vehemently when the intruders are black. This, no doubt, is a consequence of the old paternalistic doctrine which was and still is so strong among some liberals. They know the black; his desires and shortcomings better than blacks themselves.

Papers like the *Sunday Telegraph,* the *Sunday People*, and the *Evening Standard* are, I found in my experience, the few exceptions in this regard. The white 'black experts' on the *Sunday Telegraph* were no woolly-footed liberals, nor pretended to be, and in line with earlier observations did not see in me a threat. Instead they welcomed and respected my expertise, and my viewpoint.

A similar atmosphere has prevailed at the *Evening Standard,* a Beaverbrook paper and the evening stable-mate of the right-wing *Daily Express.* The *Evening Standard,* to the surprise of the black community, has pioneered reports on blacks by a black journalist himself. Not just the odd feature, which is the discerning, mark among the 'liberal' papers, but constant, regular reports. There is no doubt that the stand taken by the *Evening Standard* has helped tremendously in introducing a new element in the thorny field of community and race relations as far as Fleet Street is concerned.

Fleet Street on the whole always tends to look for the problems accompanying blacks.

Sometimes to such an extent that people start believing that every social and economic problem facing this country is in one way or another there because of the black presence in this country. And worse still some blacks start to think like that. Fortunately papers like the *Evening Standard,* although not sweeping discussion of grass-roots discontent relating to community and race relations under the carpet, have started to project over the past three years blacks as ordinary people with ordinary desires, fears and ambitions.

There is no doubt that the editor of the *Evening Standard, Charles Wintour,* has committed himself and his papers to this task. It Is therefore, in this light that *Mr Wintour's* viewpoint that the greatest contribution the media can make to peace and harmony is by the *quietness* with which it speaks, becomes extremely relevant. Continual treatment of racial matters on a crisis scale discourages the view that racial crisis can be avoided. Crisis treatment encourages a crisis attitude.

On 14 August 1970, *Richard Crossman,* the editor of the *New Statesman,* discussed the clashes between the police and the black community in Notting Hill on 9 August. What he found distressing was the fact that none of Fleet Street had any black reporters on their staff who could report the clashes. The report caused great interest in the black community and I decided to reply to Dick Crossman months later when the *New Statesman* had replied with great gusto to *Enoch Powell,* after one of his periodic outbursts. The letter challenged the *New Statesman* to do something about the lack of black reporters on its own staff. Because of the pertinence of the issue involved, this letter is reproduced as it essentially reinforces my arguments about the media.

Mr. Richard Crossman,
Editor,
The New Statesman,
Great Turnstile
London WC1V 7HJ

19th February 1971

Dear Mr. Crossman,
For some months I have been hesitating whether I should write you this letter or not. At one time I had persuaded myself that I should forget it all in case I seemed as if I was carrying a chip on my shoulder. But alas, the recent outburst by Mr. Enoch Powell and the predictable response by socialist like yourself and others reluctantly decided me to write this letter to you and The Statesman. I hope I am not too pertinent or bitter. It is just disappointingly angry.

I am coloured and have been a journalist for the past 14 years, having worked in South Africa, Indonesia, China, Vietnam and Zambia as a reporter, newscaster, and executive editor of a magazine and sub-editor. I have travelled extensively in nearly all African and Asian countries and can with all modesty and sincerity claim that I am fairly well keyed-up with events in the developing countries. I am presently freelancing in Britain, specialising in race relations.

Having been forced to leave South Africa ten years ago, because of my anti-apartheid views, I came to this country and after a year registered as a British subject. I was proud to become a citizen of this country. But that was ten years ago. I am not so sure whether I am so today.

Racism has popped its ugly head with telling results in this country. Powell I understand and can cope with. But what I can't cope with is the response by his opponents and especially those in Fleet Street. I am not writing about those editors and papers who covertly support Powell. I mean those who oppose him and go so far as to become the advocates of the Black man. They are more soul destroying and in Labour MP Eric Heffer's unparliamentary words 'bloody hypocritical'.

You, Sir wrote in the New Statesman of August 14th, 1970, when you discussed the clashes between the police and the coloured community in Notting Hill on the 9th August, that what was distressing was the fact that none of Fleet Street had any black reporters on their staff. You were dead right.

But unfortunately you did not go further. During that week, I was called on by some Fleet Street editors to report on what had happened. Two papers, The People and the Evening Standard carried articles by me and gave me a by-line stating plainly that I was a coloured reporter and had been living in the area. Now that was a rare thing to do in Fleet Street and I appreciated it. The People have subsequently carried articles by me on a freelance basis. This generosity I can only attribute to the sensitive and non-hypocritical attitude of its editor, Bob Edwards. Now and then some other editors has done the same. But only a freelance basis.

I have written to and made over 50 applications for jobs in the newspaper field in London and the Provinces. Many of them sounded very interested. They were very reasonable in their replies and over the phone. When they actually saw me, they realised they had been carried away by my surname which is as Scottish as roast beef in English. It was then that all professional interest disappeared and sweet reasonable hypocrisy set in.

The first thought I am sure that went through their mind was: Blimey, he is black. What does he know about Britain? And it would not do for a black man to report on matters, which effect black people in this country at all. All these editors have their white 'black experts', whom I am given to understand, know Africa better than the Africans, Asia better than the Asians, black homes better than black men and women, and what it means to be black in a predominantly white society. I have been verbally told time and again that I will not fit in as the particular paper has its own race relations expert who knows everything that is happening in the black world here and abroad.

But worse still. Being black I therefore cannot report on anything that is British and therefore white (an inverse powellism). I do not disagree that Fleet Street is generally saturated, but when you read the UK Press Gazette, you are amazed at the number of new appointments, which are taking place in Fleet Street and the provinces. It is as difficult for a black journalist to get on to Fleet Street papers as it is for the biblical rich man to get into heaven. I was once told by a black militant that reporting was a 'white concern'.

Yet I know many white South Africans who have migrated to this country, and who have less reporting and journalistic experience but because (and so I must unfortunately assume) they are white get a job immediately and without difficulty in Fleet Street and on so-called liberal papers.

My worst experience was with a daily liberal paper. I wrote to them, they invited me over for a chat. At the reception I waited for the night editor, who passed me twice and was searching the passage for a Mr. Morrison. White I suppose. He approached his reception and was told that is the gentleman he was looking for. At that moment I knew I would not get the job. Later, together with the chief sub we had a discussion and I was told emphatically that there would be a vacancy in two weeks' time and that I would be called and given the job on a three month probation period. Needless to say I never got the job. I was never called, but I did see a subsequent advert two weeks after I had applied for the job, for applicants. And that from a paper which writes the most anti-racist leaders and articles and takes a very moral attitude towards injustice.

But, Sir, what about The Statesman? Does it employ any coloured writers on its staff? My experience with The Statesman is also not a happy one and has indeed added to my disillusionment. About this time last year I sent two articles to your paper – granted you were not editor then. The first was returned with a note which said that recent events had outstripped the contents. Yet the matter was discussed in the media for another month and was important. The second feature was returned after a month with a terse note that it could not be used, that is after I had been on the phone for more than five times to find out what was happening to it. Maybe I annoyed the gentleman-journalist in charge. I do know that The Statesman also has its African and 'black experts' and can only surmise, since the articles dealt with Africa that, in the absence of any explanation whatsoever they were not held up because they were not up to standard. Because an article on the same theme, and not as good as mine I was told by others, was published not long afterwards in the Statesman.

It makes me sad to write this letter. I worked in many parts of the world. I successfully fought against and ended the special relationship, which existed at one time between the NUJ and the Society of South African Journalists, and prevented the latter from being recognised by the International Federation of Journalists. I did this because of the racism practised by the Society and the South African press as a whole. That is why it gave me such pleasure to become a full member of the NUJ, which is so steeped in non-racialism.

But unfortunately I cannot say the same about the media except for a privileged few.

I have settled here in Britain, married to an English girl and hoped in one way or the other to contribute towards bettering race relations in this country, through the only weapon I can effectively use – the pen. But this is not to be. Together with the small number of black journalists who are struggling in this country, I am a sad and disillusioned black man.

Journalism in this country seems to be the preserve of whites only. The black journalist is only good enough for the occasional piece of freelance reportage, but alas, not good enough to enjoy the full advantage of staff jobs. I wonder where The New Statesman stands on this matter? Please forgive me for taking your time, but with apologies, it was your article, which set me off. All that I can finally say is that I am a disillusioned, nearly disgusted and sadly becoming an angry and bitter black nigger journalist.

I remain, Yours Sincerely,

Lionel Morrison.

My letter caused some consternation to Dick Crossman who seemed on the whole quite eager to help, but was unable to appreciate the various points raised in it.

Those working for *The Statesman,* he said in his 26 February 1971 reply, were mostly occasional contributors, with a tiny staff of literally three or four people.

In view of my letter he hesitated to ask me for reportage of the 'immigrant community', but felt this was something the paper lacked. So that practically he could not think of anything better at that moment than the suggestion that I should do articles on the 'immigrant community'.

In spite of his reply, my attempts at having features published in the *New Statesman* came to naught.

And than on about 20 December 1971, the Liberal peer, *Lord (Ted) Willis* in a *World at One* talk attacked the lack of black journalists actually employed on the mass media. I wrote to him hoping that the whole issue would be given some more public airing and action. Since the letter was essentially along the same lines as the one written to Dick Crossman, extracts only are reproduced.

Lord Willis
C/o Liberal Party Organisation,
7 Exchange Court,
London WC2 20th

December 1971

Dear Lord Willis,

It was with great relief and indeed pleasure that I listened to you on The World at One the other day on the lack of coloured journalists actually employed on the mass media. The other points you raised about 'coloured' jokes were good but I would like to single out your very pertinent criticism of the lack of coloured journalists in Fleet Street.

Some of us black reporters and writers have been saying the same for quite a time. And in my experience it is not the so-called liberal papers whom are prepared to give black journalists a chance. It is papers who in some eyes are not so liberal. They have been less hypocritical. They do not speak of non-racialism in high sounding phrases – they rather act on it more positively than papers who have a so-called liberal tradition.

We are not asking for special favours. Many of us have the ability. What we ask for is just a chance. We are sure we will not upset staff relations, nor will our presence result in any problems.

I am sorry for this letter, but when I heard you over the radio the other day I thought 'here was a man who knows what it is all about'. Maybe when you have some time in the future we could meet. I would like to tell you all about how we black journalists see things in this country.

With best regards and a Merry Christmas to you,

Yours sincerely,
Lionel Morrison.

Needless to say I received no acknowledgement to my letter which was not wholly surprising. I had long learnt that it was easy for people to rave and rant about injustice and racism and then do little about it practically.

In *Race and the Press,* published by the *Runnymede Trust* in 1971, four distinguished journalists – *Clement Jones,* then editor of the *Wolverhampton Express and Star; Hugo Young,* assistant editor and chief leader writer of the *Sunday Times; Peter Harland,* Editor of the *Bradford Telegraph and Argus;* and *Harold Evans,* Editor of the *Sunday Times* – pleaded for special treatment in the press for race relations. They argue their cases eloquently, but, except for *Peter Harland,* editor of the *Telegraph and Argus of Bradford,* none of them predictably think it of any importance to raise the question of employing 'immigrant' reporters.

Harland, on the other hand, raises the danger of reporting about blacks in crisis situations only and rightly concludes that the impression is soon gained that blacks are problematic.

What is required is conscious editing, the paper going out to find other kinds of news from among the immigrants community, good news as well as bad: meetings, dinners, celebrations, speeches, presentations, retirements, sport and so on.

And quite rightly he naturally concludes what the others do not, that '*One way of helping towards this end is to employ immigrants reporters*' (author's emphasis). There can be difficulties, arising out of different standards of education, training and qualifications between one country and another, but they are not insurmountable. And in any case, as immigrant children leave English schools, they should, provided they have the necessary five "O" levels, make suitable candidates for the training scheme operated across the country by the National Council for the Training of Journalists. *'It is up to the editors begin to employ them'* (author's emphasis).

The four contributors to the publication all come to the conclusion as a whole that objectivity in race relations reporting is not achieved without a positive commitment to seek it. This conclusion all editors of British papers would swear they agree with. They might even go so far as to support the need for specialized skills and training in journalism when it comes to this sensitive area of race relations. But how many of them would agree (and act on this agreement) that the training and employment of black journalists would help tremendously to meet this situation? The absence of black journalists in the British press is proof of this hypocrisy which has so befuddled our press to date. A sad epitaph for a country with some of the greatest newspapers in the world.

-* excerpt from 'White Media and Black Britain' a critical look at the role of the Media in Race Relations today. Edited by Charles Husband published by Arrow Books,1975.

PART II

Race and Media Selected Articles

***The Press is often a distorting mirror, which deforms the people and events it represents, making them seem bigger or smaller than they really are* – Marguerite Yourcenar (1903-1987), novelist.**

***Can one really distinguish between the mass media as instruments of information and entertainment, and as agents of manipulation and indoctrination?* – Herbert Marcuse, 'One Dimensional Man'. 1964**

THE GOOD POLICEMAN PULLEY

- Why we say he should be moved from Notting Hill (1970)

ONE SIMPLE measure would significantly ease the tension between police and immigrants in the Notting Hill area of London – the posting of one policeman to some other district. He is P.C. Frank Pulley.

And there are a number of other officers whose transfer should be considered.

Transfers were suggested on Friday by Dr. David Pitt, deputy chairman of the government sponsored Community Relations Commission.

And in a statement to The People last week the same proposal was made by Lord Gifford, an outspoken barrister who lives in Notting Hill and has frequently appeared for the defence in cases involving immigrants.

Lord Gifford actually named Frank Pulley, who is pictured on the right.

Like ourselves, Lord Gifford has no criticism to offer of P.C. Pulley's conduct on or off the beat. He is indeed regarded as a first-class policeman by his superiors. He has been awarded the British Empire Medal for disarming a gunman.

But he is the object of such widespread hostility that his effectiveness as an officer in this area with its very special problems is gravely prejudiced.

And while he and a number of his colleagues patrol the streets of Notting Hill there will be little confidence in the police among the 12,000 coloured people who live in the area.

Move plan

Lord Gifford put it this way: *"I have heard P.C. Pulley's name mentioned in a number of cases and in a number of complaints made by the coloured community. I think it would be a good thing to move him and others whom the coloured people have come to mistrust."*

How that dangerous mistrust came to exist – and produce such ugly incidents as last Sunday's riot in which 17 policemen were injured – is the question we investigated in close on 100 interviews with white and black residents of Notting Hill.

The allegations made against the police were hair-raising. Harassment, insults, beatings, persecution of almost every sort.

We were unable to verify a single one of those charges. But there is not the slightest doubt that they are sincerely believed throughout the area.

And the name most frequently quoted with fear and loathing was that of Frank Pulley, who is a Drugs Squad officer.

Stainless as his reputation is, he has become a symbol of white oppression

It may even be that he and some other policemen on the beat are hated precisely because they carry out their duties without fear or favour in a district with a fringe population of law breakers.

But we heard strong general criticism of police methods from law-abiding people, too.

One of them is Australian-born, Mr. Chris Leonard, the white leader of a club for l,400 coloured youngsters called the Metro.

Last January, said Leonard, the club was raided for the second time by police seeking drugs.

"There were 70 of them. Outside the club I pleaded with two or three senior officers to come in alone and make their inquiries. I assured them they would have freedom to go around and would find nothing amiss.

"They would not listen. All 70 came in. They started to frisk young members. They pushed people around. It led to fights and arrests."

Mr. Leonard said this was just one of many incidents that rankled with the coloured community. It was not a case of police officers showing colour prejudice. Most of them didn't. But these were policemen who felt that they should rule the streets.

"My members complain that they are constantly being confronted by the police as they go home from the club," he said. "We have been given verbal guarantees by senior police officers that efforts would be made to stop this kind of thing. And there has been a genuine attempt to make things better.

"But young and less experienced officers continue to make unnecessary approaches to coloured people."

Almost every coloured person we interviewed was convinced that the police picked on blacks rather than whites for searching in the streets – nearly always for drugs. And then made them the victims of police station beatings and planted drugs on them.

One of the youth club members told a typical story.

"I was pulled in by a police officer for alleged obstruction in a street," he said. *"He claimed that I deliberately stood on a path and would not let him go past me.*

"But it was not a case of obstruction when I got to court. I found instead that I was facing a charge of having drugs in my possession. When I got to the police station and was being interviewed by a police sergeant he suddenly pushed his hand under my eyes with cannabis resin on it.

"He said: 'You know where this came from?' I told him that I had never seen drugs before in my life and that I did not even smoke cigarettes.

"But it was no good. I was stripped naked. I finished up with a conviction for having drugs."

We emphasise that there is no corroboration of this story. But we heard many like it. Even if every one is false –and many certainly are – they are evidence of utter distrust of policemen.

Several spoke of police raids on what they claimed to be perfectly innocent parties.

Mr. Duke Vin – a "soul" musician, who lives in a basement flat at 55a Acran Road, told us of a raid by about 40 policemen – one of whom was P.C. Pulley – on a birthday party he gave for his child. We spoke to several people who said they were at the party. All complained of rough behaviour by some of the policemen.

It seems that the police were searching for illegally sold drinks and drugs. That is the one point we were able to establish with a fair degree of certainty.

As for the allegations of improper police conduct, there is no reliable evidence to sustain them. Yet the belief is widely held that any social get-together of black people is liable to be disrupted.

"We dare not hold any parties in this area any more", said Mrs. Gwen Davids, also of Acran Road. *"We are too afraid."*

Even wedding celebrations are believed to be unwise.

With NUJ Barnsley Branch members – giving life membership cards to members (1987).

With Neil Kenlock during his photo exhibition of women of colour during the 1970s.

The News Line Thursday April 7, 1988

Media unions discuss S. African censorship

TWO hundred trade unionists, opponents of apartheid and supporters of the liberation struggle in South Africa attended a conference on censorship yesterday in London.

The gathering called 'White Lies' was organised by the media unions, the NUJ, NGA, SOGAT, BETA, ACTT, the Writers Guild, Anti-Apartheid and the Namibia Support Committee.

NORMA KITSON

As Lionel Morrison, the President of the National Union of Journalists explained in opening the conference, 'White Lies', addressed itself to the censorship and disinformation under apartheid in South Africa and Namibia.

He said: 'Disinformation is disseminated overseas, especially in this country.'

He told the meeting that journalists had the responsibility to ensure that 'the media does not become silent on South Africa'.

Outlining who was taking part in the conference and workshops he said that the ANC would be addressing the audience from the platform and the PAC would have a chance to speak from the floor.

A church leader who had been invited to attend the conference had been prevented from obtaining a passport to travel to Britain.

Joe Thloloe, a former NEC member of the media union in South Africa, MWASA, explained how something he had written was considered to be dangerous because it 'legitimised the symbols of banned organisations, the ANC and PAC'.

Banned

He said that the racist regime was trying to find scapegoats for the continuing uprising and blamed the media.

He described how ANC side the country were being sung within a few days in Soweto and other townships.

'Newspapers are not responsible for this. We are banned from publishing anything that could be construed as promoting the ANC and PAC.'

'The people have found their own ways of communicating.'

Sakhela Buhlungu from the Paper, Wood and Allied Workers of South Africa, which is affiliated to the COSATU trade union federation, said that in South Africa they could not limit themselves to 'pure trade unionism'.

LIONEL MORRISON discusses with Bishop HUDDLESTON

He said: 'We have learnt that in addition to fighting for a living wage we must fight for liberation.

'Censorship is part of a bigger plan to keep the people of South Africa in perpetual oppression.'

He called upon trade unions in Britain to form fraternal ties with COSATU and asked journalists to stop using reports from the censored newspapers of South Africa.

Archbishop Trevor Huddleston, President of Anti-Apartheid, spoke of the way the British press would attend a press conference where people from South Africa spoke and yet editors would cut stories produced by the journalists.

Huddleston added: 'Inside South Africa the expression of truth has been restricted in a draconian way.

'The only place where it can be spoken is in the pulpits.'

Huddleston called upon media trade unionists to 'support the alternative press by promoting its news materials and those of the liberation movements'.

He concluded: 'Total abolition of apartheid is the purpose of our commitment. We cannot afford to be disunited in the battle to destroy apartheid.'

Other speakers from the platform included Essop Pahad of the ANC, Victoria Brittain from the 'Guardian' and a speaker from SWAPO.

Amongst those attending the conference were a delegation from the PAC, led by the UK representative Rodwell Mzotane, Norma Kitson whose husband David spent 20 years in the apartheid state's jails, a group from City of London Anti-Apartheid and Mike Hicks the SOGAT member jailed during the Wapping dispute.

Workshops on Broadcasting, national newspapers and book publishing were held in the afternoon.

Discussing with bishop Huddlestone during the "White Lies' conference – which addressed itself to the censorship and disinformation under Apartheid in South Africa and Namibia.

During my presidential meetings with NUJ Belfast Branch colleagues.

Chinese Culture and Media Ministers in Beijing, hosting a banquet for the Afro-Asian Journalists Association in 1965.

With Harry Conroy, NUJ Gen Secretary and Arnold Hadwin, President of the Guild of Editors at a meeting organised by the RRWP (1987).

George Viner Memorial Trust Fund ceremony award of students and Trustees.

With Bill Morris, former General Secretary of the TGWU – sponsor of the GVMFT during a student ceremony award.

Bill Morris presenting awards to the GVMFT students (2003)

With Indonesian and Vietnamese AAJA bureau colleagues in Hanoi, (1964)

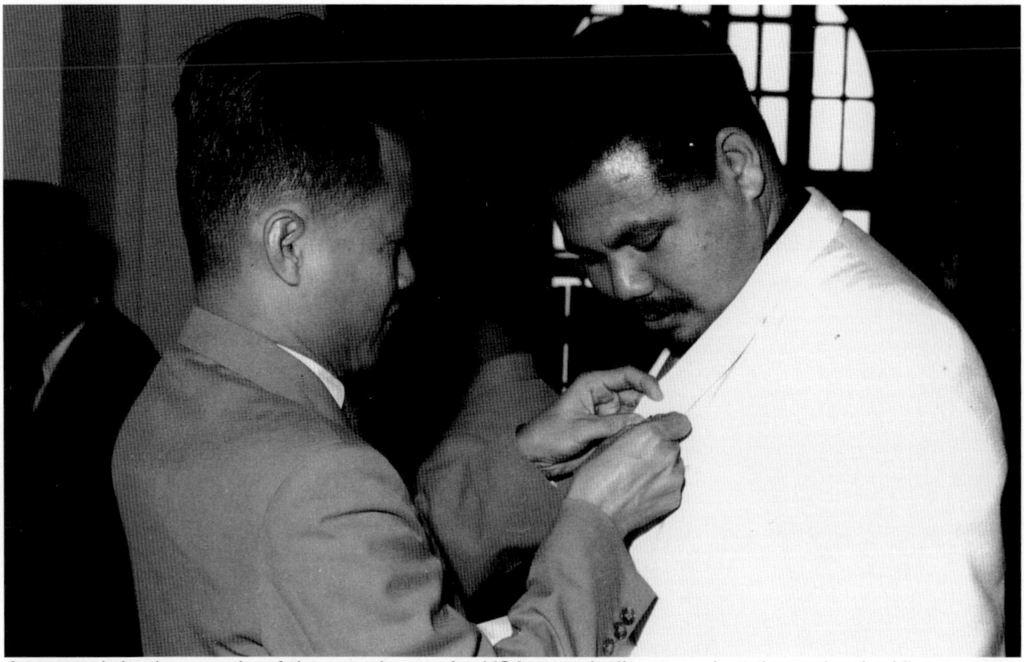

A souvenir badge, made of the wreckage of a USA army helicopter shot dowm by the Vietnamese Liberation Army, beiing pinned on the coat by Vietnamese colleagues in Hanoi (1964).

Addressing the Inaugural Conference of the AAJA in Djakarta (1963).

With President Sukarno and AAJA bureau members in Djakarta (1963).

With Zanzibar colleagues and AAJA bureau members in Zanzibar (1966).

With Mao Zedong and AAJA Conference members and bureau members in the Great Hall Beijing, 1964. Mao Zedong – front line, fourth number to the right.

With Chinese journalists at the Martyrs' Monument, Nanking, 1963.

During a journalists Conference with Nepalese colleague, Shyan Prassed and East Berlin journalists colleagues (1962).

Wedding shock

Mr. Anthony Mohipp, secretary of the Universal Black Peoples Improvement Organisation, has even written to the Home Secretary about a wedding reception he claims to have been disrupted by the police.

On a recent Saturday night, he claims, a police van, two squad cars and two other cars unloaded officers outside l04 Chesterton Road.

"The young people were shocked." Mr. Mohipp's letter asserts, *"and the entire evening was ruined for everyone."*

No illegal drinks or drugs were found, according to Mr. Mohipp and no arrests were made.

We heard similar allegations from other people. Most of those we interviewed refused to give their names. They said they feared police persecution.

This fear and this insistence on remaining unidentified was, we found, shared even by those who take a far more balanced view of police behaviour than the majority of black residents.

There was, for example, the man who said he had no personal experience of police "brutality". But he had been stopped on a number of occasions and asked to turn his pockets out.

"After eleven at night if I go for a walk across the road near Notting Hill Gate tube station, it's ten to one that I'll be stopped."

Picked on

"But let's get the situation right. Police also stop white people if they suspect them. Though with a predominantly coloured community it would appear that it is the coloureds who are picked on.

"The coloured people have let their fear of the police grow to exaggerated proportions, and the police do nothing to dispel this fear."

One young man who has been l2 years in Britain told us that he was picked up in a betting shop while he was speaking to another coloured man.

"I learned later that he had pinched a car or something like that," he said. "But though he had done wrong, I hadn't. It didn't matter about that. I was taken to the station with him.

"I was stripped, why I don't know. I protested my innocence, but it made no difference. I got a backhander across the face. And was kicked and punched"

This, too, was a story that could not be corroborated but is typical of what is firmly believed.

We sought, but were unable to interview P.C. Pulley. But we did speak to Commander Peter Nievens, head of the Community Relations Department at the Yard.

"We are of course aware of some reaction to certain policemen in that area." He said cautiously.

But his department had no complaints about P.C. Pulley. And he did not agree that any police officer should be transferred.

"We have been raised in the Police Force since l829 on the principle that everyone is entitled to the same treatment", he said. "And we in the force perform our duties without reference to race, creed or colour."

We suggested a round table conference where people with complaints could –

without fear of legal action – speak up and put their allegations.

Commander Nievens was encouraging. *"I think it would be a very good idea"*, he said. In our view, an essential preliminary to such a conference would be to transfer some men to other areas.

However, upright they are as policemen, it is a fact that confidence in them among a large segment of the community has sunk to zero.

by Sydney Foxcroft, Lionel Morrison and Mervyn Pamment in *The People* Sunday I6 August 1970

PC Pulley and the Sunday People (1972

In April a police officer was awarded £5,000 libel damages and costs by a High Court jury against a Sunday newspaper and three of its journalists. Clive Mellors looks at the view each side held of the other.

If ever there was a case which demonstrated the opposing viewpoints held by the police and the media about race relations, the case of PC Frank Pulley and the *Sunday People* plus three journalists is a classic.

PC Pulley sued the *Sunday People* for libel, claiming that an article which had been written after the now famous Portnall Road clashes in Notting Hill in August 1970, which led to the equally famous Mangrove Nine trial, had "pilloried" him He was awarded £5,000 damages and costs by a jury (eleven whites and one Asian) in a ten day trial in the High Court.

The newspaper, its then editor, Mr. Bob Edwards, and the journalists denied libel and contended that the article was an in-depth enquiry into the causes of a predominantly black protest march which had taken place and that it was fair comment, written without malice, on a matter of public interest.

PC Pulley was supported financially in his case by the Police Federation and as witnesses in support of his case had two senior policemen to give evidence.

The Police Viewpoint

He complained that in the article, which was published under the headline "The Good Policeman Pulley" and called for his posting to another area, he had been *'pilloried by irresponsible journalists acting at the behest of political agitators and criminals'. The "irresponsible"* journalists were Mervyn Pamment, Sidney Foxcroft and Lionel Morrison. The "political agitators," it was established during cross examination, were Roy Sawh, Jeff Crawford, Michael Malik and others.

PC Pulley and his two police witnesses looked upon the Mangrove Restaurant as *"a den of iniquity and evil which was frequented by pimps, prostitutes and criminals"* – a place which was the source of the trouble in the area.

All denied that there was a breakdown in relations between the black community and the police; the only problem, if there were any, was with the criminal element who were responsible for all the anti-police feeling in the area. PC Pulley was a man who loved and cared for blacks, was well thought of in the area and had a good reputation among the black community in the area.

Inspector Robert Aldritt of Notting Hill police station (one of PC Pulley's witnesses) said that he had found Mr. Pulley a very fine officer, devoted to his work and held in high regard by all his senior officers. Mr. Pulley was a humane man and had a great deal of sympathy towards coloured people by whom he was extremely well liked. Inspector Aldritt said, *"It is officers like Pulley who have done so much for race relations in mixed communities."* He further said that he regarded the way Black Power had conducted itself in Notting Hill as dangerous to race relations and public order.

All the witnesses claimed that the Press had grossly over exaggerated any problems in the area, and that the bad police black relations were a figment of the Press's imagination.

PC Pulley went on record as saying that the local MP, Bruce Douglas-Mann, was *"irresponsible"* when it came to race relations in the area. And so was the popular local newspaper, the *Kensington Post.* He agreed that he was indignant and amazed, but not embittered, by the acquittal of a number of the Mangrove Nine at the Old Bailey – a case in which he featured prominently for the prosecution.

The Press Viewpoint

Of the journalists, Mervyn Pamment is an experienced *Sunday People* reporter who has a reputation for his thoroughness and fairness and who had never been to Notting Hill; Sidney Foxcroft is a one-time front line journalist with the Eighth Army who has had the singular distinction of being commended in Parliament for an enquiry he did on Borstal conditions. He has been a journalist for over twenty years, had been brought specially from Newcastle for this enquiry and knew nothing of the area. Lionel Morrison, a black freelance journalist of sixteen years' experience, had lived in Notting Hill and specialises in race relations. He had worked for the *Sunday People* among other Fleet Street papers, has wide experience in newspaper work and has worked in various Third World countries.

Despite its history or race riots, Notting Hill was an area where relations between white and black were quite good. However, there was definitely a breakdown in relations between the police and the black community. The march in question had visited the police stations in the area to protest at the bad relations which had developed.

The journalists had interviewed about one hundred people, both black and white, and the conclusion they reached was that all was not rosy in the police-black garden. Relationships had broken down: the one name which frequently cropped up was that of PC Pulley.

The Mangrove, in the eyes of the journalists, especially Lionel Morrison, was and is a centre for the local black community where both black and white can meet and eat together and learn to understand each other. It was a respectable place owned and run by blacks. Though it had been watched by the police and had frequently been raided, no customer of the Mangrove had ever been charged or convicted for untoward behaviour on the premises. The black leaders interviewed by the reporters represented the viewpoint of a section of the black community, and it was thought that they had the right to be heard.

On the other hand the police refused permission for the *Sunday People* to interview Pulley. However the following week Scotland Yard, in an attempt to present a reply to the paper's article, arranged for the *Sunday Mirror* to do a public relations article on him. But the evidence given by the *Mirror* reporter, Peter Seeds, clearly showed that he had discovered the hostile reaction that PC Pulley's name elicited (although he could not understand why) from all the blacks he spoke to on his assignment and that relations between blacks and the police had broken down.

The *Sunday People* had articles and features by other newspapers (*The Times*, the *Sunday Mirror*, the *Sunday Times*, etc.) admitted as evidence. These articles clearly supported the viewpoint that relations had broken down between the police and blacks in the area, that it was an explosive situation and that something had to be done.

Observations

A disturbing feature of the case was the length the police were prepared to go to in getting background material on the reporters. This was commented on by Mr. James Comyn, QC for the *Sunday People*. The police had made intensive enquiries and investigations into the political and professional part of the reporters. They especially tried to make Lionel Morrison appear a "man of violence" because of articles he had written in the *Afro Asian Journalist* six years ago while working in South East Asia. They unsuccessfully tried to link him with Michael X and questioned his politics on South Africa. This line of questioning provoked the judge, Mr. Justice Bean, in a remarkable summing up, to say that one of the features of the case was possibly the innuendo that Morrison (who was born in South Africa) had been prejudiced, not least because of an article he had written six years ago when secretary of the Afro-Asian Journalists' Association. *"I doubt whether you will get much help from that", he was driven to say.*

The judge added: *"Mr. Morrison has never sought to hide that he was naturally biased by reason of his colour and by his experiences in South Africa, where he had had the distinction and misfortune to be one of the defendants in the infamous treason trial in which I56 defendants were happily acquitted after a tremendous ordeal."*

It is interesting that this case should come up at a time when evidence given to the Parliamentary Select Committee on Immigration and Race Relations by the Jamaican High Commission, the NCCL and various other bodies and individuals has shown overwhelmingly that relations between police and blacks have broken down and that the police must take much of the responsibility for this. This, needless to say, supports the case made by the *Sunday People*. The paper is considering an appeal.

***"Race Today"* June 1972 by**
Clive Mellors (pseudonym for Lionel Morrison)

THE EFFECT OF THE BLACK PRESENCE AND THE RISE OF BLACK AWARENESS ON THE BRITISH MEDIA. (1974)

The Press must first recognise that what it prints or broadcasts about ethnic groups can directly affect ethnic tension. Any organisation not in league with the devil, which makes this first positive recognition, must then recognise the commitment which follows. It must have a positive policy to avoid unnecessary damage. These are responsibilities which many in the Press refuse to acknowledge. They do so basically, since none of them profess to like the devil, by insisting that they are mere mirrors and that news is neutral.

There is no doubt the attitude of the British media has profoundly been affected firstly by the black presence in the country and secondly by the rising awareness of this de facto presence. No other institution in this country has been so fundamentally shaken or has played such an important role in assisting in the scapegoating of black people in the country, despite all the contrary protestations which are so readily forthcoming from the Fourth Estate.

In saying this I do not for one moment suggest that 'conflict' racial stories and news which are uncomplimentary to blacks should be swept under the carpet or suppressed, only that when 'racial' stories are reported the prevailing cultural assumptions about colour and 'the colour problem' should not be a criterion at all. In other words 'racial' stories should be presented in such a way that the readers do not read into it any racial connotations.

There must be an honest attempt to tell the whole story, a decision to set individuals and events in their historical, economic and social contexts and not just expose them to the arbitrary glare of publicity when the media decides that they are newsworthy. 'New value', is a capricious rule of thumb; as Harold Evans, Editor of *The Sunday Times* put it: *We in communication cannot meet our challenge by telling less than the truth. We can only meet it by striving to tell more of the truth.*

Fighting words indeed, but then even the liberal *Sunday Times* with its all white editorial teams are wont, like the rest of the British media, to place more emphasis on talking than on acting. This is evidenced in the famous METRO 4, Old Bailey Trial, summed up in an editorial of *West Indian World* of which I was then leader writer and Deputy Editor: *Two front page headlines seen in the press on 25 May 1971, read "None Police hurt in Club Riot", and "Screaming Mob in London Court Demo". They referred to an incident which occurred outside the Metro Youth Club in Notting Hill, London when police laid siege of the club and which finally resulted in the arrest of the 'Metro 4".*

Other Fleet Street papers carried full reports of the incident. They gave it full coverage. And quite rightly so. It was a matter of public concern and needed reporting.

One year later those arrested during that eventful day were finally acquitted by a jury in the Old Bailey of all 21 counts. Their trial lasted one month and over 30 policemen gave evidence in a trial which cost thousands of pounds of tax payers' money. The jury verdict was of great importance.

Yet not one Fleet Street paper reported the outcome of the trial – and except for a single and short report in one paper absolutely nothing appeared in the National press during the four week trial. A blanket silence it seems had been imposed on the trial and its outcome – a complete reversal to the treatment of the incident at the time. Why this silence, many ask? Is it perhaps that when black people are involved Fleet Street is only interested in 'trouble reports'? And that the not guilty verdict of the jury was not of importance at all? Would the press have kept silent if a guilty verdict had been recorded and heavy sentences imposed? The position of the media is still, with a handful of exceptions, the same.

A status seeking and competitive society, lately emerged from its colonial heyday and on the lookout for scapegoats to explain and atone for its doubts, deficiencies and past activities, is by its very nature bound to throw up individuals, organisations and institutions whose frame of reference is racist.

The media has often enough pointed accusatory pens at the police (and others) in this respect, but newsmen are just as much as the police, the products of society and are as prone to reflect its atavism in their work.

The days of the apocryphal, *"Small Earthquake in Argentine: Not Many Dead"*, type headline may be past but for many editors good news is no news. This reinforces society's pressures to play up the real or imagined conflict content of race stories which creates a recipe which guarantees distortion and bias, as so eloquently illustrated by Louis Kuchnick, when he discussed the media's treatment of a purported Black Power take-over of the Manchester City Council in September 1970. Since Black is a threat it smacks of conflict and violence. There is little need to understand correctly Black Power or Black awareness as a concept or to relate it to the place of black people in Britain. The less information presented about the reality of Black awareness the better. Since Black Power has news value the story made headlines in places as far away from Manchester as Bristol (*Western Daily Press*) Middlesborough (*Evening Gazette*) and Scotland (*Scottish Daily Express*) as well as in the national press and on Television.

In looking at the treatment of this story, Kuchnick found a number of interesting points emerging:

Most of the conclusions reached by Halloran and his colleagues at Leicester about the functioning of the media are supported. Secondly, we can see the tenacity of the consonance factor – so much so, that even when the original interpretation of the event was called into question, the media either totally ignored the conflicting evidence or, after presenting the contrary information, quickly reverted to the original more familiar presentation.

The story of this purported Black Power bid to rule Manchester first broke on 4 September in The Guardian and the Manchester edition of The Daily Telegraph. The Guardian headline read 'Black Power bid to rule Manchester' and the Telegraph's 'Black Power Attempt Poll Sabotage'. The Guardian story left no doubt as to the Black Power character of the plot, fully supporting its dramatic headline. "THE Black Power movement which claims that by today it will have 100 candidates standing in a Manchester municipal by-election on 24 September, has plans to take almost all the thirty-eight city council seats which become vacant next May.'

It is interesting to note *The Guardian's* and *The Telegraph's* view that the movement is supported by THE 'Black Power' organisation assumes that there is a THE Black Power movement or organisation – a theme picked up by the rest of the media. Anyone familiar with the black community would have had doubts immediately about the validity of this story, for there is no ONE Black Power organisation and the Black Power movement is divided into a large number of small groups.

When it was later proven beyond any doubt that the group – the Campaign for Action for the Relief of Need (CARN) which had put up the 19 candidates, was instead a right wing group which had shared office in London with the fascist Immigration Control Association which advocates the repatriation of all black people and that the whole story was a plot to discredit black people. The media, except for the *Sunday Times* and *The World This Weekend*, blandly ignored the new facts and continued on this 'Black Power' line of reporting. The main culprit in this issue was *The Guardian,* the guardian of the liberal conscience. The BBC in their 5.50 pm television news bulletin a day or two after *The World This Weekend* and *The Sunday Times* expose talked about a black power bid to take over Manchester.

Kushnick observes that: *The press uniformly fitted the new situation into the earlier presentation by ignoring the new. Perhaps the headline which best illustrated this approach was that of the Sun of 9 September:* '94 BLACK POWER MEN "IN ONE HOUSE" GET POLL BAN.' *That is certainly a technically sweet headline – it gets across the themes of black power while at the same time relating the story, even if supposedly facetiously, to earlier stories of houses full of immigrants. The story had no indication that there was any doubt as the authenticity of the black power plot: 'A top-level inquiry was started yesterday into a Black Power bid to swamp a city by-election with candidates'*.

The coverage of the media in this instance raised interesting points because it clearly expressed the framework of attitudes held by the British press about Black Power, and how they reported to their white readers a black phenomenon, ensconced as they saw it in mystery and fear.

It was playing to the same fears of black domination that have been the basis of Enoch Powell's appeal and his emphasis on black birth rates and black percentages in selected cities, and the media's reverential treatment of those who clamour loudest, however shaky their claim to accuracy or expertise. Enoch Powell's obiter dicta apart, probably the most striking examples of this genre were the *Yorkshire Post's* headline in 1962 during a smallpox outbreak in Bradford which provided the paper with an example of conflicting reporting. The paper's front page carried the headline: *Pakistani's blamed in smallpox city: Anger in Bradford*. This headline immediately directed attention onto the Pakistani community and in no uncertain terms made clear as to who should be blamed and who were pointing the accusing finger. In fact the outbreak originated with a nine year old Pakistani girl who died of the disease. She had been vaccinated. Although the headline spoke of a "Smallpox City" there were only I4 cases in the entire outbreak and there was no proof that Pakistani's were the cause. The text of the story was more outrightly inflammatory than informative; and was intended to incite. For example:

Bradford was an uneasy city last night.... *It was an angry city too, and all over the city, in public houses, clubs and on the buses, there was open evidence that the public as a whole was blaming the Pakistani population. Up to last night there had been no physical incidents involving whites and coloured in Bradford – a town long noted for its tolerance towards coloured immigrants – but conversation was mainly centred on the lines of 'send them home'.*

The Post's allegation of anger was challenged by the *Bradford Telegraph and Argus, The Post* could not have sent out sufficient reporters to justify such a definite and inciting statement of feeling in Bradford. As an indication of lack of panic in Bradford it mentioned there had been seven letters on the subject and 2,000 entries for the *Telegraph and Argus quiz*.

But *The Post's* reporting which was in line with its general anti-immigration stance, resulted in isolated instances of violence in Bradford. Windows were broken, the words 'smallpox' and 'wog' were painted on a Pakistani shop and white youths attacked Asians.

The *Daily Telegraph's* front page headline on 14 Feb 1968 screamed: *Kenyan Asian exodus numbers double – 100,000 may enter Britain by the end of year*. This story was based not on any official projections, as one would have expected since it was such a serious matter, not even on the estimate of the paper's own correspondent in Nairobi, where the story came from. Low down in the story this menacing estimate was credited to unnamed 'airline officials'.

The *Daily Express* on Thursday, 6 April 1972, carried the headline, *"Stay-on 'illegal' visitors start a row'*, and began the l8 column inch article, according to Hartmann and Husband, with: *Immigration officials were up in arms last night over what they regard as a New Government policy that could allow thousands of illegal immigrants with Britain without fear of deportation*.

That same day *the Guardian* ran a similar story with the headline *Kenya Asians slip through Britain's net*. The 24 column inch article authoritatively stated that: *'Immigration officers are concerned at the number of Kenyan Asians being allowed into Britain. Officers have strict instructions not to talk to the press – but an "official leak" from immigration sources claimed that the British Government's attitude towards the shuffling of immigrants from one country to another would mean that thousands of immigrants would have to be let into Britain.'*

The "official leak" turned out to be a minor interpreter employed by the Home Office Heathrow.

The *London Evening News* on 4 April 19973 led their front page with the scaring headline *School Mobs in London Race Riot*. The story said that a mob of black youths had attacked mainly white pupils and that passers by cowered in shop doorways as the white and black groups clashed. It mentioned one gang of more than 100 coloured teenagers armed with weapons including a shot gun, stiletto, iron bar and milk bottles and quoted the Headmaster of Kingsdale School, one of the schools involved as saying, *'I have never seen anything like it'*. The other school was Tulse Hill.

The Headmaster denies saying that. Indeed he was so disturbed that he immediately issued a statement emphasising that no white pupils had been involved. This was an undisputed fact which all other papers accepted. Accounts of the numbers of children and police involved, of the number and nature of the weapons, of the damages, varied widely. What was commonly accepted by all except the *Evening News* was that the fight was between black pupils from both schools.

The Daily Mail's headline blamed *'The Outsiders bussed in to keep a racial balance'.* The headmaster of both Tulse Hill and Kingsdale supported by the Inner London Education Authority, deny that any of their pupils are bussed in. *'Nor is there any policy regarding racial balance'*, the Headmaster of Tulse Hill said.

The Mail also said the children involved were *all truants from their respective schools*, an allegation both Headmasters vehemently denied.

Following the *consonance factor, the Evening News* the next days ignored all the new facts and authoritative denials and claimed: *Hundreds of parents decided not to send their children to Kingsdale School today*. It added that the school bore the signs of the violence: *More than 20 windows are smashed. Locked doors can be seen to have been broken and blinds wrenched off.*

The headmaster immediately replied that attendance that day was, *absolutely normal* and that *no damage at all* had been done to school property; there had been no fighting on school premises.

The chief Information officer of ILEA complained to the *Evening News* about both stories, but with particular reference to the headline *"Race Riots"*. The News replied that it stood by its story and undertook to reply to the accusations of misreporting which it has not done satisfactorily up to now. A week later ILEA referred the *Evening News* to the Press Council.

On the April 4.74 the Press Council which is not known for its radicalism, upheld the complaint by the ILEA that the *Evening News* published an inaccurate story under an unjustified headline. It also ruled that although the editor invited the complainants to write a letter for publication he declined to publish a correction and apology.

The Press Council in the adjudication said the story was inaccurate in a number of details and incomplete in so far as it did not include the headmaster's denial that a fight took place on the school premises: *'The words "race riot" in the headline were unjustified and in the conditions existing in the area they were irresponsible. The newspaper should have published a retraction and the complaint is upheld'.*

The Press Council's decision was immediately welcomed by the Black community which was as surprised as was the *Evening News* at the outcome.

The two *Evening News* reporters immediately complained to the NEC of the National Union of Journalists (NUJ) that they were unfairly criticised in the Press Council's adjudication. The National Executive Committee's (NEC's) sub committee reported to the July NEC that the Press Council's finding was based on the headline, its accusation that the story was inaccurate was not justified.

According to a report in *The Journalist:*

Deputy General Secretary Eric Blott said there was nothing in the story that was not repeated in stories published in the following day's Fleet Street papers. The reason a complaint was laid against the Evening News was that an editorial executive 'dressed up' the copy and put an irresponsible headline on it. The sub committee went on to recommend the NEC to accept that the criticism of O'Kill and Joseph was unwarranted. It was agreed that the NEC decision should be conveyed to the Press Council.

How the NEC reached such a decision, especially since only the *Evening News* described the fracas between black pupils of the two schools as a Race Riot only becomes possible if one is aware of the hostile attitude the NEC and the NUJ as a whole took to a motion submitted by the London Freelance Branch of the NUJ to the Wexford Annual Delegates Meeting of the NUJ in 1974. Moved by myself.

The motion was partly rejected by the NEC which argued that it should be referred back to it for action. Arguments against the motion at the ADM ranged from those who felt it was the wrong way to go about it. Many journalists actually argued that racism just did not exist in the media and among the ranks of the NUJ. The attitude to the London Freelance Branch motion was not the first time the NUJ had taken such a stand. In 1966 the Central London Branch passed a similar resolution calling for a code of conduct covering race relations. It was rejected by the annual conference.

However, all does not seem to be lost with the NUJ. Immediately after the Wexford ADM a London Liaison NUJ Committee of various London branches was set to look at the whole question of racism in the media. Although unofficially it geared various people into action, as a Sub Committee. The black community itself has taken up the whole matter by holding various seminars and meetings to discuss the issues involved.

As long as the media and journalists are prepared to condemn racism in others, like the police and Black people and not look at the dirt in their own forecourt, then we will nurture an institution which guarantees distortion and lies as far as its race related stories are concerned.

Apart from the racism in the media which manifests itself in the actual handling of the news with the all too familiar end product of stories which irrelevantly report a defendant's ethnic group, and so foster a popular identification of blacks with crime; stories which are published simply because of their subject's race; or a reluctance to question established values as in the handling of "Paki" bashing, and the blatant emphasis on the most imaginary increases in the size of the black population and coverage so slender as to be almost invisible of the reverse, there is the additional form of racism found in the employment or rather lack of employment of black people in the communications industry.

How many black journalists are there in the British media today? Of the 28,000 journalists working on newspapers and magazines less than two dozen (.09%) are black. This small percentage is not for want of trying or for the non-availability of young blacks ready to be trained for journalism.

Most of those already in the field have been trained elsewhere and the rest are on placement in Britain for foreign newspapers. There are now a number of alert, young blacks who would make every bit as good a showing as some of the white youngsters who offer themselves for selection and subsequent training as journalists. These last words are not mine but those of Clement Jones, former Editor of the *Wolverhampton Express* and *Star* and Life President of the Guild of British Newspaper Editors.

In a letter of reply to a race journal, he goes further and says, *'Much of the trouble is that dissuasion for blacks starts well before the selection stage – in fact by school careers masters and youth employment officers. I have had first hand evidence of this negative attitude at the advisory stage.*

That the majority of editors who are in the market for trainees certainly are not racist is happily true. But the majority are content to take a passive line and to duck out from; underneath, with the familiar formula, 'of course, if the right black boy or girl came along.. 'etc... And in this they are aided by the career advisory systems, to preserve status quo ante immigration.'

And a further comment by another editor, Peter Harland of the *Bradford Telegraph* and *Argus*:

What is required is conscious editing, the paper going out to find other kinds of news from among the immigrant community – the same kind of news as the paper prints about the host community, good news as well as bad: meetings, dinners, celebrations, speeches, presentations, retirements, sport and so on.

One way of helping towards this end is to employ immigrant reporters. There can be difficulties, arising out of the different standards of education, training and qualification between one country and another, but they are not insurmountable. And in any case, as immigrant children leave English schools, they should provided they have the necessary five 'O' levels make suitable candidates for the training scheme operated across the country by the National Council for the Training of Journalists. It is up to the editors to begin to employ them.

That was nearly three years ago and needless to say there has been no noticeable change. Why?

One of the problems black journalists face in the British media is the white "black expert", the race relations experts.

These experts are the ones who have fashioned to a great extent the stand of their various papers on race relations. They are "the experts" on blacks. They jealously guard their position and resist any newcomers and intruders in the field. They react even more vehemently when the intruders are black. This no doubt is a consequence of the old paternalistic doctrine which was and still is so strong among some liberals. They know the black, his desires and shortcomings better than blacks themselves. So that whatever the British media has to say, the media image we, both black and white, have of ourselves is written or broadcast by a pure lily- white hand with all its dire consequences.

It follows, emphasises Colin McGlashan who won the Campaigning Journalist of the Year Award for articles on black teenagers and the homeless in 1967, that newspaper staff ought to contain the variety of views, life-styles and groupings within the changing society they allegedly seek to reflect. And of course they don't.

The newspapers that are praised for their attitude to race relations still operate in a framework of liberal paternalism; for example they are careful not to employ black writers or reporters, except as freelances and then usually insist they work with a white reporter, or check every fact they write.

And further

What is needed is an honest portrayal of conflicts and an informed discussion of the issues they raise. That means that the views and attitudes of black teenagers, policemen and indeed the National Front, should be represented in the British Press, not what those views and attitudes ought to be, not merely when they're supported by 'facts' or quotes from 'responsible spokesmen' but what they are. They haven't been, they aren't and they won't be until the people who decide what goes in newspapers and the people who put it there are no longer an ethnocentric elite.

One outcome of the general hostility of press, its playing up of what it thinks is the interest of Black people and its misrepresentation of what actually goes on in the black British world, has been a reciprocal hostility on the part of the Black people towards the mainstream media.

This hostility is twofold. Either no information is forthcoming at all or the media is taken for a ride with tall stories which most white journalists swallow hook line and sinker. One of the best examples is the merry go round Michael X led the media in this country.

Michael X's claim that he had stacks of arms hidden away and had an army of Karate trained black guerrillas was snapped up by the Press from the *Express* to the *Guardian*, who not only reported whatever he said, no matter how ridiculous, but in fact believed what he had told them. In this way the British media could be held responsible for building up Michael X.

It is this desire, this temptation for the media to make of race as a topic that even normally responsible organs find difficult to resist. For race ranks with sex, drugs and 'permissiveness' as sure fire sensations material.

The great British tradition of tolerance so often presented via the media is an essential element of British self image. Indeed it is a British dilemma that tolerance should be so highly prized whilst discrimination is so widely practised.

One solution, argues Husband, is determinedly to deny its existence by constant verbal expression of British tolerance and refusal to acknowledge discrimination when it occurs. This has a double benefit, for not only does it sustain the national conceit of British liberalism vis-a-vis other nations, but by obscuring the reality beneath a consensus acceptance of British tolerance it provides a screen for the practice of discriminatory behaviour which by popular judgement and official utterance is impossible in a tolerant society.

Paul Hartman on the other hand reflects that *"because the mass media are social institutions and part of our social system, one of their functions is to reflect our culture and current social concerns. And where norms and values are concerned, they are more likely to reflect than to innovate".*

There is also an area in which they help to structure people's perceptions of social reality, to create *"pictures in our heads"* of what the situation is, he argues. In the relationship to the attitudes of the white public the effect lies in the image of black people that the news media project and the way they define the race relations situation and structure perceptions and expectations. Their contribution here is almost bound to be negative, without a deliberate effort to avoid creating erroneous impressions.

Clearly in important respects the effects of the mass media are to some degree determined by characteristics found in the audience and at another stage removed these characteristics can be seen to be related to features of the society itself. However, though we should be critical of mass media performance, we must not expect too much of the mass media if we fail to criticise the society in which the media operates.

(Speech and Paper to a Conference of Community Activists in London)

THE EMPLOYMENT OF BLACK PEOPLE IN THE BRITISH MEDIA - (1975)

At present the news media, like the British white population, has still to accept that Britain is a multi-racial society. For this reason it has, for example, been able to give emphasis to "immigration" and "immigrants" while ignoring the fact that increasingly the people characteristically labeled "immigrants" are in fact British.

What it prints or broadcasts about ethnic groups can directly affect ethnic tension. Any organisation not in league with the devil, which makes this first positive recognition, must then recognise the commitment which follows. It must have a positive policy to avoid unnecessary damage. These are responsibilities which many in the press refuse to acknowledge. They do so basically – since none of them profess to like the devil – by insisting that they are mere mirrors and that news is neutral.

There is no doubt that the attitude of the British media has been profoundly affected, firstly by the black presence in this country and secondly by the rising awareness of this de facto presence. No other institution in this country has been so fundamentally shaken or has played such an important role in assisting in the scapegoating of blacks in the country, despite all the contrary protestations which are so readily forthcoming from the Fourth Estate.

In saying this I do not for one moment suggest that "conflict" racist stories and news not complimentary to blacks should be swept under the carpet or suppressed, only that when racist stories are reported the prevailing cultural assumptions about colour and "the colour problem", should not be a criterion at all. In other words "racial" stories should be presented in such a way that the readers should not read into them any racial connotations. There must be an honest attempt to tell the whole story, a decision to set individuals and events in their historical, economic and social contexts and not just expose them to the arbitrary glare of publicity when the media decides that they are newsworthy. "News value" is a capricious rule of thumb; as one Fleet Street Editor put it: "We in communication cannot meet our challenge by telling less than the truth. We can only meet it by striving to tell more of the truth".

But this desire to tell more of the truth about the black presence in this country is greatly circumscribed by the absence of journalists who are well informed about blacks, about their desires, their hopes, their shortcomings and their successes. White journalists can only "interpret what Black people feel and think – and let there be no doubt, some do succeed quite well. However, in-spite of these few, an even smaller number manage to capture the "gut" feeling of minorities.

What is needed, and here I am sure every practitioner in this field would vigorously agree, is an honest portrayal of conflict and an informed discussion of the issues they raise. That means that the views and attitudes of black teenagers, policemen, and indeed the British National Front, should be represented in the British Press – not what those views and attitudes ought to be, not merely when they're supported by "facts" or quotes from "responsible spokesmen" *but what they are.* They haven't been, they aren't, and they won't be, until the people who decide what goes in newspapers and the people who put it there are no longer an ethno-centric elite.

In other words what it means is that newspaper staffs ought to contain the variety of views, life-styles and groupings within the changing society they seek to reflect.

And of course, they don't and for various reasons.

There is no doubt that the majority of newspapers that are praised for their attitude to race relations still operate in a framework of liberal paternalism; for example, they are careful not to employ black writers or reporters, except as freelances – and then usually insist they work with white reporters or check every fact they write.

Many editors, when explaining the absence of ethnic minority journalists in the staffrooms of their papers, make the following points:

1. Few, if any, black youngsters with the right "O" and "A" levels approach them for jobs.
2. They are not prepared to lower educational standards just to employ ethnic minorities.
3. Those ethnic minorities with the right qualifications who have arrived in this country as journalists need years to get to know the nuances of white Britain, and would therefore not make good journalists on British papers.

It is understandably true that, with the education system as it is for ethnic minorities today, and the poor performance rate it results in for ethnic minority youngsters, there are very few suitably qualified youngsters.

But I know of a few Black and Asian youngsters who have the necessary qualification and who have disappointingly made the rounds to local papers. I also personally know of one or two local editors who have actually told me that they have never been approached by suitably qualified black youngsters, and who when approached by such suitably qualified youngsters, when there was a vacancy on their papers conveniently found excuses not to employ them.

No-one expects editors to lower their educational requirements – not even Black people. What Black people do want is to be employed because they are capable and have the correct qualifications. They don't want concessions, what they want is just a fair chance.

On the last point. That argument has been used in my case a few times, inspite of the fact that the sort of education I and other Black people had received in our countries of birth was as British as it is here. Yet this argument, I know, has not prevented editors from employing whites from South Africa, Rhodesia (*now Zimbabwe*) and the other "Old" Commonwealth countries, who have had a similar education to mine and who know as little or as much of this country as I do.

Another, albeit, minor reason black youngsters are not forthcoming is the lack of encouragement they get to enter journalism from the school careers system. Now this is true of both black and white youngsters. But I have on record numerous cases where black youngsters were actually discouraged by school careers officers to think about journalism as a profession, let alone entering it. Another reason is the lack of encouragement from black parents themselves, who in many an instance look upon journalism as a "white preserve"

It would do well for me to recount, at this stage, my own experiences in this field, as it illustrates the problems and frustrations even a journalist, like myself, with a recognised university education and journalistic experience, had when I applied for staff jobs in this country.

Between late 1968 and early 1969 I applied for over 90 jobs. Over 80 of these were advertised vacancies and the remainder applied to a cross-section of Fleet Street papers which I thought or had heard might have a vacancy. Between the two, I virtually covered the whole of Fleet Street except for about three or four papers. The papers covered North, East, West and South England, the Midlands and most of the Greater London papers and I was told (after informing them that I was black):

- that the posts were filled, although ads for the same post in most instances appeared subsequently;
- that the posts were filled and that my application would be retained in their files should a review of the position or another vacancy arise in the future. None ever contacted me again, although similar vacancies arose;
- that professionals from UK papers only were wanted. White South African, Rhodesians and Australians who had never actually worked on UK papers and knew as much or as little as myself about this country, got jobs on these papers with no apparent difficulty.

One editor actually asked me to come and see him. In fact all he told me when I saw him was; "It is the first time I"ve had the pleasure of speaking to a coloured journalist who was resident in this country". He didn't offer me the job; it was already taken.

I will not go further into these personal experiences as they have been recounted in finer detail in the book WHITE MEDIA AND BLACK BRITAIN and the Commission's NEW COMMUNITY, both of which are available at this seminar. Also my two black colleagues on the platform will go in detail into their experiences which in essence are similar to mine.

Of the 29,000 odd journalists working on British newspapers and magazines and in radio and television, less than two dozen (under 1%) are black. The majority are here to-day. Compare this to the country's black population percentage of about 3% and the fact that over 40% of black youngsters are now second generation. These include a few Black subs (when I speak of Black, I mean West Indians, Africans and Asians) and one or two TV and radio reporters.

A survey on employment of black journalists carried out last year by the NUJ's Birmingham Branch shows that Birmingham had no black journalists despite a large black population.

There is yet another obstacle facing Black people who want to enter the world of British Journalism. That is the white "black expert" journalist – the race relations experts. These "experts" are the ones who have fashioned to a great extent the stand of their various papers on race relations. They are "the experts" on Black issues. They jealously guard their position and resist any newcomers and intruders in the field. They react even more vehemently when the intruder is black. No doubt this is a consequence of the old paternalistic doctrine which was and still is so strong among some liberals. They know the Black person, his desires and shortcomings better than black people themselves. So that whatever the British media has to say, the media image we – both black and white – have of ourselves is written or broadcast by a pure white-lily hand with all its dire consequences.

One such consequence is the media's playing up of what it thinks is in the interest of Black people – and the misrepresentation of what actually goes on in the black British world – has been a reciprocal hostility on the part of ethnic minorities towards the press. This hostility is two-fold. Either no information is forthcoming at all or the media is taken for a ride with tall stories which most white journalists swallow hook, line and sinker, and which build up an erroneous, if not dangerous, picture of ethnic minorities in this country.

One of the best examples is the merry-go-round that Michael X (the Black power leader in this country) led the media in this country. Michael X's claim that he had stacks of arms hidden away and had an army of karate-trained black guerillas was snapped up by the press from the EXPRESS to the GUARDIAN who not only reported whatever he said – no matter how ridiculous – but in fact believed what he had told them, despite what I and other colleagues, close friends to him, gave contrary information to the media. In this way the British media could be held responsible for building up Michael X.

It is this desire, this temptation for the media to make race a "topic" that even normally responsible organs find it difficult to resist. For race unfortunately ranks with sex, drugs and "permissiveness", as surefire sensational material.

How does one then meet this situation?

It was Peter Harland who at another time (in the Runnymede Trust pamphlet, RACE AND THE PRESS, pinpointed the issue when he said that:

What is required is conscious editing, the paper going out to find other kinds of news from among the immigrant community – the same kind of news as the paper prints about the host community, good news as well as bad: meetings, dinners, celebrations, speeches, presentations, retirement, sport and so on.

And then quite rightly concluded that:

One way of helping towards this end is to employ immigrant reporters.

Of course what he meant was black reporters.

There can be no doubt that the physical presence of black journalists in editorial offices would be a great psychological fillip to sane race relations reporting. Their presence would neutralize, at the least, rabid racism in editorial offices, where it exists, and they could be on hand to provide the necessary background material, nuances and subtleties which make up the black scene. I am not saying that black journalists should be employed solely for reporting about Black people. *No, what we should press for is the employment of black staff per se, not just to be employed in areas with large black populations, but even on papers operating in all-white areas.*

Of course, for a short time, it might be necessary for Black people to report about black people and issues as the occasion arises, but that is not something which should be a permanent feature and criterion for the employment of black journalists, as many black journalists, including myself, can testify is the usual practice.

The employment of black journalists also makes, apart from good race relations – sound economic sense, especially for papers which circulate in areas where there is a substantial black population and thus black readership.

No newspaper will and can deny its desire to increase its circulation, nor can and will the broadcasting and TV companies equally deny their quest for better viewing and listening ratings.

Black viewers *identify* more with "News at Ten", because of the possibilities of the visual appearance of Trevor MacDonald where it is known that a black journalist is obviously contributing to a paper, Black people are more inclined to buy a copy of that paper. Of course, it does not mean that they are not inclined to buy papers which have good and sane race relations reportage.

But let us not stop at the doorstep of editors. White journalists – and even NUJ chapels – themselves are in many an instance just as great an obstacle to the employment of black reporters. I have earlier mentioned the role of the white "black experts". I also know of at least two chapels who in fact made life hell for their black colleagues, so much so that in one instance that the black reporter, after a few months, left in disgust.

Last year, as one of our first practical steps, the NUJ Race Relations Sub-Committee sent a questionnaire to all NUJ branches seeking information about the discrimination on grounds of race and colour.

The questionnaire covered the number of black journalists employed; sizes of immigrant communities; possible reasons why few black people apply to be journalists and whether concern was felt about this; coverage of ethnic minority group stories; attitudes about positive discrimination against black people in employment or news coverage; how chapels and branches were contributing and promoting racial harmony; unfair reporting or unnecessary mention of race or colour; and omission of relevant information, unfair selection of material, or omitting to publish at all.

The response was quite good. About 72 per cent of the branches replied. A preliminary analysis of the replies confirm our fears on the question of employment, that only a handful of black journalists were employed. What emerged from the replies were:

(i) Despairingly few journalists had any idea whether there was a black presence of any size in their areas, or whether their papers were carrying any racially biased stories.

(ii) With a few exceptions, journalists showed that they themselves were not inclined to produce or originate racially-biased material.

(iii) A substantial number believed that there was evidence of discrimination against black people in employment or news coverage.

(iv) Much more must be done by chapels and branches to contribute to promoting racial harmony.

(v) Few were sure how to handle the question of "unnecessary mention of race or colour".

(vi) Little was revealed in the replies about the existence or non-existence of positive, constructive journalism.

The NUJ, in its wisdom, has at last recognised the problem we are now discussing. It is for that reason that its last Annual Delegate Meeting passed the guidelines which we have heard so much about already. The relevant one to this session, of course, is the third one, which says:

"Press for equal opportunities for employment of black staff, particularly in areas of extensive minority group settlement."

What we must in future do is to press for the inclusion of equal opportunity clauses in collective bargaining agreements, and for the implementation of procedures designed to *ensure* that equal opportunity policies are actively pursued and, here I want to emphasise, *regularly monitored* by newspaper proprietors. Only by monitoring, will we be able to see whether we are really making progress in this field.

What we must also be aware of is the acute danger of proprietors employing one or more *token* black reporters and then effectively segregating them in a reportorial ghetto of writing on "black community affairs". The old parallel with women journalists being confined to knitting, fashion and cookery is probably a salutary reminder, even if it is less true nowadays. Nevertheless, I am sure this is something the Equal Opportunities Commission, when it comes into being, will seriously consider.

In words that are as applicable and as pertinent to Britain as to the USA, and to reporting of foreign as well as domestic conflicts, the National Advisory Commission on Civil Disorders (popularly known as the Kerner Commission) which was appointed by President Johnson following the race riots which took place in the summer of 1967, said it all:

"Along with the country as a whole, the press has too long basked in a white world, looked out of it, if at all, with white men's eyes and white perspective. that is no longer good enough."

Indeed it isn't, especially if the media as a whole accepts, which I am sure it does, that Britain is a multi-racial and multi-cultural society.

If here, too, it should take the terrible and unforgivable nature of race riots to change things, the British communications media industry will indeed be deeply culpable unless we all in this marvelous profession of ours, do something positively **now** and stop pretending that there is no problem in our indefatigable British way of determinedly denying its existence by constant verbal expression of British tolerance and refusal to acknowledge discrimination in our own journalistic backyard when it occurs. I have said "communications media industry" deliberately, because I am aware that not only the press and broadcasting, also the "other side of the fence" – PR, advertising, etc. – are all involved.

By obscuring the reality beneath a consensus acceptance of British tolerance, a screen is provided for the practice of discriminating behaviour, which by popular judgment and official utterance is unacceptable in a tolerant society. The steps that we in the media must take on this issue are nothing but clear.

This paper, which is seminal and still germane to the issues involved in the 1999 Media Minority's Message Conference, in Barcelona was presented to the first held Race and the Media Seminar on l7 October 1975 organised by the Race Relations Working Party of the National Union of Journalists (NUJ) of Britain and Ireland and the Community Relations Commission-CRC- (UK)

FACE TO FACE WITH RACE - (1976)

I accept whole-heartedly the thesis developed by concerned academics, some senior practising journalists, race relations experts and others that journalists have to take special care in reporting race relations matters, especially in a multi-racial community which Britain undoubtedly is.

But, whether one likes it or not, the news media, like the British white population has still to accept that Britain is a multi-racial society. For this reason is has been able to give emphasis to "immigration" and "immigrants" while ignoring the fact that increasingly the people characteristically labelled "immigrants" are in fact British and that interestingly enough 40 per cent of the black youngsters in Britain today are those born in this country.

The Press must first recognise that what it prints or broadcasts about ethnic groups can directly affect ethnic tension. The mass media are among the many sources of information and interpretation from which people build up a picture of their world. On matters where the knowledge or information required is not available within local cultures, the media may become the main or indeed the only source. Race in Britain is such a case. A large proportion of the white populations live outside areas of black settlement, and much of the information in terms of which the subject has come to be to discussed is not of a kind that can become available at a local level.

Mass communications do not haphazardly impinge on social life from outside. The mass media are social institutions integral to the society in which they operate. Their location within the structure of society they occupy is an indication of their relevance and the influence of their output. In the case of newspapers, the things that help to shape their content and how this content is presented depends among other things on the procedures by which they obtain and process their copy, the professional ideologies of their staffs, and the know or assumed characteristics and preferences of their readers.

Events are reported because they are thought to be important; they are thought important because they appear in the news. What it would also do well to state now is that newspapers are not entirely independent of each other or of the other news media for what they print. Stories relating to an event first reported in one newspaper are usually picked up and developed by others and the television news services, if they accept that they are newsworthy.

But what sort of information about race and colour do newspapers and broadcasting regard as newsworthy? There is no doubt that over the years anything about race and colour that could be discussed in terms of immigration, of numbers, of the relations between white and black – particularly animosity between black and white – or of discriminations has increasingly come to be looked upon as more newsworthy than material that requires a different frame of reference.

As Paul Hartmann and others in their study on attitude change and the British national press concludes that as a result of the foregoing, a developing structure of assumptions and inferences about the significance of race in Britain has emerged. *"That is part of the reason why material of this kind has increased so much over the years as the coloured populations has increased, and why other kinds of material – particularly about housing, education and employment and what we have called 'normal' material – has not*", they reported.

How far these news values derive from the direction that public policy over race and immigration has taken and how far the operation of these news values may have helped shape public policy is difficult to answer. But what can be noted is the relationship between race as it is defined in official policy and race as it is presented in the press.

Race, as the press sees it, is predominantly about immigration, and immigration is not only a matter of people coming into the country, it is about keeping them out. Race is also about the relations between white and black which is presented as a matter of grave concern; black people appear as the objects and victims of hostility and discrimination by whites, and particularly of late there is an indication of reciprocal hostility from the black side.

Both immigration and the relations between white and black are the subjects of legislation and statutory machinery and of debate and controversy. The picture of race in the press has been like this for some time and there is little doubt that this news framework has resulted in the perspective wherein black people are presented as ordinary members of society becoming increasingly overshadowed by news perspective in which they are presented as a problem.

As the number of black people and the social concern over race relations has increased, so attention has moved away from the relations of black people to the major social resources of housing, education and employment – which must by all counts be regarded as an important part of the underlying basis of inter-racial hostility in the country – towards the hostility itself and its manifestations, including the concern to keep blacks out of the country and the concern to regulate hostility, by the various laws and machinery set up to this end.

We thus end up with a situation in which the press has reflected pressure that on the one hand have sought to exclude blacks from British society and on the other hand aimed to reduce discrimination against them; but has not at the same time paid proportionate attention to those factors that must be regarded as at least part of the underlying cause of anti immigration feeling and discrimination.

Negativity is also another factor which contributes to the newsworthiness of an event or issue. The more negative an event, the more likely is it to be thought newsworthy. This particularly applies to situations that are culturally distant from the society in which the news is being reported. The fact that inter-group hostility and discrimination finds easier expression, is a factor in this direction. Material which fits existing expectations and that can be reported within existing frames of reference is more likely to make news than material that does not all this of course becomes relevant if it is recognised that what is written in the British press is as a whole written by a lily white hand.

News production, it can be argued, in itself entails the generation of news frameworks which result in a selective emphasis on particular aspects of society and the world and on aspects of particular areas of subject matter. The particular kind of selectivity that operates in any given situation will be found to be articulated to the dominant value system of the society as a whole.

Now this is understandable in a white value dominated society. But does it fit into a multi-racial society which Britain also is? And does it fit into our press which ought to tell us ALL we want to know about our society. The media as a whole, unfortunately, has not a happy record at all.

When "racist" stories are reported the prevailing cultural assumptions about colour and the"colour problem" is in many an instance the criterion. Is there seriously an honest attempt to tell the whole story, or a decision to set individuals and events in their historical and economic context and not just expose them to the arbitrary glare of publicity when the media decides that they are newsworthy? "*New value*" is a capricious rule of thumb; and as one prominent Editor put it: "*We in communications cannot meet our challenge by telling less than the truth. We can only meet it by striving to tell more of the truth*".

But this desire to tell more of the truth about the black presence in this country is greatly circumscribed by the absence of journalists who are well informed about black people, about their desires, their hopes, their shortcomings and their successes. White journalists can only "interpret" what blacks feel and think – and let there be no doubt, some do succeed quite well. However, in-spite of these few, an even smaller number manage to capture the "gut" feelings of black people.

What is needed and here I am sure every practitioner in this field would agree is an honest portrayal of conflict and an informed discussion of the issues they raise. That means that the views and attitudes of black teenagers, policemen, and indeed the National Front, should be represented in the British Press – not what those views and attitudes ought to be, not merely when they're supported by "facts" or quotes from "responsible spokesmen" but what they are. They haven't been, they aren't, and they won't be until the people who decide what goes in newspapers and the people who put it there are no longer an ethnocentric elite. In others words what it means is that newspaper staff ought to contain the variety of views, life-styles and groupings within the changing society they seek to reflect. Of course, they don't.

One answer is training of journalists. Here a well prepared race relations course could be of value in journalists training courses. Another and more obvious one is the training and employment of black journalists.

Journalists are jealous of their liberal beliefs. An accusation of prejudice can arouse as much indignation as a claim that they are bad reporters. We are all experts on the subject – with no special knowledge or experience. The result is that the reporter and sub-editor can happily produce a story for publication which is potentially harmful to good community relations because it is supported by the claim that the normal criteria of news value and public interest apply.

It is becoming increasingly obvious that these "normal" criteria must be suspended if the continuing improvement in community relations is to be considered. And before I hear murmurs of censorship let me add that the newspapers job is tell it – but to make sure to tell it as it is. Which can mean that extreme care is taken in presenting the story on a factual, often low-key, basis which might offend normal journalistic practice but without stirring up racial feeling when this could be avoided.

I must confess that as a Union, the NUJ has been diffident, almost nervous about venturing into territory not directly concerned with the economic well-being of our members, for that is what our Race Relations Guidelines are all about.

News stories, headlines, and the odd adjective within a story, have their beginnings far below the editor's office, although it is he who is held responsible for everything that appears in his power. It is the reporter, the copy-taster, the sub-editor, the news-editor, the radio and TV script writer who makes key decisions.

It would force newspaper and broadcasting managements to look hard at every story with a race angle in it and ask themselves:

Is this story or broadcast going to do more harm than good?

Is it going to worsen race relations in our multi- racial society? and

is it going to stir up the consuming fires of race hatred?

I must admit that I once thought it would not happen. For reasons of protocol, for worry that the general scorn that greets do-gooding rules and regulations and that natural distrust that all journalists have for anything that smacks of control or censorship.

Now with our guidelines and the Race Relations Sub-Committee our members are complaining about the coverage of race stories in their papers. There is an awareness slowly developing that conscious editing does not necessarily mean censorship or is unnatural to what we as journalists hold so dear – the right to investigate, probe, make public, without fear or favour.

The inevitable question: are we asking for special treatment for race issues? Yes and No! No because much of the critique of race news can be applied to news generally, and changing the news portrait of race must involve alterations in the more general conception of news.

Yes, because race as an issue is indelibly different from any other contemporary group relationship. In the ability of practising journalists, editors and proprietors to face up to these problems may lie the future sensitivity and competence of white society to respond to the needs of its black citizens, and aid the dimension of boldly standing up to be counted, for when it comes down to racism there can be no impartiality.

Speaking at the Conference on the Media, Loughborough University, October 4/5 1976.

THE MEDIA AS A MESSENGER OF POLITICAL CHANGE (1981)

What is the function of the Press? It has been described at different times by different people. The major functions of communication could be summed up, I suggest, as:

1 *Surveillance* – The sentinel or lookout role of the media, watching the society and horizon for threats to establishment order and information on people or places of public interest.

2 *Correlation* – The interpretation and linking function of the media which helps their readers, the audience, understand, interpret and comprehend the different things that are happening in and out of society and how they affect each other, as well as stay in touch with others in society.

3 *Transmission* – The socialisation function of the media, which defines the society, its norms and its values to its audience and through their portrayals and coverage, assists members of society in adopting, using and acting on those values.

4 *Entertainment* – The function of the media for diversion and enjoyment, which provides stories, features, music and films designed to make the audiences laugh, cry, ridicule, relax, reflect, rather than gain information.

5 *Economic Service* – The role of the media within the economic system of the society which in Britain means that most media function as corporations serving the needs of their shareholders and other corporations by attracting audiences that will either pay for the media products or serve as the target for advertising messages. In short the media is there to make money as well.

Advertisers, generally, demand mass audiences to advertise and market their products. The communication media responds by adopting news and entertainment strategies that would attract the largest numbers of readers. Since the majority in Britain are white, this means that the Black minority are treated as fringe audiences, not important enough in numbers to dictate the content that would be directed to the majority white audience.

The media therefore reinforce a collective consciousness in the members of the audience that is necessary to attract large numbers of undifferentiated people. It follows that the task of the media to look for commonality among members of the audience, common themes, values, ideas, interest, areas that would attract and not offend the majority white audience. With few exceptions, this means that the content of the media reinforces, rather than challenges the established norms and attitudes of the society.

To do otherwise would be to risk offending significant numbers in the majority audience and, in the process, losing the large audience demanded by the advertisers.

British society, characterised by the assimilative mentality through which immigrants are expected to be integrated into British society and culture, has often treated members of groups who have not blended or completely integrated into the mainstream as outsiders. Racial minorities that can be identified by colour are often 'beyond' integration, unable to blend over a period of a generation because of physical characteristics. They are not only beyond 'integration' but outside the focus of the mass audience so necessary for the survival of the media. Their numbers are relatively small compared with the white majority and, as a result, they are not considered important components of the mass audience. For the most part, the British media treat groups who are not in the main stream audience either by ignoring them or stereotyping them.

Films, TV, radio programmes, newspapers and news magazines generally ignore the issue confronting Black people in Britain, as well as their culture and traditions. When they are treated it is often in stereotypical roles, such as violent Black youth or sinister Asian landlords. These characterisations of Blacks are largely based on the perception and preconceptions of those outside the group, rather than the realities of the groups themselves. They are pictures of racial minorities as seen through white eyes.

The media in Britain rarely covers activities of Black communities unless in accordance with their surveillance function, they are perceived as posing a threat 'to the established order' or, in accordance with their correlation function when they are covered during colourful cultural festivals such as Notting Hill Carnival. Thus the audience see only a slice of the minorities, one that does not jar their preconceptions of these groups. In fact the media portrayals help legitimise and reinforce such preconceptions. In the absence of alternative portrayals and broadened news coverage, one sided portrayals and news articles easily become the reality in the minds of the white audience.

Whites are to be seen in a wide range of roles, ranging from villains to heroes. Blacks are seen only as lazy violent thugs or scroungers. There are not real alternative portrayals to counter the stereotype.

The media has its greatest effect when it is used in a manner that reinforces and channels attitudes and opinions consistent with the psychological make up of the person and the social structure of the groups with which he or she identifies.

This reinforcement and channelling effect of the media, when coupled with the content analysis that has been made on coverage and portrayals of minorities in news and entertainment media, provides an insight into the negative effects of one-sided media images on Black groups portrayed.

The public language of journalism is a statement about what is "normal". It conveys messages through the complex associations and implications of its metaphors and unstated assumptions. If a journalist's language violates the experiential reality of a minority or identifiable group within society, it creates a conflict between reality and the personal experience of those people who come to be identified as deviant. Such a cognitive conflict easily contributes to actual conflict between members of a group that has been so singled out and stereotyped and the public, the dominant group at large. Excreta was put through the door flaps of Black people in parts of Britain and many were subjected to racial attacks and harassment after Enoch Powell made his notorious "Rivers of Blood" speech in which he warned the British people (white) that the Black presence in Britain was against their interest. His speech of course received wide and uncritical reporting in the British press.

Studies also show that bigoted persons watching television programmes ridiculing bigotry interpret such programmes as reinforcing their pre-existing beliefs. Studies show that children, both Black and White, are especially affected by entertainment characters that portray minority groups and that the media is a significant source from which they got their opinions or knowledge of Black people.

The British media have not just expressed general opinions and feelings, but have themselves significantly, through their editorials and comment pieces, contributed to such negative feelings.

Most items are about crime and human interest, followed by the national issues of immigration and the debate about legislation against such immigration.

The actions of the neo fascist National Front received much attention and although there is a space devoted to the "white" side of the "problem", namely discrimination, this is typically portrayed as incidental, as the act of extremist individuals, and not, no not, as a structural manifestation of British racism.

Young Black West Indians tend to be associated with crimes in general and mugging in particular.

Another way the British media connives and fosters the racism prevalent in society is by not seeking out Black views.

Blacks, both in Britain and in African countries, are seldom asked to give their opinions. The media prefer to invite a white "minority specialist", usually male, to give his views. Additionally the Black experts on British papers are usually white reporters. Have you ever listened to a Black "White expert"?. When I started in British journalism I always found myself marginalised and only got stories when Black groups refused to speak to White journalists.

When Black people are present it is only in "non speaking" roles, even for events that directly involve them. This is not only time for their role in press stories, but also for their participation in the media themselves. Especially in higher positions, there are virtually no Black journalists. What does become obvious is the fact that there are a number of prevailing and persisting commonalities:

1 Ethnic minorities in Britain are also minorities in the press, they are less employed and less represented.
2 Many of the dominant topics are directly or subtly associated with problems, difficulties or threats to the dominant values, interests, goals or culture.
3 Black events are consistently described from a White majority point of view, in which the authorities are given more space and credibility than minority spokespersons.
4 Topics that are relevant for the ordinary daily life of Black groups in Britain, such as work, housing, health education, political life, and culture, as well as discrimination in these areas, are hardly discussed in the media unless they lead to "problems" for society as a whole or when they are spectacular.
5 Racism is systematically under reported, reduced to incidents or individual discrimination, or attributed to small right wing parties and located in poor city areas.

Racism of the elite or the various institutions is seldom reported. It therefore goes without saying that against this background, the media have been reluctant, to say the least, to discuss publicly its own role in the reproduction of racism in society. Critical analysis is censured and my own experience of the press suggests that critics are often personally discredited or prevented from collecting data in fieldwork.

The role of the media in what takes place in our society is highly relevant. It provides the main 'data' and the issues people may use for every day conversation. This does not mean that most newspapers explicitly formulate racist opinions. Many editors and journalists will maintain that they are against racism and generally loathe extremist racist parties.

Their role is more subtle and indirect. Negative reporting is partly, but only partly, a consequence of routine conditions of news production and news values. Negative spectacular events tend to get more attention and any group without power and influence will have less access to the news media.

The many "neutral" topics that are present for the white majority in Britain (such as political organisation, culture, the arts) are not there when they are about Black groups.

The problems for the majority (economic recession, unemployment, lack of housing, crime) are not paralleled by those problems that are relevant for the minority. On the contrary, the majority problems are often subtly attributed to the very presence of Black people. Deeper social causes, contexts and consequences such as the role of discrimination in housing etc are seldom discussed.

Even when the media does not formulate negative opinions, it provides a definition of the Black situation that makes such negative references not only possible but plausible. In this way, it both pre-formulates prejudice and reinforces the partial models of the Black situation that is acquired by personal experiences, hearsay and socialisation.

In conclusion can I therefore reaffirm that the primary role in the construction of a dominant (white) consensus in Britain is played by the media and that this role is defined not only in terms of its vast mass-mediated scope and by the assumed representational goals of the print or broadcast media in the reporting of social events. The media also play an intermediary role in the reproduction of other types of public discourse. Much of news, as I indicated earlier, is not so much about happenings or events, but about what other people, typically the powerful and the elite, say or write.

Speech to a Race and the Media Meeting organised by the RRWP - local Cardiff journalists and broadcasters, race relations activitists and black community organisations.

BLACK RESPONSES IN A MULTIRACIAL SOCIETY – democracy, minorities and racism. (1981)

For even outside the realm of government we regard it desirable to evaluate institutions from the point of view of the degree to which controlling decisions are determined by the consent of the participants. – Prof Sidney Hook.

Black politics in Britain in the main are the politics of those at the bottom of society. And, although forming not much over 2% of the population, the blacks are coming to see themselves as potentially part of a revolutionary vanguard and justifiably for two reasons. First, they are identifiable and so subjected to the recurrent spur of social discrimination from a powerful white majority. Secondly, they are on the whole inspired with the pride of the revolutionary heroes of America, Africa and the rest of the Tiers Monde. Added to this is the fact that the scenario is also set in a country where the democratic process is a much extolled platform creed, manifesting itself in bursts of legislative manoeuvres to meet a growing or waning (the choice depends on who are the protagonists) racist tide.

But the reasonableness of the democratic process does not, as any serious minded student of discriminatory practices will vouch, lie in any specific piece of legislation, but in the rationale of the method by which majority (re white) decisions, like the Race Relations Act, are reached.

The philosophy of democracy rests not on the belief in the natural goodness of man, but in his educability; not in the inevitability of social progress, but in the potentialities of human nature and intelligence of both the majority and the minorities.

The history of race relations in Britain serves to show that the most reliable check upon what de Tocqueville called the '*legitimate tyranny of holy injustice*' of majorities is, not any absolute veto by a white majority, but the development of appreciation of the constructive function of black minority dissent in a world where we cannot achieve final truth.

The moral that may be drawn from this is that where majority rule on racial lines prevails its decision will reflect the degree of enlightenment or of race bigotry, the ways of thought, and habits of action which are characteristic of the community. Governments may sink to depths lower than their source; they cannot rise higher.

A functioning democracy presupposes that it is possible to find in any community a degree of common interest among all the groups sufficient to make resort to internal strife, in whatever form, whether peaceful or violent as manifested recently in Lewisham, Bristol, Ladywood or Notting Hill unnecessary.

Intelligent democratic programmes of action, therefore, will aim, among other things, at introducing those institutional changes that will permit even those who lose in the peaceful processes of democratic struggle to lead lives of usefulness, dignity and responsibility – a prerequisite absent in the estimation of blacks themselves.

It is in this context that Britain's blacks will not go on accepting the false doctrine that other individuals can be better trusted to discover and administer to their needs than their own imperfect selves.

They have come to believe in themselves, albeit slowly. And having begun to believe, have made this very belief an ethos – an integrated complex of social values which determines the status, responsibility and duty of each of them.

To some this ethos may be a myth about this world or the next accompanied by a hope for greater peace on earth or in heaven. To the majority it has become a sense of identity and an intense resentment against discrimination, rationalised as a demand for justice, fair play and equality of opportunity, which is the well publicised tradition of British society.

This now naturally poses another question which needs looking at. What alternative method can be embraced by a society like ours which permits and encourages plural values and plural associations? The more intelligence is liberated in a democratic community, the greater its control of nature and the sources of wealth; the greater its control of nature, the greater possibility of diversifying interests, values and associations; the great diversification, the more necessary the function of intelligence to mediate, discuss, co-exist and harmonise.

But is there in Britain today such an intelligence actually being liberated to create a racial atmosphere conducive to harmony, co-existence and possibility even a genuine acceptance? To the black minority it does not seem so, and instead the opposite – a distinct evidence of a significant amount of hostility in the white majority community – is rather more evident.

The fundamental premise of the foregoing argument is naturally the assumption that the black minority in this country are here to stay, generally and intensely regard Britain as their home and share in the responsibilities expected from every citizen in a democratic state.

Give and take the ambiguity of the attitudinal loyalty the older black settlers have given to this country, it is the growing presence of the second generation (over 40% of them are born in this country) who more readily fit in with the above premise – at least in theory. But the treatment that even they are getting from the majority make this ideal difficult to sustain.

How does, and how can this black presence actually and possibly fit into the larger community here?

Britain is not a self-contained ethnically homogeneous or consensus dominated nation state, nor is it a country free from racism. To the fact that the racial frame of reference is an integral part of British history and culture going back many centuries and full of vivid examples. And here let me state categorically that this belief was not and is not the preserve of the *'ignorant, the poor and the working class'* as so many well-intentioned white liberals are wont to make us believe. For was it not none other than the ageing Queen Elizabeth I who in l601 issued a Royal Proclamation ordering all '*blackamoors*' out of the Kingdom and once and for all rid the country, badly afflicted by hunger and poverty of "*those kinds of people*".

One and a half centuries later this viewpoint received help from that well-known liberal philosopher, David Hume, which achieved wide publicity and added strength to the growing anti-black lobby: "*I am apt*", Hume argued, "*to suspect the Negroes.. to be naturally inferior to the whites. There never was a civilised nation of any other complexion than white, or even any individual eminent either in action or speculation. No ingenious manufacturer among them, no arts, no sciences. There are Negro slaves dispersed all over Europe, of which none even discovered any symptom of ingenuity.*"

That Hume, an educated, sophisticated man should contribute to the perpetuation of mythology indicates that prejudices often stemmed not from the ignorant but from the informed and 'the enlightened'.

Racism is not something which has just cropped up its ugly head in the 1970's and 1980's with the rumbling scum of the National Front and the National Party, or with the increase of the black presence since the 1950's. It has been here for centuries and later found constitutional expression in the Empire and latterly in the constitutional concept of the multi racial Commonwealth, with its emphasis on tolerance, which in itself does not mean the end of racism and race relations problems, but is merely a pre-condition for the attempt to build a racially just society.

What is not in dispute is the fact that we are a multi-racial society – a mosaic of various racial groupings all living in one society with different cultural affinities, and not a nonracial, homogeneous society.

But multi-racism and racial tolerance do not in themselves spell peace, dignity and self respect. Bernard Crick in "*The Strange Death of the American Theory of Consensus*" (Political Quarterly, Vol 43, No I 1972) together with others has reminded us that "*Tolerance is the limited acceptance that one extends, out of a mixture of policy and humanity, to those things of which one disapproves.*"

In fact both multi-racism and racial tolerance could result in strife and discord if they mean a stifling of the energy and view points of any of the units comprising society. For even if the multi-racial goal is achieved and there is a genuine tolerance of the black minority in British society, and this means the overcoming of activist racism, then we can expect the black minority to seek to combine and fight for the advancement of their position.

And it is here where the great dilemma faces a democracy. Should certain viewpoints be suppressed in the interests of the majority and in the interests of protecting the very fabric of a consensus society? Should minorities always conform to the whims, caprices and interests of the majority? For indeed here lies the predicament John Stuart Mill so blandly put that "*.. the food of feeling, is action.... Let a person have nothing to do for his country and he will not care for it....* ".

The possibilities of such a stifling becomes obvious where the various units – and in Britain's instance – the smaller units – are forced to conform to the ideals and norms of the majority. Commonly known as assimilation or integration, this process usually means the submergence of minority traditions, religions, viewpoints and the acceptance of different and stronger viewpoints with the eventual disappearance of the minority group or their traditions.

But also being a pluralistic society, there is the obvious yet simple fact that individuals who for some purposes are classified together nonetheless retain differences. For pluralism implies that societies do not always necessarily advance towards and develop into entities with a uniform way of life. Groups may be found in the same society which, although they accept and contribute to certain general features of the society of which they are part, nevertheless maintain their own identity. This is what is happening among and with a substantial majority of the minority black community in Great Britain to-day.

This separate "*identity*" is essential for many if they want to exist. This has not, as some white liberals will argue, produced massive or total separation (a kind of inverse racism). In such situations as J. Milton Yinger in "*A Minority Group in American Society*", New York, McGraw Hill, 1965 p 93) points out, "*separate groups tend to be inclusive rather than exclusive; and they are based in most instances on significant cultural differences*."

It is the lack of understanding of this development that has baffled many from the majority group and instilled an erroneous belief in many of them that they "understand" black feelings, fears and beliefs. And this is understandable for many of them associate with and know only middle-class members of the black minority, who being "deviant" identify themselves generally by class and not race (whereas the white working class has identified itself as a race and not as a class – refuting Marx's prediction of inter-racial proletarian solidarity with scarcely an exception). Thus both classes adjacent to the race barrier tend to maintain it, and the black bourgeoisie in order to lose their unwanted racial identity.

It is no good arguing that there are common interests where such issues as race relations are concerned, for the conceptions of the common interests are never common. If they were, government would be a mere administrative detail. However, the variety of interests that are always to be found make necessary that no interest be excluded from voicing its demands, even though these demands may, in the process of democratic deliberation, be compromised or rejected. The only historical alternative to the participation of the masses in the processes of government in the Western world, is, if I remember, the ancient, artful and uncertain technique of "*bread and circuses*". That the modern bread is smeared with margarine and the modern circuses are cinematic and the television makes no essential difference. Such a technique conceals differences and trouble centres; whereas the methods of participation and consultation uncover them, articulate new social needs and suggest instrumentalities for handling them.

Democratic government (in theory) implies the consent of the majority and minority in decisions affecting them directly. How true is that of race relations legislation? The rapid vocal increase in racism among the majority spells the lie to that majority's acquiescence to race relations legislation. The absence of any meaningful consultation has generated popular indifference or hostility. And it is clear that even those who believe that professionally wise men, the government experts and bureaucrats must do the governing, exclude at their own period those whom they would govern – whether majority or minority – from their counsels.

As said earlier, the wisest policy cannot succeed in face of popular indifference or hostility. And this is what is happening in the race relations field. A distinct failure so far to involve both parts of the governed whole – the white majority and the black minority – in issues that effect their daily life and their immediate future. Past race relations legislation, however "*good*" it was, was bound to meet popular indifference or hostility, precisely because those who govern excluded from their counsel those affected by such legislation. And here I mean grass-roots involvement. Beyond a certain point, the longer the delay in seeking such counsel, the more costly in tears and suffering will be the process of equality for everyone concerned, but especially for those who have so far endured the greatest indignities. For a basic; human and democratic right is violated whenever and wherever racial discrimination is practiced.

Present legislation, the Race Relations Act 1976 has to a certain extent sought such counsel. Not enough may be argued, but the tide of advance of such consultation in the final analysis measures the authentic growth of the democratic idea, and the effectiveness of any race legislation.

A talk given at a seminar to community activists in London.

THE MEDIA, SOCIETY AND RACE RELATIONS IN BRITAIN – (1984)

When examining the media, society and race relations, it is relevant in order to deal with the press and race relations to look at our society more generally.

A few basics suffice. No matter what day, what paper we open we will always find a report which deals with immigration, racism, or with asylum seekers. These are important matters because they are issues the press always seems to be involved in.

Migration is not new, and has gone on for centuries. There has been a steady flow of people to and from Britain over the last 500 years, to and from a wide variety of countries, Jews, Poles, Hungarians in the 1930's and further back to the Norman Conquest, the Roman Empire and Viking settlements.

Daniel Defoe (author of Robinson Crusoe) wrote accurately in l761:

A true brown Englishman is a contradiction,
In speech, an irony, in fact, a fiction,
It's well that virtue gives nobility,
How shall we else the want of birth and blood supply?
Since scarce one family is left alive which does not from some foreigner derive?
Thus from a mixture of all kinds began
That heterogeneous thing, an Englishman.

What is new is measurable Black immigration.

One of the first records of a black immigrant can be found in the time of Queen Elizabeth I. But so also can be found an early case of racial discrimination, as legend has it that she took a dislike to this settler and banished him from this land never to return and expressed strong disapproval of the presence of black people in her realm and indeed ordering that *those kind* of people should be deported forthwith. On l July l596 Elizabeth I caused an open letter to be sent to the Lord Major of London, his Aldermen and to the Mayors and Sheriffs of other towns in the following terms:

"Her Majestie understanding that there are of late divers blackmoores brought into this realme, of which kinde of people there are already here to manie... Her Majesty's pleasure therefore ys that those kinde of people should be sent forth of the lande, and for that purpose there ys direction given to this bearer Edwarde Banes to take of those blackmoores that in this last voyage.. we brought into this realme the number of tenn, to be transported by him out of the realme... "

Immigration since World War II

Troops stationed in Britain during World War II came from every part of the Empire, for instance, Clifton Robinson, former Deputy Chairperson of the Commission for Racial Equality, came with many other Jamaicans to serve in the RAF. There were some 7000 West Indians in the RAF. There were others working in factories – encouraged by the Ministry of Labour until the scheme ended in 1947. Further, there were Indians who went to fight in North Africa and Gurkhas who fought in the Far East. After the war most returned to their country of origin but some remained.

Immigration from the West Indies began in the late 1940's. For example, the "Empire Windrush", the first ship from Jamaica came in June 1948. Until 1951 the immigration totalled less than 1000 people a year. The pattern of migration was characterised by its responsiveness to British Labour market requirements, eg. it slowed down in the mid-fifties during the recession and it again grew in the early 1960's during the boom. But no attempt was made to match skills required and people.

Why did people want to come?

It is important that we know why people did come to Britain. Most immigrants came from the Indian sub-continent and the West Indies.

From the Indian Sub-continent they came for various reasons. There was a period of internal political upheaval in the later 1940's; there was the question of independence; civil strife; there was partition; there was enforced internal migration leading to 4 million refugees (Sikhs and Hindus); there was a shortage of land – the maximum size of farms in Eastern Punjab was 30 acres; and there was great efforts by both British and Indian to travel abroad to encourage immigration to Britain (who helped overcome Indian regulations).

From the West Indies, the Islands were experiencing some economic difficulties. But major efforts were made by British employers to encourage West Indians to come to Britain; most notably the National Health (then headed by Enoch Powell) and London Transport. Big posters were used in Barbados saying: "*You are welcome to come and work in Britain*", and "*London Transport welcomes you*". Then there was the establishment of the Commonwealth and the concept of the "Mother Country" with freedom and access for all members. These were the factors that made people come over here.

During the 1950's and 1960's immigration continued, reaching a peak in 1960/61 but even then the total number was less than l00,000. This created a desire for control. It led to the Commonwealth Immigration Act, 1962, and the voucher system which meant:

a) Only those who had jobs to come here
b) Only those with specific skills
c) Only those with good employment prospects

In 1965 category (c) was discontinued, and the number were restricted to 8,500 per annum. In 1968 the numbers were restricted to 5000. Since then the majority have been the immediate dependants of immigrants, people who had come over a long, long period. The situation at present is that primary immigration is stopped, its only fiancees and dependants who are waiting to come here.

Discrimination

Discrimination against the new arrivals began almost immediately. They were expected to take on unsocial, unpleasant jobs; they were expected to have the worse housing – signs reading "*no children, no dogs, no Coloureds*" were not uncommon; they were barred from numerous clubs, pubs, restaurants. etc.

And of course discrimination still exists today. It may not be so blatant but it is alive and well. For instance in

Employment

50 per cent of employers discriminate against black job seekers; black youth unemployment in some inner cities is 60 per cent, compared with 40 per cent white unemployment; blacks remain in junior posts; employers are uncompromising of black religious and cultural needs; and there is indirect and often unintended discrimination.

Housing

If you look at the national Housing and Dwelling Survey and take shared amenities as an example, the figures are 3 per cent white, 9 per cent Afro Caribbean, l3 per cent Asian. If you take overcrowding (2 + to a bedroom) the figures are 5 per cent white, l8 per cent Afro Caribbean, 30 per cent Asian. If you take the ages of property (pre 1919) 27 per cent white, 47 per cent Afro Caribbean, 62 per cent Asian. The CRE report on Race and the Public Sector indicated that white families are 3 times more likely to be given a house than a flat or maisonette than identical black families; white families are 8 times more likely to be offered new property than black families; and there is a massive over representation of black families on certain estates.

RACIST ATTACKS, LEISURE AND SERVICES

Although figures are not available (and not many people complain), there is a stream of complaints about clubs, discos, insurance brokers, estate agents, landlords and banks. Do you know that it is estimated by Home Office figures that one racially motivated attack takes place every hour each day.

Race Relations legislation

The existence of discrimination has, at least half heartily been acknowledged by Government since the early sixties. There have been three separate acts of Parliament: 1966 Act, 1968 Act, and 1976 Act – The latter combined the Race Relations Board and the Community Relations Commission to establish the Commission for Racial Equality (CRE). It also recognised and made unlawful indirect discrimination.

Is racism everywhere?

A Daily Mail reporter once complained to me that the CRE finds discrimination under every stone. He was right. But he had missed the point.

Prejudice against foreigners in general and against black people in particular is deeply embedded in British life. Its most obvious manifestation is in our British history of slavery which was justified on the basis of white superiority.

If you combine prejudice and power you have racism which in turn will, unless stopped, lead to discrimination. Given the nature of British Society we do, indeed, believe that discrimination occurs in almost every aspect of British life.

The Role of the Media

What is the role of the media in all of this? The first point to be made is that the media is made up of different medium and we have to deal with the press and broadcasting separately and the individual components of the media treat race in different ways. But the central argument applies to a greater or lesser extent to all.

Statements made by journalists in the print and electronic (broadcasting) media show that both contribute to and validate the general public's world view. Most people are uncritical and unsophisticated about what they read, hear or see in the press. If they heard it on the radio, saw it on TV or read it in the paper, "*It must be true*". A Journalist language creates and validates the viewer's, listener's or reader's assumptive world. As an important agent of "journalisation", it establishes public and accepted standards of a taken-for granted reality.

I believe that the media presents black Britons as different and a problem to white Britons. As a white population accounts for 96 per cent of the population and therefore seldom has direct personal relations with their fellow black (Briton) citizens and gain most of their information through the media. I also believe that this is profoundly damaging to race relations in that it both perpetuates the racist attitudes of white people and encourages black people to believe that they are a temporary and unwanted part of the British society. It must, of course, be stressed that the media's treatment of black Britons has improved over the years, particularly in broadcasting, and I would like to deal with the broadcasting first.

Until the last few years *broadcasting* coverage was characterised by what the Americans describe as the *invisible man theory*. Blacks, were simply not seen on television or heard on radio. Further, there was nothing about black culture, there was nothing about the black contribution to the economy, and blacks never appeared in soap operas, plays or serials. The only time they did appear was when white editors perceived that they were creating problems. For example, with immigration, with social security fiddles or with street disturbances such as those that occurred in Notting Hill in the late sixties and in Brixton. I had experience of this when I was working freelance in Fleet Street. I was never called in to do ordinary stories, only when there were disturbances, so called riots, when a black youngster threw a brick through a window, was I 'discovered' all of a sudden.

The position has, of course, improved, "*Coronation Street*" which is set in an area with a black population of around l5 per cent, took its first tentative step by employing a black actor. "*Crossroads*" introduced black actors in 1980 and have a number of them now. The BBC had black nurses in "*Angels*". Central Television ran a police series a couple of years ago which featured a black detective, although the detective was depicted in a bad light. Trevor MacDonald has been employed by ITN and is now its anchorman and so have others. And now if you switch on "*East Enders*" you do see black faces. And Ethnic Minority programmes have emerged, although they are broadcasting at times that they are off-putting to white audiences.

There has also been a number of programmes recently which have tried to deal honestly with the problems faced by black Britons. Despite certain misgivings voiced about the production, the BBC series "*Black and White*" did a considerable amount to raise public awareness of racial discrimination. The Wednesday screening had a viewing audience of almost 7 million. There were articles in most of the national newspapers, in the Listener and other magazines. Those 5 programmes did a great deal in a week to create a positive climate for race relations. It was a chance to put race matters clearly and visibly on the small screen and reach into the average British home. The more programmes that are produced that tackle race matters, especially the difficult areas, the most likely the climate could change for the better. But it is only a beginning.

For example, how often are black religious occasions even mentioned on radio or television? How often does a black doctor appear on phone-ins? How often do you hear a black recipe on the air? How often do you see black actors in domestically produced television material? The answer is, sadly, not often.

May I move on now to the press and I begin by stating the obvious. If broadcasting is about news, newspapers are about views. Popular newspapers in particular select and treat news in such a way that it will pander to the prejudices of their readers. This argument certainly applies to race relations. There are two factors which make up a newspaper, the way a story is treated and the item selected for coverage coupled with the amount of coverage given to a particular item. I should like to deal with these issues separately, although they are interconnected.

Language: It has long been recognised that there are dangers in mentioning the colour of a person's skin in a story unless it is an integral part of the story, such as in crime reporting. But is still goes on. *The Sun*, for example, led with a headline which read, "*Black Crime Shock*", in June last year when the police released the crime figures for London. Although mugging amounts to only around 2 per cent of London crime and it is estimated that only around 500 people are involved, the reader might well presume that *The Sun* was reporting a national situation covering all crime.

But the damage was done. For example, how many journalists automatically think that when you hear of a street crime, a house burglary or a rape, that black people are involved unless you are told otherwise. Yet there is no evidence that blacks are disproportionately involved in crime.

That leads me to my second area. The items that are selected for coverage and the amount of coverage given.

There are, I believe, two issues which illustrate a cause for concern: immigration and crime.

Immigration; Every time Parliament debates immigration, some crackpot argues that repatriation is a live issue, you can be sure that extensive coverage will follow. When Enoch Powell opened up his mouth about immigration all the papers reported about immigration. There would be heavy weight articles from learned commentators, there would be responsible leading articles and so on. Yet when we or others attempt to set out the simple facts of immigration it is usually simply ignored.

Crime: If we move on to crime, the picture is even more extreme. The simple truth is that if you are black and involved in crime you are many times more likely to be reported in the press. May I give you two examples. Some of you may remember the murder of Terry May, a young disabled motor cyclist who was stopped and subsequently murdered by a group of black youngsters. It was a horrible crime and day after day it received massive coverage. Our friends on *The Sun* ran a front page headline which read, "*Black Mob on the Rampage*". You may not, however, remember Fenton Oboga. He died on the day the Terry May trial began, whilst buying some fish and chips, he was set upon by a group of white youngsters. The National Media managed a total of l2 column inches on his murder. Whereas the amount of column inches on the Terry May came to nearly 500. Was the lack of interest in Fenton Oboga because he was black?

Let us look at child attacks. You may remember the horrid story of the black youths who set upon a mother and child. Extensive coverage followed which included a reward of £500 from *The Evening Standard*. However you may not remember the story of the black five year old child who was attacked the next day by some white youths who beat her up and threw her over a six foot wall. If you do not remember it, it is perhaps not surprising as the only paper to cover the story was *The Caribbean Times* and needless to say *The Standard* did not extend its offer to this brutal murder.

Indeed, so powerful has been this "white" perspective that events which would have been irresistible news stories had they happened in white communities, have been ignored because they occurred in black communities. Readers of *Caribbean Times, Asian Times, African Times, Jagaran, Garavi Gujerat, Des Perdes, Daily Milat, The Voice, The Journal* find themselves discovering an alternative reality, almost totally absent from the white news media. For example, large scale police action against members of a black community is ignored in the white press. Whereas, similar action directed against a white community would elicit banner headlines.

The power of the media to generate a positive or negative climate for race relations is well illustrated by the Manchester MacDonald enquiry reporting over the past few days.

The press, by and large were quick to blame Ahmed Ullah's death on the anti racist policies practised by Burnage High School. They rubbished anti-racism and one paper even suggested that instead of reducing racial conflict the anti racist policies promoted it.

A similar treatment was given to coverage of visitors from India, Bangladesh, Pakistan, Nigeria and Ghana when the Government imposed a visa requirement for entry to Britain. The visa requirement was discriminatory; a case for it had not been made out; neither the Governments concerned nor the CRE had been consulted; and no provision was made to send adequate and trained staff out to the countries concerned. With a couple of exceptions, no newspaper took up these matters. When around 2,500 Asians arrived, the tabloid newspaper were awash with picaresque and inflammatory headlines: "Asian flood swamps airport", screamed *The Express, "3,000 Asians flood Britain"*, shouted *The Sun. "Migrants flood in"* echoed *The Mail. The Sun* in a follow-up produced a banner headline, "*Liars*". Only *The Independent* and *The Guardian* agreed that the scenes at Heathrow were a "*disgrace*" to Britain.

The newspaper reports contained falsehoods and distortions. The Asians who travelled were visitors and not immigrants; a very large majority of them had a right to come; many came sooner than they had intended because of the uncertainty of the Government policy; and the chaos was a result of inadequate planning. The Asian community was subjected to a vicious moral mugging at the hands of the press. A mugging which would feed into the racial prejudices of the British people.

In terms of giving the other side of the story, vis-à-vis, Manchester it had to wait until Ian MacDonald, Gus John and Reheena Bhavnani broke their silence on the leaked report; to strongly back anti racist teaching and reject calls for a Government enquiry into the Inner London Education anti-racist policies.

Our popular culture is both developed and framed by the media. If the ethnic minorities are excluded from this process, as many would argue they are, then the realities of their lives here in Britain are ignored. Black people have become almost invisible in the entertainment side of broadcasting and highly visible, at times, in actuality broadcast. They appear in the newspapers mostly as part of the "problem" of race relations in Britain. And yet a wide range of their activities, pursuits and achievements are never reported. The media often perpetuates stereotypes of the ethnic minorities because journalists do not have contact with black British people to get the real story.

It is not surprising that the ethnic minority communities are wary of people in the media whose stock in trade seems to be stereotyping.

What we should see is more coverage of race matters, on a regular basis, and even handed approach. It is only in this way that stereotypes can be challenged and a more accurate image of our multiracial society be drawn.

Mechanism of Social Control

The longer I have been in journalism the more I have become involved in the political aspects of the media. I have come to see it, not part of our freedom, which I think it should be and originally was. The media has become, or is becoming more and more a part of the mechanism of social control over society, particularly in the last l0 to l5 years, perhaps longer. As Britain's economic strength has declined the necessity for social control has become greater, looking at this in terms of press and broadcasting freedom and I think that our freedom as a society in terms of our ability to speak to each other has diminished.

I will give you one example of which you may not feel is very relevant, but I think a symptom. Six years ago the Government passed a law called The Contempt of Court Act. It was supposed to tidy up, for the benefit of all journalists, what is a difficult and dangerous area, and quite properly difficult because the administration of justice in any society is an important business and it should not be held in contempt. The difficulty is that the Government allowed a clause to go through in that Act which allowed Courts to impose restrictions on what could be reported. The NUJ warned about the dangers of this sort of thing, but were ignored and what has happened now, up and down the country is that Magistrates and Higher Courts are using the Act to prevent the reporting of trials. Now you may say it is not very important if the local paper cannot report what is happening about a local burglar; but if you uphold this principle you can apply it to any kind of trial and you start to get closed off. That is just one example of the problems of social control that trade unions are fighting against.

There is a need now for journalists to become much more critical of their performance in reporting race relations. I doubt that many journalists would wish to continue in the profession if they felt their only function in life was to reflect the concerns of society. Journalists and journalism rightly is jealous of its prerogative to challenge and analyse events; to dig beneath the veneer, to reveal the reality. This is a valued and necessary function of journalism; and it is one which has been only weakly exercised in the reporting of race relations. It is vital for the future of race relations in multiracial Britain that journalists resist the temptation of the ready made news category and actively question and analyse the assumptions beneath popular and partly political discussions on race relations. The Five Point Guidelines for the Reporting on Race Relations adopted by the NUJ represents the basis for an improvement. At least they are a minimal sanction against the inept or racist journalist; at best they may help to defend the conscientious journalist who is hindered by editorial policy. They may of course expose an unwillingness on the part of journalists or proprietors to take the issue much more seriously.

It is important, however, to reiterate that there is no suggestion being implied that news which is critical of issues which affect racial minorities should be suppressed. This, indeed, would constitute a threat to press freedom. Moreover, efforts to improve race relations would be damaged if the public were to feel that information was being hidden from them. A healthy democracy depends on the availability of facts and the clash of opinions about them.

Prejudice and racism are a community concern and not just a concern of the group that are the targets of prejudice and racism. It is a concern of all the members of our society. We all pay the price, whatever it is in the destruction of property, civil unrest or practical instability.

Racial minorities are part of the fabric of our society and racist attacks upon them can delay or prevent their participation as full and equal participants. As well, such attacks have a direct impact on the total community as they encourage inter-group tensions and conflicts. The recent experiences demonstrate the potential destructive role the media can play in lengthening racism and discrimination and creating a fertile environment for the eruption of racist conflict. These costs are social, but there are also the individual costs; the individual effects of prejudice and racism.

The press have freedoms and responsibilities, and so does the community. The community has the right to fair representation in the media and the right and responsibility to address what they believe is unfair and racist reporting.

There is, however, a crucial difference between the portrayal of fads from differing viewpoints so that the readers can make up their own minds about them, and the distortion of information that stereotypes black people as has happened in our national tabloids today.

Racial tolerance and equality depend in a large measure upon the pursuit of knowledge and understanding. Journalists and editors, I insist, have an obligation to provide that understanding.

Speaking at a Race and Community Relations Seminar in London

STUDIOS WILL BURN, 'RACIST' MEDIA WARNED (1985)

BROADCASTING unions and employers were told at a meeting that unless they were serious about eradicating discrimination and ceased to foster society's racism in news reports, frustrated blacks would probably continue to react towards them as they did during the civil disturbances in Handsworth, Brixton and Tottenham.

"*Must we wait until studios are burnt down, before you realise the anger and frustration many blacks have against the media*," a black graduate told a packed conference on Broadcasting and Black People.

The conference, the first of its kind, was organised by the Race Relations Working Party of the NUJ and jointly sponsored by the ACTT, BETA, Equity, the Writers Guild and Society of Authors.

Earlier the Conference heard from Jake Ecclestone, NUJ Deputy General Secretary, on the NUJ's concern about the effect media coverage of blacks had on the safety of journalists. "*What has become clear to our union is the terrible effect racist reporting has on our members, and the anger it evokes from the black community*," he said.

Representatives from the BBC and Independent Broadcasting stations heard complaints about discrimination by the industry in training, recruitment and employment from black participants from all over Britain.

A call was made for recruitment policies which would outlaw internal advertising or word-of-mouth recruitment as well as the inclusion of unnecessary qualifications or excessive years of experience.

One woman with two 'A' and six 'O' levels vividly recounted her experiences of applying for a job with the BBC: "*I was told that I did not have the necessary experience although this was for a job which entailed me being trained. I had the required educational qualifications. I was also told that they needed a 'BBC sort of person'. The BBC has a bad image if it wants blacks to believe the industry is serious.*"

The meeting was; however, assured that the industry itself was concerned that there were such a small number (about 1%) of blacks in broadcasting.

Bob Rowlands, BBC Controller for Training, said: "*We not only declare were are equal opportunities employers in the BBC but have embarked on a training and recruitment policy, which will show we are.*"

What became clear during discussions at the four workshops (training employment/recruitment, the writer's role in broadcasting and the role of the unions) and the report-back sessions was the need for the industry and unions to reflect the multiracial make up of the British society. Only through a proportionate influx of black workers could the racial prejudice obvious in the workplace be broken down, the conference was told. But this demand for equality in employment could not be detached from the struggle against racist images and negative coverage in the media.

Stereo-typical

Strong feelings against stereotyping of blacks on television were expressed. Black actors and actresses instanced plays which both consciously and unconsciously portrayed blacks in stereo-typical roles.

"*What we need is a concentrated effort to improve and increase the adoption of integrated casting*," said Louis Mahoney, from Equity.

The unions came in for considerable criticism, There was a belief that the membership rules of some unions which require that you first have a union card before getting employment in a particular industry was discriminating against black workers.

How many black members were there in the unions? Why aren't the unions attracting black members? Do unions encourage black participation in all levels? Of all the unions there it was pointed out that only the NUJ has a black NEC member. Do unions provide anti-racist courses for their own members? These were some of the questions asked and discussed.

Summing up the conference proceedings, Shiv Ayer, chairman of the NUJ Race Relations Working Party said a concerted campaign to get more black journalist trained, recruited and employed in broadcasting was necessary. At the same time it was vitally important for the broadcasting unions to open their doors and encourage black workers to join and participate fully and equally. "*It all boils down to translating commitment into action on behalf of black people in broadcasting*," he said.

A 'Charter for Action' highlighting the following points was agreed:

- That the unions and employers adopt a firm position on ethnic record keeping; monitoring their workplace and committing themselves to equality targeting – which should be included in all house agreements.
- An assurance that negotiations on equal opportunities are an integral part of the bargaining framework with employers.
- That union should carry out a proper and extensive recruitment campaign among black media workers.
- That there should be concentrated efforts to improve and increase the adoption of integrated casting.
- That it is important that the broadcasting media improve its image among the black community by taking drastic steps against racial stereotyping and racist reporting and that the various codes of conduct be enforced.
- That union prepare a register of black media workers and make these available to employers whenever job vacancies occur.
- Employers should review their training schemes to take black media workers' needs into account.
- That media unions set up joint machinery which would monitor all house agreements to make sure the equal opportunity clauses are being implemented. This joint machinery should also monitor general progress on the implementation of all equal opportunities policies.

UK Press Gazette,1985

BLACK JOURNALISTS FIGHTS FOR HIGH STAKES (1987)

Unless the National Union of Journalists (NUJ) changes its public image and translates its equal opportunity commitments into action, then it will continue to be perceived by black journalists as a white trade union for white journalists. This was the message which came over loud and clear at the NUJ-sponsored conference "Print Journalism and Black People", held at the University of London Union last December.

The conference, which had an attendance of about l00 black journalists, was the first of its kind held by the NUJ to discuss union organisation, recruitment, training and employment in print journalism.

General Secretary Harry Conroy urged black journalists to join the Union and "make it work for black members"

Unequal Opportunity?

"You cannot stand outside and criticism what is not taking place within the Union. Get in, and make our Union a truly multi-racial organisation. Help us transform our Equal Opportunity Policy into a working policy," he told delegates, who came from all parts of Great Britain.

"Black people are generally in lower-paid jobs or unemployed. There is no equal opportunity in applying for jobs in the first place. We have to encourage more open advertising. We have to encourage employers to go to under-represented areas and give people the opportunity to apply.

"There is no point in pious statements. Practical problems need practical solutions and suggestions."

He said the NUJ wanted active black members throughout the Union structure.

The Conference heard publisher and editor of Third World Communications Kofi Buenor Hadjor, describe the role of the British press as "reinforcing racist images of black people".

"What does this mean in practical terms for us as black and anti-racist journalists?" asked Hadjor, who was a UNESCO communications adviser and founder of the Tanzania School of Journalism.

"It means," he asserted "That much of what we have done so far, and perhaps been satisfied with is becoming more and more irrelevant. The scale of the attack on the black community if so enormous, the stakes are so high, that we must now start to respond accordingly. We can no longer be content to remain a miniscule and largely ineffectual pressure group on the establishment media. WE must set our sights much, much higher."

And that is exactly what the delegates did. The conference discussed union organisation, recruitment, training and employment issues in detail in working sessions, and highlighted matters which the NUJ should act on:

a) The NUJ should take note of the fact it comes over to the black community as a white trade union for white only. It has to change its image and live up to its equal opportunities policies.

b) It has to respond quickly and positively to racist attacks by the media on the black community. Black people look to the Union also to champion their cause against racism and discrimination.

c) *The Union should publicise its activities more. Union structures have to be better exposed and publicised.*

d) *It should establish a membership record of all its black members so as to ensure that they received equal treatment from all the Union's services.*

The Conference heard details from various participants on the discriminatory practices they had to go through. One delegate highlighted the problem of training. *"Employers want high educational standards even if these are an unnecessary requirement for the job. Yet when you do have these qualifications you are still faced with discrimination. As a black person you have to be ten times better than a white candidate."*

What became clear was that there were many black youngsters with the necessary educational qualifications who because of their colour were not given training or jobs. What could the Union do, delegates asked.

Commenting on the British university system generally, it was said there was a relatively high rate of drop-out form courses by black students. This reflected not so much on the quality of the students as on the fact that the system was not designed for black people but for the white middle class.

The answer?

In this context support was expressed for "Black only" courses, such as the Radio Journalism Course at the Polytechnic of Central London. However, such courses were seen only as a short term expedient to be followed until the balance between black and white on general courses had been rectified.

Disillusionment with the system spilled over into disillusionment with the unions.

But the answer did not lie in being outside the Union. *"Black journalists must get inside the Union, and shake things up. We must show the way in fighting for basic solidarity. More, much more, can still and should still be done to aid the struggle against apartheid, as well as the fight against racism closer to home. The best place to do that from is inside the Union, not from the sidelines",* one speaker said.

Chaired the Conference and reported it in The Journalist and West Indian Digest – 1987.

A CHALLENGING YEAR FOR THE NUJ (1988)

The National Union of Journalists of Great Britain and Ireland is about to embark on a new year – its 82nd – one in which it will cope with the effects of challenge and confrontation of closures and cutbacks. Of gross government interference and attacks, of all of which has been the bannerol of a hectic 81st term.

It has been a most complicated, vocal and challenging year for the union. In looking back, as its first black President, I have also tried to look forward, and at the end of this week, with a fresh set of targets firmly and determinedly mapped out, the NUJ ought to be allowed some room for optimism, if only on the basis that after a year as frustrated and challenging as 1987, the next 12 months can only get better.

Whether it will, depends entirely on ourselves. Clearly this is a time for frank and serious discussion, particularly for honest and searching examination of our relations with other media unions and our own members, our methods of work an obviously some of our policies. But it is not a time for defeatism or division in our ranks or for deserting our basic principles as trade unionists.

Calls to examine various facets of our policies should not be interpreted by those outside and indeed by some inside our ranks as betraying a lack of confidence in our basic purpose: the organisation of collective strength and collective action to promote and defend the professional and financial interests and welfare of our members.

Inevitably the biggest threat to our profession has been the government, either directly or through its agencies – the courts and the police.

The seriousness of this government attack cannot be stressed too much. The Government's Employment Bill, which carries through all the proposals of the Green Paper 'Trades Unions and their Members' published last year, is due to become law in the summer of this year.

If ever there was an iniquitous and prohibitive piece of legislation, then here is one. It strikes at the very heart of trade unionism. It is intended to ban unions from disciplining members who defy a strike call, even when a majority of members have given their support for the strike in a secret ballot, and the closed shop is effectively outlawed. Unions seeking a mandate for industrial action will have to conduct separate ballots where the membership is spread among several workplaces and majorities will have to be achieved in each.

The Secretary of State for Employment refers to this provision as an "anti-rigging" device to prevent unions from selective balloting to bring out a group of key workers against the wishes of the majority. Of course, in reality, it is simply another device with the sole aim of making sure that unions cannot easily take industrial action.

Where does that leave democracy? Do ballots only mean something when the result goes the right way – that is, it rejects action?

The Bill aims to create and ferment divisions within our ranks by encouraging individual members to use the law against their own colleagues. It creates financial incentives for individual union members to stab their colleagues in the back. It will break up group chapels and the collectivity they embody. It will place onerous financial and administrative burdens on us, which are clearly intended to maximise costs and minimise efficiency.

But what is even more disturbing is the lack of outcry by the trade union movement generally against this concerted attack. This Bill must be taken seriously by all in the Trade Union and labour movement – its aim is nothing less than the destruction of union effectiveness and hence eventually of the need for unions. The NUJ must play an important role in this fight. We must step up our campaign. We must not give the green light to employers and allow this government to decimate our union.

But that is only one example of what Tory rule over the past nine years has meant.

A few years ago we could still speak of the increasing encroachment by government on press and broadcasting freedom. Today the pace and the extent of that encroachment has reached alarming proportions. Both the police and the courts have demonstrated their willingness to be the handmaiden of this government.

Our member *Jeremy Warner,* a business news writer on *The Independent,* was fined £20,000 for refusing to name his sources for two stories on company take-overs. The court's action demonstrates that the protection offered to journalists with confidential sources by the Contempt Act was not only largely imaginary, but also sheer tommy-rot.

During the past year, with the Spycatcher case, the extension of injunctions against one newspaper to bind and thus paralyse all newspapers to report fearlessly, the mischievous and maleficent introduction of prior restraint on the press, the all embracing injunctions against the BBC, the dawn raids on newsrooms, the discovery that the D-Notice Committee is a one-way government patrolled street, the threat of imprisoning a journalist for protecting his source, the virulent government opposition to the Shepherd Bill and the order of *Sir James Miskin,* Recorder of London, that the police were to arrest any photographer attempting to take photographs near the courts, is a clear indication that this government had dragged Britain into the league of nations where press freedom is noticeable by the subservience of the press to government, the number of journalists imprisoned and the myraid anti-press freedom laws on the statute books. We have indeed reached a stage where press freedom is barely understood, disturbingly disappearing and manifestly being attacked.

An added challenge to our union comes from the changing pattern of employment – the move away from traditional journalism to electronic journalism, the much greater emphasis in certain sectors on short term contract work, the considerable difficulties in achieving recognition from employers on new sites, and the attempts by some managements to deunionise some newsrooms and grades of staff.

If the onslaught by government has been fierce, then the attempts by managements to undermine our collective bargaining power has been equally so.

Our ability to continue to organise, represent and defend the interest of our members is being placed in jeopardy by the personal contract offerings of certain managements. These "personal contracts" not only undermine our collective bargaining strength; it hits at the very heart of what the union is all about. There is no doubt that as a union we are partly to be blamed simply because we were slow to recognise the warning signs and then slow to react; and some of our chapels have allowed house agreements, hard won in the late 1960s and early 1970s to fall into decay.

How we stop this threat to our collective bargaining power depends on our ability to alert our membership not to sign and how we prosecute the campaign we have started. Our campaign will inevitably lead to a wave of industrial action. Are we as a union in a position to support, maintain and defend our members if they are penalised by managements for refusing to sign away their existing rights?

When we launch campaigns we must ensure that we have the resources to carry them out, and that we secure the participation of our members in those campaigns.

Colleagues, not only do we have to face the challenge of the changing structures and patterns of employment, we must also recognise the changing patterns of habits and attitudes of our members.

The more rapid the technological changes in the pattern of employment in the media become, the more job insecurity grows; the more our members face the arbitrary and often drastic decisions of management, the more vulnerable and anxious they become about the commitments they have assumed and the improved standard of living they have achieved and seek to maintain.

What we as a union must do is to persuade those members that now especially, they need the benefits of union membership.

I am not going to claim that the NUJ is able to prevent all closures and redundancies, nor can the NUJ prevent all the uncertainty and hardships which changes in the industry and the working practices can bring.

But what I can claim and must assert is that those in membership of the NUJ are less vulnerable to those dangers and anxieties than those who stand alone as individuals waiting to be picked off one by one.

To be able to tackle all these problems, we need an organisationally strong NUJ. Each sector in the union is interdependent on the other. For too long have we been shooting ourselves in the feet?

In the same way that News International's original move to Wapping caused problems throughout the industry, further erosion of the NUJ position in that company, which employs over 1,000 journalists, will only weaken our union, lead to de-recognition and all the industrial horrors it entails. We must put the dispute behind us. We must.

Some colleagues have refused to examine the appropriateness of their attitude to our members at Wapping. A crucial question is whether this attitude has become retrogressive, a fetter which is restraining the full development of an effective union organisation emerging at News International.

This attitude needs to be honestly and openly examined. It most probably was the correct stand to take at one time. But adopting a particular stand does not mean it would be applicable in all situations and forever.

Practical experience has or should have taught us that a particular form of struggle and action will be highly effective under certain conditions, whereas under changed circumstances it can become totally counter-productive.

What we need to do at this critical stage in our history is to recognise that the contradictions lie not with our fellow union members. These contradictions are, however, of a different nature and their resolution requires totally different methods of organisation and relationship. This is what the threats of the government and media employers on our profession and on trade union rights demand from us: to painstakingly examine the prevailing contradictions in our industry and in our union in order to forge the broadest united front. The one-sided view from some union members, albeit a small but articulate and active number has and will only result in serious setbacks to advance the cause of broad unity in our union. The historical challenge facing our union is whether we dare to adopt this realistic approach.

The critical stage, which our trade union struggle has reached, makes it imperative that these matters be approached with the utmost seriousness. Sadly such seriousness has not been too forthcoming. We cannot anymore afford to be guided by emotional superficialities.

But the function of the NUJ is not only to be protective. We seek to be positive, to play our full part in adaptation to change and to eradicate any Luddite, to press for equal opportunities, to combat racism, to secure a better and healthier working environment, and in every way to strengthen our members in their workplaces.

The industry itself has changed. Newspaper managements have expanded their interests. The days when a successful newspaper used to be the sole property of a media organisation are long gone. Maxwell and Murdoch preside over a conglomerate of media interests – newspapers, cable, satellite, books, magazines Along with these new media interests, managements are moving towards treating the communications industry as one. In the broadcasting sector, casualisation is increasing and more freelance based as traditional areas break down.

In this atmosphere of electronic advancement and a multi-facet media industry, the NUJ with only 32,000 members will soon find it difficult to continue to exist effectively as a union. As the recent TV AM experience shows, the contradictory nature of inter-union relations has become clearer. The tough line of TV AM's management reveals the need for greater union solidarity, as did the Wapping experience.

Under the banner of freedom of the market place, and because the communications industry is expanding profitable fields, the government – supported by the majority of Fleet Street proprietors – is now arguing that market place principles should apply to the media as a whole. This means deregulation in the broadcasting field and the opening of the floodgates which will enable the press barons to swallow up broadcasting.

Our response to all this must be positive and decisive – for too long have the NUJ simply reacted defensively to issues. We need to sharpen our strategy of traditional, industrial campaigning but that is simply not enough. There is, fortunately, a real alternative. But that desperately needs a new input of political energy and skill to move forward, and start the process of meaningful inter-union relations leading to a federation of all the media print and broadcasting unions namely NGA, SOGAT, ACTT, BETA and EQUITY. That is the only answer to our survival in the future, and I am glad to say that I have helped start that process in the union.

Like Martin Luther King, I too have a dream. A dream that within the next five years we will be part of a single media union with over 500,000 members – where with all the resources such a formidable combination of workers will have at its disposal, could be used to more effectively defend our professional codes of conduct; oppose the growing legislative restrictions on journalists and broadcasters; meet the onslaught of antagonistic managements, and offer some more tangible industrial strength to support individual members in all aspects of the media. If we do not start to grasp the nettle now and decide with whom we want to join forces, then heaven forbids we may well be forced – out of sheer desperation – to join with large unions which have no media interest, and where media issues would receive little priority.

Colleagues, what has saddened and worried me during my year, as President is the rapidly declining media standards. There is no doubt that public confidence in the media, particularly in the tabloid press, has sunk to an all-time low. Fabrication, gross distortion and sensationalisation of news has increased, to a point where even the Press Council has acknowledged that voluntary 'restraint' has broken down. Media attacks on Black people, lesbians and gay men have increased. And what is worse is that when government plans for broadcasting are allowed to go ahead then we will see how TV companies will be forced to compete with the tabloids for a niche in the gutter. Our members have been forced to write lies and an atmosphere has been created where journalistic ethics is low on the agenda. Standards have dropped so badly and inaccuracy is so widespread, that we desperately need a law like Anne Clwyd's ill-fated Right of Reply Bill to enforce consumer rights on editors who deliberately misinform their readers. What it comes down to is trying to reconcile the endless and avaricious pursuit of profit with the pursuit of truth.

But despite this terrible avalanche of bad reporting, I contend that it is not the NUJ's main role to clean up British journalism. We can try, but the primary object of the Union is to get better pay and conditions for its members. And that is our dilemma. This might seem to be a counsel of despair, but it is not and cannot be bearing in mind our historical concern and fight to maintain ethical standards in our profession – a concern of which we can take great pride.

I believe that we must seriously embrace the proposals which were so central to the Right of Reply Bill – the establishment of a Media Commission, which would replace the Press Council and Broadcasting Complaints Commission. The establishment of such a body, genuinely representing consumers, would have the bite the Press Council lacks and the representativeness our Ethics Council need. Legislation on media standards is, I believe, inevitable. Government threats point menacingly towards such a move. Clearly what we should do is to ensure, with all the media unions, that legislation does become a reality – but on our terms.

One of the highlights of being President is the fact that you have the opportunity to go about the country and meet members in their chapels, branches and area councils. You are exposed to the views and opinions and concerns of members. During my term I have visited 50 branches, chapels and area councils. What has come over clearly to me is the high morale, fierce loyalty to the Union and good attendance at small branches right round the country.

What branches away from London feel is a desperate isolation from the centre, and a feeling that London is too remote, bureaucratic and does not serve them. Having visited every Scottish and nearly every Irish branch, I have been struck by the high degree of organisation and responsibility of our members in those countries.

There will be debate in this conference about what restructuring of the Union should take place and if so, when. It is right that such a debate should take place, but what I hope delegates will bear in mind when they so debate the issue is the message which was signalled to me clearly – what members need is a greater feeling of commitment and value for money. The role and presence of the Irish Council has helped to fill this gap in Ireland where links between the sectors are manifestly better than anywhere else in the Union.

We are one of the most democratic unions, but one of the worst organisationally. We are all aware of the realities of our work and our concerns in this area. Our biggest worries, and those of colleagues at branch and regional level, are invariably: How can we get more of our members to play an active part in the democratic structures of the Union? How can we get a clearer feedback about our policies? How can we do more to satisfy the members' needs? These were the questions put to me by those branches I visited and which I have relayed to my colleagues on the Executive and at Acorn House.

I believe that internally we have to get our priorities right. We have to cut out the messing that occasionally takes place in our union, either because of offended egos or macho images. We have too much serious and urgent work to undertake; so we can ill afford internal hiccups. I have sometimes been surprised at the bitterness and vitriol, which go into our internal battles. This year has not been different. There are those in our union, whether in branches or on the NEC, who believe there are two sides to every question: the view taken by all good trade unionists; and the view taken by reactionary scum, hell bent on selling out the membership. Conversely, there are those who believe that the Union consists on the one hand on devout, responsible men and women, and on the other, of the frenzied power maniacs determined to wreck it from sinister political motives.

The propaganda of the participants tends to obscure the fact that there are not many of them. What proportion of your branch and chapel – especially the big ones – regularly attends meetings? Generally the answer is 4-5% and sometimes there are not enough for a quorum. Look at the appalling election result turnouts. Even despite our workplace ballot magic formula!

What is clearly obvious is that a climate has been created in which the mass of the membership feels unable or unwilling to participate. The individual finds it hard to operate in a situation where the major battles are set-pieces involving heavy artillery. The result therefore, is that at branch and chapel level, with notable exceptions of smaller branches and those outside London, there is insufficient participation in decision making; and at the top, we are positively stifled by participation in decision making. For our overweight democratic structures at the top frequently threaten to engulf Acorn House in paperwork. We are becoming so querulous, litigious, introverted and intolerant, that we are in danger of killing off the weakened union we still possess, and if we are not careful, fighting for the political control of a corpse.

These are hard things to say. But as I said at the beginning, this is a time for frank, honest and serious discussion. The message that I have positively got from my year in office and from my visit to branches is that what the NUJ needs is fewer slogans and more thought; less bureaucratic democracy at the top and more participatory democracy at the bottom; less viciousness internally and more determination externally; and a great deal more thought about how to win friends and influence people in the rest of the trade union movement.

Having established our policies, priorities and our campaigns, we have to engage seriously in the task of finding common, uniting issues and of education and communication with our members in order to demonstrate the links between the policies we evolve, the priorities we set and their needs and interests. The message from the many branches I visited and the numerous letters I have received from members is that there are factors which can and have united the membership, principally press freedom and the government's attacks on trade union rights. Let us use our defence of those two issues to bring more members in the Union and to strengthen it organisationally. That is why I believe that a major membership drive is necessary and that 1988 should be the NUJ Recruitment Year.

In any one year of office there are certain things, which gives one great pleasure as well as concern. Mine has been the fact that I have not been marginalised into being looked upon as *the* NUJ Black President. Branches and chapels have called on me as President of the Union to visit and discuss with them various aspects of union policy.

As a Black person I felt relief at not being patronised and expected to talk just about Black issues. I was accepted as a trade unionist in the NUJ. My concern, however, was the feeling that by having me as President, a belief had developed that the NUJ had now come to grips with racism and discrimination that is prevalent. Racism in the media has reached unprecedented heights. Discrimination is still rife.

The Union itself must put into effect, at a greater speed, its comprehensive equal opportunities policies. It must attract more Black journalists and that can only be done if it changes its 'white' image. I can, however, say that attempts are being made and more Black journalists have joined the Union during my term than any other time. The setting up of the *George Viner Memorial Trust Fund* has added to this increasing credibility of the Union among Black journalists and the Black press.

As a union which has played a long and honourable part in developing relations with journalist organisations in all parts of the world, we have to condemn the government's appalling record on South Africa – a record about which we must all feel a sense of shame, just as we express our admiration for the magnificent spirit of the South African trade union movement, and MWASA in particular.

Being South African born and having lived half my life in that country, with parts of my roots still there, I am proud of the NUJ's position on South Africa and its solidarity with the struggle there. We have similarly during the year cemented our relations with journalists and their unions world-wide, in particular with our Palestinian colleagues. In the international debate this solidarity and support will be spelt out more.

In conclusion, can I say that in our self-examination we must not abandon the spirit that has always distinguished our Union. That spirit has never been better expressed than it was by *George Loveless,* one of the Tolpuddle Martyrs, when over 150 years ago he returned from enforced labour in Australia. He said then: *"I call upon every working man in England to shake off that supineness and indifference to their interest which leaves them in the situation of slaves. Has not the working man as much right to preserve and protect his labour as the rich man his capital?*

Let the working classes of Britain, seeing the necessity of acting upon such a principle, remembering that union is power, listen to nothing that might be presented before them to draw their attention from the subject, alike despising and conquering party disputes and personal bickering; and they will accomplish their own salvation and that of the world".

Our world, colleagues, might be different from the world of George Loveless, but it's still a world in which journalists, men and women, need to combine work together and recognise that **Union is Strength.**

Presidential Address to The National Union of Journalists (NUJ) of Britain and Ireland's Annual Delegate Conference, Sheffield 19 April,1988

DOES THE MEDIA PRE-FORMULATE PREJUDICE AND RACISM? (1990)

The primary role in the construction of a dominant (white) consensus in this country is played by the news media.

This Role is defined not only in terms of its vast mass-mediated scope, and by the assumed representational goals of the print or broadcast media in the reporting of social events; the media also plays an intermediary role in the reproduction of other types of public discourse. Much of the news is not so much about happenings or events, but about what other people typically the powerful and the elite, say or write.

By altering perception, modifying expectations, and transforming communication behaviour, to-day's electronic mass media – especially TV is changing social life.

Research shows as it did in America *(David L. Altheide* – Media Power, Arizona State University) how the mass media 'mediate' relationship between time, place and manner of events by providing communication formats for ordering everyday social reality. Most people read or hear about the discourses of institutions, government, politicians, business people, unions, churches through the media. And news production is organised to access such source discourses routinely in the most effective way.

These news production strategies involve ideologically shared values and routines of attention allocation, stylistic formulation and exclusion. This holds a fortiori for socially and ideologically prominent topics such as various minority groups and ethnic relations. And because the media provide the daily discourse input for most adult citizens, their role as a prevailing discourse and attitude context for thought and talk about black groups is probably unsurpassed by any institutional or public source of communication.

Hartman and Husband (1974) in their seminal study of racism and mass media, have explicitly paid attention to these information sources for what people know and find about ethnic groups. In standard interviews and written questionnaires, they asked children and adults from which sources they got their opinions or knowledge of black people. As expected, the media score high in areas with no or few black groups, followed by personal experiences and what they heard from other people. Yet, in high contact areas, both adults and children attribute most of their belief to personal experience. In general, the media are especially given credit for information about national issues such as immigration, the number of immigrants, violent conflicts, and the occurrence of discrimination. Personal experiences are especially mentioned for information about cultural differences.

These findings should be interpreted with caution, since the research method was the well-known survey type. The relatively low score on media information in low-contact areas does not necessarily mean that people have actually had much less information from the media in such areas as opposed to high-contact areas, but only that in many kinds of beliefs are rather attributed to more reliable or more concrete personal information. For most categories, it is highly unlikely that people have acquired information by personal experience only. It is probable that personal experiences often also include things they have heard *"from other people".* For instance the fact that many people say they know about *"resentment"* or *"prejudice"* against minorities suggests that they heard about this from others, or from the media.

The press did pay attention to conflicts, tensions, and resentment against the new citizens, but hardly discussed the underlying causes and consequences of this resentment, such as black prejudice and racism, or discrimination against Black people. On the whole, minority groups were not represented as being part of British society, but as outsiders who preferably should be *"kept out".* Racist statements of someone such as *Powell* received wide coverage in these years. The authors conclude that the media have not just expressed general opinions and feelings, but have themselves contributed to such negative feelings.

Other British studies confirm these conclusions. *Critcher, Parker and Sondhi* (1977) and Troyna (1981) in their analysis of the British regional press (Birmingham and Manchester), found that most items about crime and human interest, followed by the national issues of immigration and the debate about legislation against such immigration.

The actions of the neo-fascist National Front receive much attention, and thought there is space devoted to the *"White"* side of the *"problem"* namely discrimination, this is typically portrayed as incidental, as the act of extremist individuals, and not as a structural manifestation of British racism. *Hall et al.* (1978) in their extensive study of the political, legal, social and media reactions to the *"mugging crisis"* also found that young Black West Indians tend to be associated with crimes in general and with mugging in particular.

Downing (1980) who summarises his findings from an analysis of TV programmes, stresses that Blacks, both in Britain and in African countries, are seldom allowed to give their opinions. The media rather invite a White *"minority specialist"* usually male to give his views. Immigration is the main theme, and violence against Blacks is treated as regrettable incidents.

Also *Greenberg and Atkin* (1978) and Roberts (1975) conclude that Black people are mostly present only in *"non speaking"* roles, even for events that directly involve them. This is true not only for their role in press stories, but also for their participation in the news media themselves. Especially in higher positions, there are virtually no Black journalists. *(Greenberg and Mazingo,* 1976). Although these studies are over ten years old, the situation is essentially still the same now 10 years later.

What does become obvious is the fact that there are a number of prevailing and persisting commonalities:

* Ethnic minorities are also minorities in the press – they are less employed and less represented.

* Many of the dominant topics are directly of more subtly associated with problems, difficulties, or threats to the dominant values, interests, goals or culture.

* Black events are consistently described from a White, majority point of view, in which the authorities are given more space and credibility than minority spokespersons.

* Topics that are relevant for the ordinary daily life of Black groups, such as work, housing, health, education, political life and culture, as well as discrimination in these areas, are hardly discussed in the press, unless they lead to *"problems"* for society as a whole or when they are spectacular.

Racism is systematically under-reported, reduced to incidents of individual discrimination, or attributed to small rightwing parties and located in poor city areas. Racism of the elite or the various institutions is seldom discussed.

It goes without saying that against this background, the media have been reluctant, to say the least, to discuss publicly their own role in the reproduction of racism in society. Critical analysis is censored, and my own experience of the press suggest that critics are often personally discredited or prevented from collecting data in fieldwork.

The role of the media in what takes place in our society is highly relevant. They provide the main *"data"* and the issues people may use for everyday conversation, especially for those topics of talk that cannot be inferred from personal experiences of contacts with other people: immigration policies, the number of immigrants, unemployment statistics, the role of ethnic groups in housing and education, discrimination and crime statistics.

This does not mean that most newspapers explicitly formulate racist opinions. Many editors and journalists will maintain that they are against racism and generally loathe extremist racist parties.

Their role, indeed, is more subtle and indirect. Partly, but only partly, is negative reporting a consequence of routine conditions of news production and news values: negative, spectacular events tend to get more attention, and any group without power, influence and organised spokespersons will have less access to the news media.

The many *"neutral"* topics that are present for the White majority (such as political organisation, culture, the arts) are not there when they are about minority groups. And the problems for the majority (economic recession, unemployment, lack of housing, crime) are not paralleled by those problems that are relevant for the minority. On the contrary, the majority problems are often subtly attributed to the very presence of minority groups. Deeper social causes, contexts and consequences, such as the role of discrimination in housing, everyday contacts, education and employment, are seldom discussed.

Even when the media do not formulate negative opinions themselves, they provide a definition of the black situation that makes such negative references not only possible but also plausible. In this way, they both pre-formulate prejudice and reinforce the partial models of the black situation that are acquired by personal experiences, hearsay and socialisation.

The Black Parliamentarian' vol 1. (1990)

THE CORRELATIONS BETWEEN RACISM AND THE MEDIA IN BRITAIN – (1992)

“What is the function of the media and how does it impinge on and reinforce racism. To what extent does it pre-formulate, foster prejudice and legitimise racism?

A reporter from the London *Daily Mail* once complained that as black people we see racism and discrimination under every stone. He was right. My experience makes me sensitive to any form of racism and paternalism. But he missed the point. Prejudice against foreigners in general and black people in particular are deeply embedded in British life. Its most obvious manifestation is in British history of slavery which was morally justified on the basis of white superiority.

If you combine prejudice and power you have racism which in turn will, unless stopped, lead to discrimination. Given the nature of British society I do, indeed, believe that discrimination occurs in almost every aspect of British life.

The relationship between negative impressions of black people and press reporting has been studied in several surveys. In the 1974 seminal study entitled, *“Racism and the Media”* by Paul Hartman and Charles Husband, the following results were discussed and are still pertinent and presageful after nearly 20 years’ its publication.

The study attempted to find the source of influence on people’s prejudices, attitudes or beliefs about black people in Britain. For example, when asked; *“Can you tell me what you know about black people living in Britain today”,* the most media-linked responses were: objects of prejudice, disadvantage, poor housing, causing trouble, taking jobs, taking homes and anti immigration. Replies linked to personal experience were: cultural differences, anti-stereotype, favourable, unfavourable, equality, resentment, culture clash and personal dislike.

When asked, *“Do you think there are any problems connected with black people living in this country?”* media-linked replies were greater, particularly from parents. Replies linked to media sources focussed on anti immigration, trouble numbers, poor housing and disadvantage.

Hartman and Husband state that: *“Not only did our subjects find it more difficult to think of good things about multi-racial Britain than to think of problems, but the mass media were more help to them in thinking about problems than in calling good things to mind.”* ‘Good things’ most commonly mentioned were: black people working as medical staff, doing jobs that otherwise would not get done, their contribution to keeping public transport going and simply that they were ‘nice people’ in that order. None of these were closely associated with media sources.

The study concludes: *“This media definition has two facets. On the one hand people have been kept aware of the hostility and discrimination suffered by black immigrants. In this respect in not allowing social injustice and hardship to go unnoticed and in maintaining visibility of egalitarian and anti racist values, the media have performed a valuable function. On the other hand, and simultaneously, people have derived from the media a perception of the black population as a threat and a problem, a conception more conducive to the development of hostility towards them than acceptance.”*

“The British news media has failed to report adequately on the underlying bases of racial conflict in Britain, and in doing have assisted in the scapegoating of black

immigrants: in this their conflict framework has played a facilitating role. In saying that we are not suggesting that 'conflict' racial stories and information uncomplimentary to black groups should be ignored or suppressed, only that the handling of racial news should not be based on the uncritical acceptance of prevailing cultural assumptions about colour and the 'colour problem'. 'Racial' news should be presented so as to discourage simple racist interpretations on the part of the audience."

It is vital that the news media should debate the background to conflict and not confine itself to monitoring the symptoms. Ignorance of the nature of the real sources of social tension can be countered by a more determined responsible journalism. Such a policy is, however, outside the range of cosmetic solutions, for adequate discussion of the role of immigrant labour in the British economy, or of the structural reasons for unemployment and housing shortages would ultimately remove the buffer of scapegoating and lay bare the actual inequalities.

Given the current pattern of ownership and control of the media and their close identification with those interests that gain most from social inequalities and from the 'management' of conflicts rather than their removal, it remains unlikely that such a radical change in policy can be achieved. (my emphasis)

In a media dominated society such as Great Britain, all of us depend on the media of communication to portray and define those things we have not always experienced for ourselves. Thus we 'learn' about others through radio, television, films, newspapers and magazines. This pervasive influence of the media in British society has been aptly described and documented by others who have analysed the communication media in modern society.

The functions of the media in modern society have been described in different times by different people. What I want to do is to see how these functions impinge on and correlate to the racism which is so endemic in British society.

The major functions of communication could be summed up I suggest as:

e) surveillance: the sentinel or lookout role of the media watching the society and horizon for threats to establishment order and information people or places of public interest

f) correlation: interpretation and linking function of the media, which helps their readers – the audience – understand, interpret and comprehend the different things that are happening in and out of society and how they affect each other, as well as stay in touch with others in the society.

g) transmission: the socialisation function of the media, it's norms and it's values to it's audience and, though their portrayals and coverage, assist members of society in adopting, using and acting on these values.

h) entertainment: the function of the media for diversion and enjoyment, which provides stories, features, music and films designed to make the audiences laugh, cry, ridicule, relax, reflect, rather than gain information.

i) economic service: the role of the media within the economic system of the society which in Britain means that most media function as corporations serving the needs of their shareholders and other corporations by attracting audiences that will either pay for the media products or serve as the target for advertising messages. In short the media is there to make money as well.

Advertisers generally, in Britain and elsewhere, demand mass audiences to advertise and market their products. The communication media responds by adopting news and entertainment strategies that would attract the largest numbers of readers. Since the majority in Britain are white, this means that the Black minority are treated as fringe audiences, not important enough in numbers to dictate the content that would be directed to the majority white audience.

The media therefore reinforces a collective consciousness in the members of the audience that it is necessary to attract large numbers of undifferentiated people. It follows that the task of the media to look for commonalities among members of the audience – *common themes, values, ideas, interest areas* – that would attract and not offend the majority white audience. With few exceptions, this means that the content of the media reinforces, rather than challenges the established norms and attitudes of the society. To do otherwise would be to risk offending significant numbers in the majority audience and, in the process, losing the large audience demanded by the advertisers.

British society, characterised by the assimilationist mentality through which immigrants are expected to be integrated into British society and culture, has often treated members of groups who have not blended or completely integrated into the mainstream as outsiders. Racial minorities that can be identified by colour are often 'beyond' integration, unable to blend over a period of a generation because of physical characteristics. They are not only beyond 'integration', but outside the focus of the mass audience so necessary for the survival of the media. Their numbers are relatively small compared with the white majority and, as a result, they are not considered important components of the mass audience. *For the most part, the British media treat groups not in the mainstream audience by either ignoring them or stereotyping them.*

Films, television, radio programmes, newspapers, and news magazines generally ignore the issue confronting black people in Britain, as well as their culture and traditions. When they are treated, it is often in stereotyped roles, such as violent black youths, or sinister Asian landlords. These characterisations of blacks are largely based on the perceptions and preconceptions of those outside the groups, rather than the realities of the groups themselves. They are pictures of racial minorities as seen through white eyes.

The media in Britain rarely covers activities of black communities, unless in accordance with their *surveillance* function, they were perceived as posing a threat to the established order or, in accordance with their *correlation* function, they were covered during colourful cultural festivals – like the Notting Hill Carnival. Thus the audience see only a slice of the minorities, one that does not jar their preconceptions of these groups. In fact the media portrayals help legitimise and reinforce such preconceptions. In the absence of alternative portrayals and broadened news coverage, one sided portrayals and news articles easily become reality in the minds of the white audience. Whites are seen in a wide range of roles, ranging from villains to heroes. Blacks are seem only as lazy violent thugs or scroungers. There are not real alternative portrayals to counter the stereotype.

Studies also show that the media have their greatest influence when they reinforce rather than change the opinions of those in their audience. The media have their greatest effect when they are used in a manner that reinforces and channels attitudes and opinions consistent with the psychological make up of the person and the social structures of the groups with which he or she identifies.

The reinforcement and challenging effect of the media, when coupled with the content analysis that have been made on coverage and portrayal of minorities in news and entertainment media, provide an insight into the negative effects of one-sided media images on blacks groups portrayed.

Studies that have been done show that negative, one sided, or stereotyped media portrayals and news coverage do reinforce racist attitudes in those members of the target audience who have such attitudes.

The public language of journalism is a statement about what is "normal". It conveys messages through the complex associations and implications of its metaphors and unstated assumptions. If a journalist's language violates the experiential reality of a minority or identifiable group within society, it creates a conflict between reality and the personal experience of those people who come to be identified as deviant. Such a cognitive conflict easily contributes to actual conflict between members of a group that has been so singled out and stereotyped and the public, the dominant group, at large. Excreta was put through the door flaps of black people in parts of Britain and many were subjected to racial attacks and harassment after Conservative Member of Parliament, *Enoch Powell,* made his notorious *'Rivers of Blood'* speech in which he warned the British people (white) that the black presence in Britain was against their interest. His speech of course received wide and uncritical reporting in most of the British press.

Studies also show that bigoted persons watching television programmes ridiculing bigotry interpret such programmes as reinforcing their pre-existing beliefs. Worse still, *Hartman and Husband* (1974) in their seminal and now still relevant study of racism and mass media in Britain show that children, both black and white, are especially affected by entertainment characters that portray minority groups and that the media is a significant source from which they got their opinions or knowledge of black people.

They concluded that the media had not just expressed general opinions and feelings, but had itself significantly, through editorials and comment pieces, contributed to such negative feelings.

Other British studies confirm these conclusions. *Critcher, Parker and Sondhl* (1977) and Troyna (1981) in their analyses of the British regional press (Birmingham and Manchester) found that most items are about crime and human interest, followed by the national issues of immigration and the debate about legislation against such immigration. The actions of the neo fascist National Front received much attention and although there is a space devoted to the 'white' side of the 'problem' namely discrimination, this is typically portrayed as incidental, as the act of extremist individuals, and not as a structural manifestation of British racism.

Hall et al (1978) in their extensive study of the political, legal and social media reactions to the "mugging crisis" also found that young black West Indians tend to be associated with crimes in general and mugging in particular.

Another way the British media connives and fosters the racism prevalent in society is by not seeking out blacks views. *Downing* (1980) who summarises his findings from an analysis of TV programmes, stresses that blacks, both in Britain and in African countries, are seldom asked to give their opinions.

The media rather invite a white 'minority specialist', usually male, to give his views. Additionally the black experts on British papers are usually white reporters. But have you ever listened to a black "white expert"? When I started in British journalism, I found myself always marginalised and got stories when black groups did not want to speak to white journalists.

Greenberg and Atkin (1978) Roberts (1978) and my own research in 1974, 1980, 1985 and then in 1991 shows that black people are mostly present only in 'non speaking' roles, even for events that directly involve them. This is not only true for their role in press stories, but also for their participation in the media itself. Especially in higher positions, there are virtually no black journalists.

What does become obvious is the fact that there are a number of prevailing and persisting commonalities:

1 Ethnic minorities in Britain are also minorities in the press – they are less employed and less represented.
2 Many of the dominant topics are directly or more subtly associated with problems, difficulties or threats to the dominant values, interests, goals or culture.
3 Black events are consistently described from a white majority point of view, in which white people are given more space and credibility than minority spokes persons.
4 Topics that are relevant for the ordinary daily life of blacks groups in Britain, such as work, housing, health, education, political life and culture, as well as discrimination in these areas, are hardly discussed in the media, unless they lead to 'problems' for society as a whole or when they are spectacular.
5 Racism is systematically under reported, reduced to incidents of individual discrimination or attributed to small right wing parties and located in poor city areas. Racism of the elite or the various institutions is seldom reported.

It therefore goes without saying that against this background, the media has been reluctant, to say the least, to discuss publicly its own role in the reproduction of racism in society. Critical analysis is censured and my own experience of the press suggests that critics are often personally discredited or prevented from collecting data in fieldwork.

The role of the media in what takes place in our society is highly relevant. It provides the main 'data' and the issues people may use for everyday conversation. This does not mean that most newspapers explicitly formulate racist opinions.

Many editors and journalists will maintain that they are against racism and generally loathe extremist racist parties.

Their role, indeed – could I suggest – is more subtle and indirect. Partly, but only partly is negative reporting a consequence of routine conditions of news production and news values; negative spectacular events tend to get more attention and *any group without power and influence will have less access to the news media.*

The many 'neutral' topics that are present for the white majority in Britain (such as political organisation, culture, the arts) are not there when they are about black groups.

And the problems for the majority (economic recession, unemployment, lack of housing, crime) are not paralleled by those problems that are relevant for the minority. On the contrary, the majority problems are often subtly attributed to the very presence of black people. Deeper social causes, contexts, and consequences, such as the role of discrimination in housing are seldom discussed.

And even when the media do not formulate negative opinions themselves, they provide a definition of the black situation that makes such negative references not only possible but plausible. In this way, they both pre-formulate prejudice and reinforce the partial models of the black situation that are acquired by personal experiences, hearsay and socialisation.

In conclusion, I reaffirm that the primary role in the construction of a dominant (white) consensus in Britain is played by the media and that this role is defined not only in terms of its vast mass mediated scope and by the assumed representational goals of the print of broadcast media in the reporting of social events. The media also play an intermediary role in the role in the reproduction of other types of public discourse. Much of news, as I indicated earlier, is not so much about happenings or events, but about what other people, typically the powerful and the elite and in this country the white community, say or write. By altering perception, modifying expectations and transforming communication behaviour, today's electronic mass media in Britain is drastically changing British social life, unfortunately for the worst.

A talk to journalism students at City University, London 1992.

CRE LABELLED IRRELEVANT (1992)

The Commission for Racial Equality is l5 years old today. With a welcoming message from the then Home Secretary, Roy Jenkins, ringing in my ears, I helped set up the Commission for Racial Equality (CRE). Established by the Wilson government under the Race Relations Act 1976, to promote equality of opportunity and work towards the elimination of racial discrimination, it was a watershed in race relations.

In its first annual report, chairman David (now Sir David) Lane proudly pronounced that the Commission was conscious of the fact that it had been appointed to serve the whole nation and that it needed to retain the support and confidence of ethnic minorities and the population at large.

Those fateful words have now come to haunt the present £60,000 a year chairman, Michael Day.

Instead, the CRE's l5 years of existence conversely show that the patterns of discriminatory behaviour in Britain have not only become more deeply entrenched, but has increased considerably. It also shows that during these l5 years the CRE has not only lost any support and respect it might have had among black people when it was set up, but that it has additionally become a damp squib as an effective and respected race relations agency, despite an increased budget from £3.5 million to £15 million annually.

It has been severely accused of racism and discriminatory practices by its own staff, indicated by its former deputy chairman Prof Bhikku Parekh as ineffective and without clear priorities, and taken to Industrial Tribunals for alleged discrimination.

Morale is at its lowest ebb, staff have formed a secret Black Support Group to expose what is taking place in the organisation, and the staff union – MSF – have asked the CRE's l5-strong Home Office appointed Board of Commissioners to conduct a full inquiry into all aspects of morale and working relations in the Commission.

And in a scathing and terribly indicting resignation letter, a black senior research officer, Danielle Walker, says "that stark contrast to the statutory purpose of the CRE, notions of equality of opportunity appear to play little part in the application of the Commission's internal employment practices. I feel that it is in my best interest to go to an employer where my skills and experience will be valued, rewarded and encouraged to develop".

To appreciate the organisation's prolapse under its present Chairman Michael Day, a former chief probation officer, whose knowledge and understanding of race relations pales in comparison to that of his heavyweight predecessors, Sir David Lane, a former junior Home Affairs Minister and Sir Peter Newson, a noted educationalist and administrator, it would be expedient to look at the raison d'etre, for its existence.

The Act under which the CRE was established, recognising the existence of racial discrimination, had been acknowledged by the British government since the early sixties.

A race relations law assumes that the black minority are part of the British community and that the threat to law and order comes from denying the Black minority the protection of the law. An immigration law assumes people are in the country on sufferance and if things get bad they should go and that they are a threat to law and order.

The Act went through and the CRE established on 13 June 1977. It specifically empowers the CRE to give assistance to organisations, to advise and assist individuals' complaints, to carry out research and educational activities, to issue codes of practise and to conduct formal investigations.

How successful and effective has the CRE been in combating racism and working towards equality of opportunity and how relevant is it to the nineties?

When the CRE was set up great expectations were generated that it would be able to formulate a comprehensive strategy for dealing with the related or at least equally important problem, of disadvantage and that it would as a statutory body set up with all-party support, be able to take Government along with it on this road, and in the words of its first Chairman, "retain the support and confidence of ethnic minorities and the population at large".

Although it has since its inception, investigated and then published reports on over 50 formal investigations in companies and areas where it believed racially discriminatory practices were taking place, given assistance to an average of about 700 complainants each year and financially grant aided numerous black groups, it has increasingly been criticised by the black community accusing it of being ineffective, afraid of powerful employers and powerless in its relations with central Government.

Many black and Asian people argue against the inability of the CRE to appreciate that things have changed in society and it is dealing with a much more conscious and active black and Asian community.

It is true, they argue, that now most forms of legally supported and intentional discrimination has become less frequent and that people of colour have made extraordinary achievements, despite severe obstacles. However, they argue, the effects and intentionally discriminatory practices remain long after court decisions, published formal investigations and social customs signal the reduction of overt discrimination.

Racism has instead over the past 15 years become more subtle and often unintentional. There is no doubt that the consequences or outcomes of this policy for the black minority in Britain is disastrous. It is, black people insist, not equal opportunity declarations and written codes of practices which are important and relevant, but outcomes which are manifestly absent in the race equality arena. A recent study, Buried Talents, by the Ecumenical Committee for Corporate Responsibility of 100 top firms underpins this point. The survey shows that only five firms were able to provide detailed information on the ethnic composition of their workers reported by any one company was five per cent and even then the workers were mainly employed in the lower grade jobs.

The nineties have seen a marked increase in racist attacks and harassment in levels of discriminatory practices in employment, education and housing. The softly, softly approach when dealing with employers, which bedevils the CRE together with its lack of support from the black minorities and its inability to influence the decision makers must in itself ask questions as to the relevancy of the organisation.

It is not that the CRE does not have a large enough budget and staff. It is how prudently and on what it spends its budget and how it deploys its staff. Of its £15 m annual budget it spends £10 m on salaries for CRE and Race Equality Council staff,

£4m on research, rates, printing and production and only £1m on legal cases and support. It is not that it has not got strong legal powers. It is the CRE's increasing preoccupation with bureaucratic strictures, excessive paper work and rapidly declining commitment to racial discrimination in the Asian and black communities.

They claim that 25 per cent of officers' time is taken up on their three-year plan reports; annual operating plans; strategic plans; personal job plans; budget plans; output measures and performance indicators; and appraisals. This is the equivalent of 50 of the CRE's 213 staff being engaged solely in bureaucratic form filling.

The CRE tries to be everything to everyone and as such is doing nothing for anyone. It is a law enforcement agency; a body doing promotional and educational work, a race relations research organisation and a body which purports to serve the whole nation and which at the same time needs to retain the support and confidence of ethnic minorities and of the population at large. Additionally it needs to have the listening ear and confidence of government.

In reality, however, it is not a law enforcement agency. As it is now constituted under the Race Relations Act, and the way it has used those powers, it has lost any clout it might have had as one.

Its promotional and educational work after 15 years of existence has made no real impact on altering the patterns and trends of discrimination in employment and housing, nor has it radically changed the behaviour of people. Its research programme is inconsiderable and is better done by other more capable and better funded research bodies.

It has not retained the support and confidence of the black and Asian communities, nor that of the population as a whole.

Black and Asian people ask pointedly how the CRE's investigations in Working Men's Clubs affect their daily lives?

Its lack of priorities and inability to direct its resources to areas which really matter, questions its understanding of what is really required of it and whether it should go on existing. Its management structure is overwhelmingly white and like the organisations and society it is trying to change, there exists a hierarchy of occupational roles, power and responsibilities. Black people in the organisations are disproportionately located in lower level positions, characterised by little decision making power, limited opportunities for real advancement, less autonomy and less access to information.

According to a recent confidential CRE report on equal opportunities the Commission is failing to meet targets for recruiting black and women staff, with people from India, Pakistan and Bangladesh significantly underrepresented. The Chair of the Working Group on Equal Opportunities for Women, Mrs. Shahwar Sadeque, a CRE Commissioner, has this to say about the position of black women in the CRE: "If the recommendations of this report are not implemented then the Commission, quite justifiably, can be accused of much navel gazing and little activity". Black women, she said, do not see any changes occurring unless, "the Commission does practice the solution it offers employers in general – positive action". The report further accuses the Commission of lack of understanding about what it means to be an equal opportunities employer and "reveals a great deal about the true values of the organisation".

This inability to enforce its own internal equal opportunity policies has adversely affected staff who are required to persuade firms outside to be good equal opportunity employers.

"How can we tell employers to carry out our Code of Practice in employment and require them to be good equal opportunity employers if we ourselves so flagrantly flout our own Code?", a senior CRE officer queries.

In desperation, staff have formed a Black Support Group. Out of fear of victimisation, its membership remain anonymous. The Group in its recent letter to all CRE staff accuses the CRE of nepotism, racial discrimination, financial incompetence and of management ineffectiveness. "The Commission's reputation among black people is very low, and it has become an obscene irrelevancy. Staff morale is at its lowest and the dismissal of the CRE by the black public outside is too serious not to be heeded", the letter says.

It further encourages staff to supply MPs with information about the discriminatory acts in the CRE to raise in Parliament and says, "the situation in the CRE is so desperate and as such desperate measures need to be taken to ensure that we pull this rudderless boat back on to course or sink with it.

Management's response was to dismiss and denounce the Group. "It would be tragedy if we allowed a small group of people to jeopardise all our achievements and even the continued existence of the Commission", Peter Sanders, the Chief Executive, told a staff meeting.

An Industrial tribunal is about to hear the case of the deputy legal director of the CRE, Khursid Drabu, who alleges that racial discrimination prevented him getting the post of legal director. At least three similar cases by CRE staff are also pending.

One recent example of the breakdown of staff relations was the dismissal of senior education officer Gerry German, who had been in charge of monitoring racial harassment in schools and colleges, for allegedly leaking information to the Press. He is appealing in the knowledge that four of his former colleagues have already won their appeals after criticising the CRE.

All this is not lost on the black minority and to many of them who were prepared to give the organisation a gestation period of grace.

Having seen the problems develop over many years – I helped to set up the CRE and worked for it for 14 years as its Press and Public Relations Chief Officer until I took early retirement – I know the internal problems cannot be written off as local difficulties. There is, it must be said, a lack of direction, lack of leadership and lack of priorities.

The 1990's have seen a marked increase in racist attacks and harassment and in levels of discriminatory practices in employment, education and housing. Yet the CRE has shown a singular inability to influence Government. It has also adopted a softly-softly approach when dealing with employers, which is clearly failing.

What is needed, they argue, is an entirely different kind of body than that envisaged by parliament in the seventies. Not a body with such a wide and therefore inoperable brief, but a body with clear and specific functions which will have the weight of the law behind it. However, such a change can and will only take place if government itself is fully committed and places equal opportunities and the outlawing of racial discrimination as a high priority and introduces a different kind of race relations law with a different kind of organisation.

In its present form and its present leadership the organisation, can only continue to constitute a growing insult to the black community, a drain on public funds and a gross irrelevancy to the public at large.

Taken with its failure to come up with clear strategies which will help change the life patterns and chances of those mostly affected because of their colour, the whole reason for the CRE's existence must now be drawn into question. And therefore it must go.

Regrettable, I have to say I now share that view.

"The Weekly Journal", 11 June 1992
Also see 'WHY THE RACE BOARD MUST GO – 15 years on the Black and Asian Communities are losing faith in the Commission for Racial Equality', Daily Mail, 22 May 1992

INSTITUTIONAL RACISM IN PRINT – THE SAME OLD STORY...(2003)

In Britain, last year, only over 4 percent of journalists came from ethnic backgrounds-and the rest from white middle-class families. A startling report for year 2002? No! It is not, nor is it deceptive.

This survey is a report from the august British Journalism Training Forum (JTF), which claimed at its launch in July last year, that journalism was drifting into a kind of unintended apartheid. Ian Hargreaves, chair of the JTF then enjoined that the industry needed to take action to make sure its journalists more reflected the ethnic and social mix of the population. Fighting words, indeed, but it is nearly 30 years too late. Apartheid in the lilywhite newsrooms has been there all the time. Alive, breeding and arrogant.

In a seminal *Race and the Media* seminar held on 17th October 1975 in London-organised by the National Union of Journalists (NUJ) of Britain and Ireland's *Race Relations Sub Committee* (predecessor of the *Black Members Council* – BMC) and the *Community Relations Commission* (predecessor of the *Commission for Racial Equality*) there were less that two dozen (under 0.8%) black journalists in the newsrooms and there were nearly 22,000 white journalists working on newspapers, magazines and broadcasting. It compared this to the country's black population percentage of about 3% and the fact that over 40% of black youngsters were second generation. These included a few black subeditors, reporters and one or two broadcasters. I was then one of them.

A survey on employment of black journalists carried out in 1974 by the NUJ's Birmingham Branch showed that Birmingham had no black journalists despite a large black population.

As one of its first practical step, the *Race Relations Sub Committee* sent a questionnaire to all NUJ branches seeking information about the discrimination on grounds of race and colour.

The questionnaire covered the number of black journalists employed; sizes of immigrant communities; possible reasons why few black people apply to be journalists and whether concern was felt about this; coverage of ethnic minority group stories; attitudes about positive discrimination against black people in employment or news coverage; how chapels and branches were contributing and promoting racial harmony; unfair reporting or unnecessary mention of race or colour; and omission of relevant information, unfair selection of material, or omitting to publish at all.

The response was interesting and enlightening. About 72 per cent of the branches replied. A preliminary analysis of the replies confirmed our fears on the question of employment, that only a handful of black journalists were employed. What emerged from the replies were:

(1) Despairingly few journalists had any idea whether there was a black presence of any size in their areas, or whether their papers were carrying any racially biased stories.

(ii) With a few exceptions, journalists showed that they themselves were not inclined to produce or originate racially-biased material.

(iii) A substantial number believed that there was evidence of discrimination against black people in employment or news coverage.

(iv) Much more must be done by chapels and branches to contribute to promoting racial harmony.

(v) Few were sure how to handle the question of "unnecessary mention of race or colour".

(vi) Little was revealed in the replies about the existence or non-existence of positive, constructive journalism.

It would be interesting to see how chapels will respond to a similar questionnaire, and how attitudes have changed, and whether the composition of the newsrooms have coloured?

Guardian Media Group chief executive Bob Phillis also told the Journalism Training Forum last year that the industry must confront the equality issue and "look in the mirror and ask how our organisations measure up". And when the broadcasting big chiefs emphasised that the BBC was 'hideously white. and that television is dominated by white Anglo-Saxon men and it's a disgrace'. Pugnacious? Yes! But when did they ever before look in that shiny-cleaned mirror?

At that seminar in 1975 we were also aware of the mirrors around us. The media, then, and now generally still, mirrors the way minorities are perceived, plagued by stereotypes. A black colleague at that seminar was forced to say to me: "Mirror, mirror on the wall tell me do I exist at all".

The mirror of course, was the media, polished and held up by the image-makers, commercial and public television executives, producers, editors, writers or artistic directors. And as a collective body, they helped to reinforce the artist's concept of Britain – white on white. No flies in the buttermilk. Yes, the chances of survival of a black journalist in the media white conglomerate, was as limited as a fat spider in the web of a vicious hungry tarantula.

Unlike 1975, there were only 22000 journalists in the UK. Now there are around 70,000. Of these 60,000 work in publishing and 10,000 in broadcasting. By the late 1900's, the number of black members in the NUJ had increased to about 1.9% from the 0.8% of 1975., and the national minority population is now 5.27% compared to 3% in 1975. On the face of it there are more black faces-more visible yes- but then there are also measurably more white faces.

When one compares the present status of ethnic minorities with what went before, an optimistic picture emerges it seems – more black faces on TV and some in newspapers, but when compares achievement in statistical terms as a proportion of the population, and the career ladder they are on, the picture is rather dismal and worse then what it was.

How many black and Asian journalists are there now in the media industry? In 1975 we knew the number. Eight years later the Black Media Workers Association (BMWA) in 1983 were able to publish a survey *Black Workers in the Media Industries.* The 684 black people identified working in all media, apart from the black press, represented 0.07per cent of the total media force.

And then 9 years later – 1999 :

* London-based national papers (13 in number) employed only ten ethnic minority editors, 13 writer/reporters and one columnist.

* Throughout the entire ITV network, there were fewer than 160 ethnic minority

staff in programme departments.

* The proportion, out of a total of 8100 staff employed by ITV and Channel 4, just 300 (3.7 per cent) came from ethnic minorities.

* The proportion of people from ethnic minorities employed by the BBC in London, where most of the staff is based, actually fell from 7.5 per cent in 1996-97 to 7.4 per cent in 1997-98.

* The situation in magazines and local and regional newspapers was even worse, and we could not get a number.

The major media unions, according to the BMWA in 1983, "had taken a number of theoretical steps to bring about equal opportunities for employment of more black staff, but those steps were only slowly becoming practical ones and equal opportunities clauses are still not included in all agreements with employing bodies, and unions find it difficult to enforce them".

Chairing the 1975 seminar, I had this to say about this issue:

"What we must in future do is to press for the inclusion of equal opportunity clauses in collective bargaining agreements, and for the implementation of procedures designed to ensure that equal opportunity policies are actively pursued and, here I want to emphasise, regularly monitored by newspaper proprietors. Only by monitoring, will we be able to see whether we are really making progress in this field.

In words that are as applicable and as pertinent to Britain as to the USA, and to reporting of foreign as well as domestic conflicts, the National Advisory Commission on Civil Disorders (popularly known as the Kerner Commission) which was appointed by President Johnson following the race riots which took place in the summer of 1967, said it all:

"Along with the country as a whole, the press has too long basked in a white world, looked out of it, if at all, with white men's eyes and white perspective. that is no longer good enough."

Indeed it isn't, especially if the media as a whole accepts, which I am sure it does, that Britain is a multi-racial and multi-cultural society.

If we want to do something positively **now** and stop pretending that there is no problem in our indefatigable British way of determinedly denying its existence by constant verbal expression of British tolerance and refusal to acknowledge discrimination in our own journalistic backyard when it occurs.

By obscuring the reality beneath a consensus acceptance of British tolerance, a screen is provided for the practice of discriminating behaviour, which by popular judgement and official utterance is unacceptable in a tolerant society. The steps that we in the media must take on this issue are nothing but clear.

The employment of black journalists also makes, apart from good race relations – sound economic sense, especially for papers which circulate in areas where there is a substantial black population and thus black readership.

No newspaper will and can deny its desire to increase its circulation, nor can and will the broadcasting and TV companies equally deny their quest for better viewing and listening ratings."

Twenty-eight years ago we said it all. Since then new media researchers and academics have been saying exactly what we had already said and researched. Institutional racism in print, in Britain, is not new and racism and journalists have always been bound together with the stickiest of verbal glue. What is new is the churning, inventing and regurgitating of the same wheel. What we need is the determination and strength to translate all the surveys, researches and wonderful words into action. Yes,that would definitely be journalism in action.

Published in diversity-online.org,
Feb 2003 and in The Black Journalists, June, 2003

IS THERE A CONSPIRACY AGAINST ASYLUM SEEKERS BY TABLOID NEWSPAPERS? –

Ignoring, their own Code and traditional editorial standards of reporting and handling stories on race issues? (2003)

Is there a conspiracy by some tabloid newspapers to incite their readers against asylum seekers, black people, Muslims or aliens? Have they dismally failed to uphold and defend their own Code and traditional editorial standards? If you do not understand how newspapers work, you might think there is a conspiracy to play up the issue.

Do news stories create feeing frenzies?

Utterances of politicians and others reverberate into a great tumult with news stories and speeches piling up on each other with increasing frequency, so that before the row from one dies away, it is followed by the impact of another, until the details merge into a mounting clamour that excites the senses and drowns the still small voice of reason.

Three years ago, the newspaper and periodical industry framed its own Code of Practice ratified by the Press Complaints Commission (PCC), which is charged with enforcing it.

All members of the press have a duty to maintain the highest professional, ethical, albeit traditional, editorial standards and the Code sets the benchmark for those standards. It both protects the rights of the individual and upholds the public's right to know.

The Code is the cornerstone of the system of self-regulation to which the industry has made a binding commitment. Editors and publishers must ensure that the Code is rigorously observed, not only by their staff, but also by anyone who contributes to their publication.

It is essential to the workings of an agreed code that it be honoured not only to the letter but also fully in its spirit. And it states unequivocally that the Code should not be interpreted so narrowly as to compromise its commitment to respect the rights of the individual, nor so broadly that it prevents publication in the public interest.

Commentators may feel that the Code, with its traditional editorial standards for reporting and handling stories on race relations, seem to have been suspended, submerged, or worse, intentionally flouted in the exciting roller coaster hysteria of tabloids on heat.

Whether it is the case that readers' existing prejudices are reinforced by the press, or those prejudices are actually shaped or encouraged by the media, the considerable extent of press coverage on stories to do with asylum seekers during these few weeks, as shown on our ***Media HateWatch UK*** section, (http://www.diversity-online.org)is either openly hostile or lacking interpretation and context. It must appear to many readers as an encouragement for readers to equate immigration/race relations with the exploitation of this country by asylum seekers, especially black people and Muslims in general, leading to racial violence and conflict. Additionally, we have had the recent conflation of stories about asylum seekers and terrorism.

Objective reporting need not preclude differing treatments of race relations subjects, or of issues on asylum seekers by different newspapers.

We must be aware that it is not always understood that there is merit in the way in which different newspapers look at the same facts from different angles. Properly done, that variety of coverage can contribute positively to public knowledge by enabling a searching and sceptical examination of fact and opinion. There is, however, a crucial difference between the portrayal of facts from differing viewpoints, so that people can make up their minds about them, and the distortion of them for purposes of political propaganda.

Reporting issues on asylum seekers, or on issues of race relations, is not pleading for special treatment, nor is it an attempt to stop newspapers from printing views that reflect their editorial policy. It should not require a newspaper to stop printing immigration or asylum statistics or to stop discussing calls for a reduction in future immigration in its editorial columns. But what it does require, and this is by no means inconsistent with the traditional requirements of editorial standards, is that immigration statistics should be reported accurately, with adequate interpretation and in context; that speculation or views should be attributed as such and not presented as fact. Discussion of future immigration should not be so angled as to cause or encourage hostility towards asylum seekers, black people, Muslims or other aliens already legitimately living in this country.

The hostility that can result from misunderstanding and misinformation should not be underestimated. Racial hostility, prejudice and xenophobia are not a simple expression of dislike based on personal choice, but an irrational fear, which can be fed and perverted from many unrelated sources. There is no doubt, as experience in this country and other countries has shown, that racial hostility can lead to considerable suffering and, in certain circumstance, to death. Racial hostility and xenophobia are also extremely wasteful of human resources, in that they lead to the expending of people's time and energy in misguided actions, whilst the real and basic problems of society or of the economy remain unchanged.

It is therefore important that editors should examine their editorial policy in order to ensure that the style and content of their reporting on asylum seekers and race relations issues does not encourage or reinforce racial hatred, hostility or xenophobia. Obviously the menu for a good story is what we all learned when we all sharpened our writing tools as trainee journalists.

Selectivity: Is the story really necessary? Selectivity does not necessarily imply distortion.

Objectivity: The 'bandwagon effect' and hysteria should be avoided. Stories and allegations should be ascribed to their source and their authority evaluated. Statistics should be checked, interpreted and placed in context. Speculations and rumour have no place in news columns. Fears should not be exploited by irresponsible and exaggerated reporting. Particular care should be taken when reporting violence and events which cause racial tension The agreed Code is definitive when it states that newspapers and periodicals must take care not to publish inaccurate, misleading or distorted material including pictures.

Position of story: Is it given a place as front-page lead or in small print inside?

Timing of the story: The accuracy of a story should first be checked and placed in the context of the paper's policy. Traditional press standards of accuracy should be rigorously applied to stories involving racism, religion or asylum seekers.

Method of treatment: A balanced text cannot redress the damage caused by sensational headlines. Headlines should be moderate and emotive and 'gory' references should be avoided.

The text itself should further reflect:

- a policy on identifying racial origin or religion. The Industry's Code, in no uncertain terms, states that *the press must avoid prejudicial or pejorative reference to a person's race, colour, religion, sex or sexual orientation or to any physical or mental illness or disability;*
- avoidance of reporting 'negative' qualities only;
- care should be taken over readers' letters, and editors should have responsibility for the 'tone and truth' of reader' letters printed;
- stories should be ascribed to their source and their authority evaluated.
- generalisations and stereotypes should be avoided;
- human fears should not be exploited;
- speaker's allegations should be checked for accuracy and balanced by opposing views.

Responsibility for a story's angle is often a circular one. Whilst editors take responsibility for the newspapers' line and may encourage or oblige reporters to produce material in accordance with this, reporters and journalists are not without influence and cannot avoid responsibility completely. Theirs may be the initial judgment of whether the story they are following is still newsworthy if the 'colour' is taken out of it and it is unlikely that any news editor would adhere formally to a policy that news is only news if an asylum seeker, a black person or a Muslim is involved.

The opinions expressed by columnists/contributors often receive firm editorial backing with the essence of their arguments re-iterated separately in newspaper editorials, giving them legitimacy.

On many occasions articles are supplemented with cartoons or poems in which racist and xenophobic messages are conveyed even more explicitly and where grotesque stereotypes are expressed visually or in verse. They borrow freely from the racist and xenophobic imagery that was popularised in the heyday of the British Empire to justify its subjugation and exploitation of 'natives', and bring that imagery to bear on peoples' perceptions of the issues affecting black people in Britain today. This is exactly what is being done to the latest asylum seekers.

Verse and cartoons can be a powerful source of communication both because poems are easy to understand, easy to the ear and because graphic illustrations such as cartoons can bring a dry issue to life. Both are popular and supposedly harmless weapons of humour and ridicule against their targets. Editors always argue that using stereotypes or exaggerated images and words in poems to represent individuals or groups of people is in the nature of their work, and they are merely making jokes. But behind every 'joke' a serious point is being made. It is this serious point, not the jocular verses, jokes or humour in themselves, which is objectionable. Far from being light and harmless fun, these kinds of poems and cartoons, reinforce and perpetuate popular stereotypes of asylum seekers, whether as 'illegal' asylum seekers or welfare scroungers. This identifies them as legitimate targets for hostility and its consequences.

Neutrality is not always adequate in reporting race relations or issues on asylum seekers. The Code enjoins newspapers, whilst they are free to be partisan, to distinguish clearly between comment, conjecture and fact.

Objectivity should be sought and public hysteria should not determine news coverage. It is important that official information/statistics should be handled with more sophistication and in court reporting, the racial dimension of the case should be reported only if relevant. News is not news simply because a black person/an asylum seeker/Muslim or immigrant is involved. But more importantly, the message of a story should be 'well rounded'-placed in context and accompanied by interpretation.

There must be many others, but here is a simple checklist based on the stories on http://www.diversity-online.org ***(Media HateWatch UK*** section) which was used to assess balance, objectivity and moderation – the elements of the industry's Code of Practice: The four W's and How, which were incessantly drummed into us in our training to last all our journalistic life, can now be used as our strengths in adhering to and extolling our traditional editorial standards and upholding and defending the Code.

WHERE: Is the story given as a front-page lead or as small print inside. Is the photo on the front page? How is it used? Is the story given several columns or a few inches? Headlines are an important constituent of a news item and may influence the way readers interpret the text of that item; moreover, this influence is likely to be greater on the casual reader who may not read the remainder of the item thoroughly.

WHEN: Is the story released before or after its accuracy is checked and the authority evaluated? Editors, according to their own Code, must ensure that those working for them comply with these requirements and must not publish material from other sources which does not meet these requirements.

HOW: Is it placed in the context of background facts or overall policy or is the story treated sensationally-by headlines, positions or photographs? A reasonable text cannot balance the effect of sensational headlines or editorials. Has the point of view been expressed?

WHY: Is the story only newsworthy because an asylum seeker or a black person is involved? Is the story joining a 'bandwagon' of immigration, crime, fraud stories or linking it with terrorism? Its Code stresses that publishing details of a person's race, colour, religion, sexual orientation, physical or mental illness or disability must be avoided unless these are directly relevant to the story.

The call for more interpretation, analysis and evaluation of the presence of asylum seekers is in no way contradictory to editors' or journalists' traditional responsibilities of full and balanced reporting. In many cases it may be an extension of their present practices, but it is a constructive extension not a threatening one. Adhering to the Code of Practice, and its traditional editorial standards on balanced and accurate reporting, could ensure that, in future, these issues are treated in a less explosive and more responsible manner.

Published in diversity-online.org. 2003 and the Black Journalist, Sept, 2003

THINGS DON'T CHANGE; THE SAME TARGETS, EXCUSES, JUSTIFICATIONS, DOUBLE TALK AND THE SAME SUPERFICIAL CONCERN FOR TOLERANCE. (2003)

"Asylum seekers, immigrants new faces"... whether you are a newspaper editor, columnist, broadcaster, or politician, if you choose to descend to the level of the gutter in what you publish or say in public, you should expect the worst kind of reaction from your readers or from your listeners.

On no subject is this more true at this time than on that of asylum seekers. Xenophobia and racism is based on the age-old desire of man to find a ready scapegoat, and dislike of anyone who does not readily conform, fit in, whether in behaviour, colour or religion. To perpetuate racism and xenophobia through our media is not only anti-social and grossly irresponsible, it is well nigh criminal.

The attitude of our newspapers and broadcasting stations is a crucial element in race relations and opinion forming on asylum seekers. Immigration or colour prejudice can be materially affected by the way these media handle stories concerning them. This observation is not new, and sadly, nor are racist and xenophobic articles and news reports new to our newspapers.

Things have not changed. If you visit the *Media HateWatch UK* section of http://www.diversity-online.org you can read page after page of poisonous coverage and how these stories show that 'asylum seeker' once meant 'scrounger' and now means 'terrorist'. Addition in many stories recently there is a conflation of stories about asylum seekers and terrorism.

Nearly 33 years ago it was possible to find headlines such as 'Threat to Survival-Increasing Flood of New Immigrants' above an inflammatory letter to ***The Daily Telegraph*** from the late Tory MP, Sir Cyril Osborne (18/10/67).

The Daily Express in February 14, 1971 merged fact with fantasy: "There are 200,000 Asians in East Africa' it announced in a leader on Feb 12, 'all possessing British passports, who may come here soon'. This falsification launched a series of 'floods,' 'tides,' 'stampedes,' and other connotations of a deluge into ***The Express's*** treatment.

This culminated on March 1,1971 with a headline: *'A million Chinese can arrive here next week if they want to.'*

Later the ***Daily Telegraph*** again that February, announced on page 1: 'Kenyan Asian Exodus Numbers Double – 100,000 may enter Britain by end of the year.' This was based not on any projections, nor even on the estimate of the paper's correspondent in Nairobi, where the story originated. Low down in the report it emerged that the origin of the menacing headline was the calculation of anonymous 'airline officials.'

A similar event took place in 1972, when a story originating from one man gave rise to reports that the British Government was easing its policy on the entry of unqualified immigrants into Britain. The story blew up over 41 Asians who, on arrival in Britain without the correct papers, had been allowed to remain as visitors for a period of three months after immigration office headquarters had considered their case.

The Daily Mirror front page screamed: 'Smuggling of Exiles Alarms Britain'. And

The Times leader of 14 August, 1972 said: 'Immigrants already settled here stand to suffer more than anyone else from a rate of new immigration greater than the social body of the host country can digest, or than its prejudices can tolerate.'

The Daily Express on April, 1972, carried the headline 'Stay-on 'illegal' visitors start a row' and began the 18 column inch article with: *'Immigration officials were up in arms last night over what they regard as a new Government policy that could allow thousands of illegal immigrants into Britain without fear of deportation.'*

On the same day ***The Guardian*** blazed the front-page headline: 'Kenyan-Asians slip through Britain's net.' The introduction to the 24-column inch article stated that: *'Immigration officers are concerned at the number of Kenyan Asians being allowed into Britain. Officers have strict instructions not to talk to the press-but an "official leak" from immigration sources claimed that the British Government's attitude towards the shuffling of immigrants from one country to another would mean that thousands of immigrants would have to be let into Britain'.*

These quotations show that two papers generally considered to be of different political complexions, printed similar stories which implied that there had been a shift in Government policy regarding immigration, a consequence of which would be 'thousands of "illegal" immigrants' entering Britain. However, what ***The Guardian*** chose to label 'an official leak,' originated from a Mr Bill Pryke, who was an interpreter employed by the Home Office at Heathrow.

The instant fit of this news item into the race-news framework was so compelling that the normal journalistic routine of adequately checking sources was not carried through. As a consequence these two papers gave considerable prominence to an event which was, in itself, insignificant, but which, through their acceptance of, and elaboration of it, became yet another immigration scare, a further proof that black immigration was threatening.

The Daily Express's front page in February 24, 1971 was dominated by the headline: 'Panic airlift may aid 4,000 Asians to beat ban' - a point underlined in the leader column's stern warning against 'any attempt by any transport organisation to frustrate the Government's intention to stem the flood'. The news judgment of these papers led it to play the 'influx' angle for all it was worth and some of the stories were reported against only the flimsiest background of agreed fact. A common sacrilegious abuse of facts by reporters and subs was the comment from *Frederick Whitehead's* column in the **Birmingham Post** in 1977:

'The tree-lined street where I used to live in Handsworth, Birmingham is now an alley of putrefaction. Many of its houses are pustules of social profanity, its gutters gather the jetsam of decay and the faces of the alien people who live there are a fretwork of sullen resignation'.

The newspapers of April 5 took up the ***News of World's*** cry, but not just with the £150,000 mansion ***(Daily Mail, The Sun, The Daily Express*** and ***Daily Telegraph);*** the ***Daily Mail*** also carried a feature on Asians jumping the housing queue – *'A Kenyan Asian fixed himself a council house ahead of 17,000 people on the local housing list within a week arriving in Britain'.*

It was, to use the newspapers 'own terminology, as if the floodgates had burst. General reporting on refugees, immigrants, black people and race relations increased considerably over the next few weeks, and the majority of newspapers had a field day with Asians' 'exploitation' of the social services and Asians' pouring into the country', Here are examples of headlines to major news stories or features at that time:

'Storm Over the Two-Wife Migrants' – ***The Sun,*** *6.5.76*
'Invasion of Asians Forces Borough to Call for Help' – ***Telegraph,*** *6.5.76*
'New Flood of Asians to Britain' – ***Mirror,*** *6.5.76*
'Another 20,000 Asians are on the Way' – ***The Sun,*** *6.5.76*
'Asians trick BR to enter' – ***Mail,*** *8.5.76*
'Scandal of Day-Tripper Immigrants' – ***Mirror,*** *8.5.76*
' "Queue Jumping" Rumpus' – ***Express,*** *8.5.76*
'Banda's Asians Fly In' – ***News of the World,*** *9.5.76*
'Refused Welfare – but 'I'll settle for council house' – ***Express,*** *10.5.76*
'Asians fly out of 'New Uganda' – ***The Sun,*** *17.5.76*
'Mellish cries "Enough" on Asian influx' – ***Telegraph,*** *18.5.76*

For two weeks then, readers were subjected to a barrage with constant *news coverage on Asian immigration and asylum seekers from all the newspapers, and those two weeks' period turned out to be only the precursor of a long summer in which immigration, race relations and black people provided a major portion of news coverage.'*

Then as with the Kenyan Asian story, and as with many other racist and xenophobic stories, newspapers sensed that large choices were open to them under the general umbrella of 'news' They reveled in their power to affect public opinion and political action on racist and xenophobic matters.

The point about the press handling of the coverage of the Kenya Asians in the late 1960s and early 1970s is its remarkable and prophetic similarity to the coverage first of the Jewish refugee problem in the period 1938-39: 'Aliens Pouring into Britain' was the headline of the ***Daily Mail,*** while the **Sunday Express** (June 1938) wrote: *'In Britain half a million Jews find their home. They are never persecuted and, indeed, in many respects the Jews are given favoured treatment here.*

'But just now there is a big influx of foreign Jews in Britain. They are overrunning the country. They are trying to enter the medical profession in great numbers. Worst of all, many of them are holding themselves out to the public as psychoanalysts.

'Intolerance is loathed and hated by almost everybody in this country. And by keeping a close watch on the causes which fed the intolerance of the Jews in other European countries we shall be able to continue to treat well those Jews who have made their homes among us, many of them for generations.'

In 1900, the **Daily Mail** described the flight from tsarist pogroms thus: *'There were Russian Jews, Polish Jews, German Jews, Peruvian Jews: all kinds of Jews,all manner of Jews. They fought and jostled for the foremost places at the gangways; they rushed and pushed and struggled into the troop shed, where the Mayor of Southampton....had provided free refreshments.*

'They had breakfasted well on board, but they rushed as though starving at the food. They brushed the attendant to one side. They cursed if they were not quickly served, they helped themselves at will, they thrust the children to the background, they pushed the women....they jostled and upset the weak, they spilled coffee on the ground in wanton waste'.

And then in August 1938 the ***Daily Mail*** described the refugee Jews fleeing from Nazi German: “The stateless Jews from Germany are pouring in from every port of this country in becoming an outrage”.

It is remarkable how the press coverage of the latest Asylum refugees’ plight is uncannily similar and prefigured? Nearly 70 years later the old double-talk is still being employed without embarrassment or question. The problem it seems always lies with the asylum seekers, and not in white racism. The respectability of white prejudice is sanctified in the claims that certain cities can take no more asylum seekers, for reasons that scarcely trouble to disguise outward hostility.

Theoretically the existing Race Relations Amendment Act already places some constraints on editors, columnists and journalists. It is unlawful to incite racial hatred, though, because of the difficulty of defining “incitement,” this particular piece of law has not, in fact, proved to be an effectual restraint.

The imagery of threat, of floods of asylum seekers, terrorism, crime, and of dirty and infected hordes of aliens, which was apparent in 1938 and which was developed to the state of art by journalists, politicians and cabinet ministers in the late 1960s and ’70s and now so brutally and eloquently, is once more brought forth. The presence of the alien, asylum seeker, foreigner, the black, Asian, Muslim and Jew have, time and again, been the vicious target of the prejudices of the lowest common denominator, especially when articulated and fostered by the so-called respectable Press.

In this roller coaster of hysteria, ***The Sun, The Express*** and ***Daily Mail,*** especially, are still now conveying a ‘paranoid’ definition of events through their unquestioning acceptance of the belief that the entry of asylum seekers constitutes a life-threat to our social fabric, social services, housing, health, education, security, and of course, good race relations.

Today’s tabloid newspapers are an volcanic landslip which strangles any explanation, reason and simply but torrentially rushes on, headlong into glaring headline. Their latest coverage is intentionally racist, sycophantic, sometimes bizarre, inflammatory, yes surreal as well, and a violation of most journalistic ethics taught at our journalism schools and centres.

Once again, over six decades later, our press has dismally failed to acknowledge, analyse and confront British prejudice; and instead, covertly, smugly, and smilingly hides behind the silky veil of superficial concern for tolerance. Admirably summing it up, to paraphrase Jamaican Dick Pixley, a former BBC producer: ‘The godly are not having their say. For them it’s page 4 bottom, and it’s page one lead for blood’.

Published in diversity-online.org 2003

PART III

Selected Biographical Notes

A black poet must remember the horrors
The good jobs can't last forever,
It shall come to pass that the fury
Of a token revolution will fade
Into the bank accounts of countless blacks
And freedom-loving whites.

– Conrad Kent Rivers
The Still Voice of Harlem

ONE BRAVE BLACK MAN'S HOPES FOR SOUTH AFRICA

- by Bernard Levin *The Times, London, Friday, June 3 1977.*

With every preconception pulling him in the opposite direction, he came back from South Africa believing that real progress has been made and that it is likely that it will be maintained.

On Monday *Lord Chalfont* reported on a recent visit to South Africa. Today, I want to do the same, though not in the first person. For on Sunday, there were two remarkable newspaper articles published on the subject, one in the *Mirror* and the other in the *Telegraph.* They overlapped each other substantially in subject-matter, they came to roughly the same conclusions, and they were both distinguished by a remarkable courage. All this, however, is not so much of a coincidence as you might imagine, for they were both by the same man; *Mr. Lionel Morrison.*

Of this *Morrison,* I know somewhat, and like what I know. He is a freelance journalist of distinction, and thus not only a member of the same branch of the NUJ as myself, but its treasurer, in which capacity he is to be regularly seen registering, on his expressive features, every conceivable variety of amazement and horror at some of the suggestions for spending the branch's money that are put forward. For in the branch's fiscal matters, he is of the most rigidly conservative school of economists, regarding any unbalancing of the budget with a dismay that could hardly have been excelled by *Gladstone;* in his personal political beliefs however, he is a socialist, and an active and militant one, at that. Yet he is impeccably and unwaveringly democratic withal, and in every way scrupulously fair.

He is also, and it is very relevant to my remarks today, a black man, born in South Africa. Indeed, he has the honour of having been one of the defendants in the notorious "Treason Trial" (whatever became of that professor who was the prosecution's "expert witness" on communism, and who cruelly led by defence counsel into identifying as of communist tendencies printed matter which turned out to be from one of his own books?)

After his acquittal, along with all the other defendants, when the case collapsed in ignominy and derision, *Lionel* was imprisoned, on another such charge, for two years, and later "banned" – turned, that is, into the peculiar form of Unperson that is South Africa's chief contribution to the categories of mankind. Shortly after that, he left his native land and settled in Britain, becoming a British citizen. But his large family remained in South Africa, and earlier this year he received news that his mother was very ill, and like to die.

He had never been back to the land of his birth since he left some 17 years ago; moreover, he wanted to be near his mother at the last. But as a *banneling,* a black man, a British citizen, the husband of a white woman and a former resister of South African tyranny, he could scarcely have had fewer hopes of being admitted if he had been a typhoid carrier. Nevertheless, he did get a visa from the South African authorities, and even managed to get its week's duration extended by a month when he was there. (His mother did die, and he was with her.)

Now naturally, despite the sad personal reasons for his visit, *Mr. Morrison* went about in South Africa, talking, listening and looking. In the two articles to which I have referred he sums up his feelings and conclusions, and astonishing ones they are. For remember, this is no tame guest of the South African Foundation or any similar propaganda organisation, no businessman seeking lucrative contracts there, no apostle of apartheid. His credentials, as an unwavering opponent of that vile state are absolutely impeccable and his suffering in that capacity a matter of record.

Now I am not about the reveal that so doughty a champion of democracy and equality (he has, incidentally, served most valuably on several bodies in this country concerned with race relations and allied matters) has become converted to, or in any way an apologies for the brutal and morally corrupt philosophical foundation of South African rule, or a defender of its conduct in maintaining that rule. Indeed, he was not concerned in his two articles to offer his opinion of the character of South African society at all. What he was doing was offering a prognosis. And the reason I regard the articles as of such exceptional interest and importance is that his prognosis was hopeful; very hopeful. Of course he was wary; of course, he made clear that the South African rulers have yet to demonstrate their good faith, and – even more – to concede the fundamental principle which they have lived, and still live, by denying. But despite all this, he – with every preconception pulling him in the opposite direction – came back from South Africa believing that real progress has been made, however casually, quietly and pragmatically, and that it is very likely that it will be maintained.

He sees the signs which lead him to this conclusion in many places and many happenings. In, for instance, the relaxation of "petty apartheid" that has led to the disappearance not of the laws requiring separate facilities for blacks and whites, but – in many instances – of their provision. He sees it in the greater affluence among urban blacks. He sees it in the amount of attention devoted to black problems that would once have been simply ignored in the increasing politeness used to many blacks by many whites (the positively Martian atmosphere of South Africa can be poignantly sensed in *Lionel's* astonishment that he was referred to, both in the white newspapers and to his face, as *"Mr" Morrison,* which would have been inconceivable at the time of his departure), in the fact that he was allowed to attend a white service in a Dutch Reformed church, in the attitude he found among blacks – an attitude based on the demand for their rights coupled with a turning away from the violent road to their attainment.

I said that *Lionel Morrison's* articles were courageous as well as astonishing, and so they are. I know well, and he better, what reactions are bound to follow their publication. On the one hand, they will be used by scoundrels both here and in South Africa not for the purpose for which they were written – which was simply to record an honest man's experiences – but to claim his support for their own argument that south Africa is a happy, decent and racially harmonious nation. (I can just imagine some of the letters the *Sunday Telegraph* will publish next week – and some of those they will receive but not print.) And on the other hand, *Lionel's* articles and *Lionel* will be attacked by the liberal establishment not – which would be perfectly legitimate – as giving a limited and unrepresentative account of conditions in South Africa, but as a betrayal of his cause and his people, as a sell-out to apartheid, as the fawning of an "Uncle Tom" on those whose approbation he seeks.

In the circumstances, I must emphasize for those who have not read the articles in question that they do *not,* directly or by implication, concede that there is good in the odious creed of apartheid; nor do they fail to draw attention to the vast amount of cruelty and suffering produced by it; nor do they omit comment on the remarkable frequency with which those arrested by the South African police tend, during questioning, to fall accidentally out of high windows. Nor do they forget the just aspirations of the vast majority of South Africans for a place in their own land and society denied them solely on account of the colour of their skins.

Lionel Morrison went back to South Africa. He saw and heard; and what he saw and heard he has now described. It is not necessary for anybody to agree with his tentatively hopeful conclusions (I do not myself); it *is* necessary, I can assure you as one who knows him well, to agree that he is both a shrewd observer and a man of complete integrity. Time will show whether he is right to be hopeful, or whether all he has seen is yet another false dawn. Meanwhile, because so many of those who attack him do so because they hope he is wrong, let me say that I hope he is right.

THE SOUTH AFRICAN LION THAT NEVER SLEEP

by Benson Turay, *African Times, London.24 August,1987*

There is more to the National Union of Journalists (NUJ), that soliciting support for trade union activities against bosses, especially in the case of black newspapers, says *Mr. Lionel Morrison,* the first black person to head Britain's most powerful journalists trade union.

Therefore he wants to see more black journalists become members of the union and make use of the facilities that are available.

Employers too must do all in their power to help because he believes that it is the only way out to correct the current imbalance in the profession and indeed the union.

Mr. Morrison, a South African exile, told the *African Times* in an interview shortly after the announcement of his election in April 1987 to the titular position that he is very pleased with his election to the NUJ's presidency. He hopes it will serve as an encouragement for black journalists in the country. He said it proves that with determinations and active participation within the union you can get somewhere.

HIGH ESTEEM

"As a black person you've got to be more determined, better than others and get the support of your community," he said. What his election does " spell out is that there is commitment in the NUJ. It has got its equal opportunity, anti-racism and anti apartheid policies. It shows that there is a market in the area of policies where the union can go."

His determination and relentless participation have earned him a high esteem in the journalistic world. His involvement in British trade unionism has seen him as a treasurer of a branch, chair of an area council and participant in union negotiations.

And what he has done is to simply bring in his wealth of trade union experience from Africa and Asia to the NUJ. This, he said, has helped him tremendously.

He advised black journalists not to be disillusioned, and insisted that the fact that he can make an impact in journalism should serve as an encouragement and inspiration to them. *"It shows that if you join the union, participate in the main stream events of the union and not stand outside, you can do something within the structure that can change things. It's difficult, but it's possible",* he said.

Mr. Morrison's career in journalism started in his teens when he became the editor of his school magazine in South Africa. Since then, he has been in and out of prison because of his anti-apartheid beliefs. One of the reasons for his many arrests by the South Africa authorities was because he was in "possession of banned literature" and for painting political graffiti on important public building walls, for which he was jailed for five months At the age of 21 he became the youngest person to be charged with high treason.

It was after he and the other 156 "traitors" were acquitted after the Sharpeville massacre took place. He then fled the country. But, before that, he pioneered the formation of the first multi racial journalist's trade union in South Africa – NUSAJ. "We were all supposed to be members of the South African Society of Journalists but black people were not full members of the union and we were very dissatisfied with conditions", he revealed.

In 1960 *Mr. Morrison* arrived in Britain to become the Anti-Apartheid Movement's press officer and also to solicit the support of the NUJ for his union in South Africa. "I also made representation to the International Federation of Journalists and the International Organisation of Journalists and they all supported us."

In 1963, he and some other African journalists formed the Pan African Union of Journalists in Accra, Ghana, to which he became a member of the steering committee. In the same year, the Afro-Asian Journalist's Association was also formed in Indonesia and *Mr. Morrison* became the African representative and editor of the magazine The Afro-Asian *Journalists.* Adding to his glittering professional record, he later became press adviser to the black activist *Michael X* and the *Black House.*

He has been closely involved with helping in setting up trade unions in Africa and Asia, training African and Asian journalists and running the association's monthly magazine. The magazine was translated into different languages especially during the Chinese and Vietnamese war to reach a wider audience.

Mr. Morrison has no faith in the white media in this country because of the racism that is prevalent within it. "The whole theory of publish and be damned is one of the terrible things that continuously rears its head in British journalism and the British press generally suffers from a monopoly situation. That is not healthy because it means press control is in the hands of a very small number of people.

NEGATIVE PERCEPTIONS

"Journalists themselves – we have a code of conduct – we try very hard to make them adhere to it," he pointed out. But he knows this code has been abused in many cases, because: "Journalists have been educated in a tradition and system which is not multiracial in its proper context."

Most, if not all of the journalists who claim to be experts on black issues, he said, were educated in a system where racism is still festering in schools, view points are still very prejudiced, black people are looked upon as troublesome and negative and the terminology "the devil is black and angels are white" is in common use. "All this, and more form part of the education which white journalists have gone through and are still going through", he said.

These negative perceptions are what people in the profession should begin to change. They should begin to think about the effects of what they write on a changing society rather than wait until the damage has been caused. *"But I think what is more important is that they must not present reports on race as they do on sex."*

Here, he sees the relevance of the Black press in Britain. What gave way to the emergence of these papers is dissatisfaction by black people with the white press. Black people felt that the white media does not represent their views fairly, he said.

"It is a healthy sign that we must have a diverging press. I think black papers are playing an important role in putting forward black points of view correctly but also help in educating the white community and press".

BAROMETER

"The black press also plays a vital role in providing a barometer for black activities. It makes it easier, for black people who face problems in trying to get jobs in white papers. Black papers are the only places where they can get employment. Of course, these papers too have problems. They don't have the money and facilities like the

white press. But I think also that journalists working in these places must have at least fair deals," he said.

Mr. Morrison had his share of British racism when he decided to get a job. He said that a friend tipped him about a job in a "liberal" daily newspaper. He applied and he was asked to come along for an interview. He got to the receptionist and asked for the night editor, when he came to fetch him he walked past him three times before he finally asked the receptionist where *Mr. Morrison* was. She then indicated to the only person at the reception.

During the interview, though, the night editor was 'nice' to him and he offered him a job within two weeks. The two weeks came and went and there was no word. That was it. In some cases, he said, editors were only interested in seeing this black journalist. *"The assumption then, and it's still true now, was that black journalists were only useful where there is a riot."*

He has plenty of faith in the NUJ, anyway, and he revealed that it is about to set up a fund that will benefit black journalists in terms of training. *"So the union can do a lot. But it will do more if black people join to push things further. We all know that if we are not united, we don't speak as one, we're not going to get anywhere".*

He admitted that the union is "Lilly-white-male dominated and so on", but if we stand outside and don't take part we will shout for the rest of our life and nothing will come to us.

Black people in Britain often say that what they are going through is similar to what is happening in South Africa, but for most South Africans Apartheid in Britain is subtle and at least people can operate openly whilst in his country you can't. And *Mr. Morrison* believes that "we must fight discrimination and apartheid anywhere, whatever country you are in. If we fight it here, we'll make it less possible for this country to support apartheid in South Africa.

I am not an expert on the South African issues to be quite honest, but my main bone of contention is the fact that whilst the South African forces are killing innocent people in the country, the ANC and PAC are engaged in ideological differences. The situation is so frustrating that both parties hardly share the same platform. I put this question to *Mr. Morrison* who is equally concerned.

He said, *"As the struggle intensifies in South Africa unity will be forced on people. These differences will go because at the end of the day it is the people inside the country who are going to change things. Exile politics are the worse politics.*

"Whatever happens within the next ten years we are going to be in a hell of a battle. There is no other way out. What we outside can do is to help make the job of those in the country a lot easier. We must make it difficult for this government, and indeed any other government to give support to the South African apartheid government. And the British people must give moral support. That's our job here, and not to direct the struggle in the country," said a concerned *Mr. Morrison.*

PRESIDENT'S 'THINK FIRST' FORMULA FOR SURVIVAL

By Jean Morgan – UK Press Gazette 1st June 1987

Lionel Morrison has become president of the National Union of Journalists in a year when it is broke and divided over Wapping. A committed trade unionist and a far-sighted man, he is intent on fundamental changes in his year of office to revitalise the union for the 21st century. Jean Morgan finds out what they are.

Lionel Morrison pored through his morning post at Acorn House and told me: "Nothing there to rush off for". As we settled back for our talk, I thought it would be hard to envisage Morrison rushing into anything.

He has learned in a hard school to think before action.

A black South African, he was one of the first anti-apartheid fighters against *Dr. Verwoerd's* unsympathetic regime and was tried for treason when he was 21. He was acquitted of a plot to overthrow the State but his trial and that of l56 others provoked the Sharpeville massacre.

Out of Africa in 1960, he continued the fight by becoming Press officer for the anti-apartheid organisation in this country.

Today he is principal information officer at the Commission for Racial Equality. In between he has had periods in international trades unionism in Indonesia and China and a PR job for *Michael X,* one time black movement Messiah, later hanged for murder.

But if he thinks first, it is not to say *Morrison* is indecisive. He has clear-cut views on the way the union should go.

He is the first man at a high level in the NUJ I have heard ready to say the union should take some blame for the way in which the Wapping dispute developed.

"The advent of new technology has shown us in the union that we were not prepared for the consequences of new technology. That is the lesson of Wapping," Morrison admitted.

"We, as a union, had many years to plan a proper strategy on new technology. We really wasted six or seven years. We should have had a strategy which took into account the domino effect of Wapping on new technology in other areas."

Nor is the battle over in his eyes. *"I think it is important that we prepare ourselves for the 21st century. I'm afraid the union reacted, as always. It is time for us to take the lead. And that does not mean we have to be at loggerheads with management."*

Just now, *Morrison* and general secretary *Harry Conroy* are talking of building bridges with the Wapping chapels. Yet the union's conference delegates voted for more punishment for News International journalists (95 have already been fined £1,000 each), and the chapels themselves demand no less than a complete climb-down by the union. How can all these viewpoints be reconciled?

Morrison is a staunch proponent of sticking by the rule-book

"I have encouraged the people at Wapping to make use of union rules and structure. Our rule book is a democratic one and we should be bending over backwards to see its procedures are carried out properly. If not, we are subject to the appeals Tribunal and the courts of the land.

The union had to act in the circumstances. Whether the issued instructions (to NI journalists, not to cross picket lines) were wrong becomes an academic question. What we have got to do now the dispute has ended is to sit down and say how do we

really pick up the pieces at Wapping. It's going to be done through patience, better understanding, being more honest with each other, and a clearer strategy. I do understand the desire of the chapels to have their way in this instance, but they must be realistic. At the end of the day some may feel the rules are still acting against them and they will take the union to court. That's up to them."

What sanctions can the union effectively impose at Murdoch's papers now?

"There is a tendency in the union to look at the strike weapon as the first weapon. It is not. It is the ultimate weapon. First, you must analyse the situation, work out a plan and you may find you have to negotiate issues even if it is not palatable.

We must not get involved in industrial action that we cannot sustain. That is the most debilitating thing that can happen."

Morrison is looking for strength for the "articulate but small" NUJ from other unions, to create one union for the newspaper industry. Natural affiliates are the print, broadcasting and electricians' unions. Talks are under way with both broadcasting unions but the NUJ, £407,000 in the red, is not in a strong bargaining position.

"I don't think we're a very attractive bride."

"As one union we have not been able seriously to meet the onslaught of the employers. The new Government Green Paper on trades unions should bring us more closely together. It is one of the most vicious attacks on trade unionism ever."

He is pinning his faith on the complete restructuring of the NUJ – *"nothing can be sacrosanct: feathers are going to be ruffled."*

"The union is in financial straits – it's broke – and we have an organisational structure that is in danger of total collapse."

The membership must decide now whether branches are old hat and can be replaced by chapel power; whether the annual conference can be held instead every two or three years; whether NEC members must be elected for one year or can stay for three.

The union has to stop budgeting for 34,000 members instead of the true figure of 31,000 (90 branches were disbarred from ADM for failing to make proper financial returns) and find some way to check expenditure on elections (more than 130 places for 16 branches contested every year).

Without dismantling what the membership supports, *Morrison* hopes that a summer debate will bring change to a more efficient, effective, democratic and cost-effective union.

And once again – *"It must take us right into the 21st century."*

There is a good response already. By September, *Morrison* wants the NEC to be formulating recommendations for the next ADM.

While this is going on *Morrison* will be doing his best so see that the cause of black journalists in the union and in British journalism is championed. The former is his first priority. He sees himself as a symbol *"pour encourager les autres."*

"Britain is a multi-racial society. It's no good the NUJ adopting a colour-blind approach. We have to say 'Come into the union. This is the sort of thing we can help you with'."

Training is top of the list. *"Today you see more black faces in the regional Press, though not enough, but black journalists still have difficulty getting jobs on Fleet Street papers. Editors will find it difficult to sustain the old argument that there are no trained black journalists if we help them train."*

For the man who helped found the first South African multi-racial journalists' union, the censorship on news and news men there is bad news The union has taken a strong stand with money, moral support and plans for an alternative news agency in the Cape.

But *Morrison* is critical of people who support the black struggle in South Africa and forget the struggle against racial intolerance here. *"There is a Third World in this country."*

He is banned from going home. Would he rather be there fighting, than here?

"Yes. The work is really there. But if I were, I would most probably be in jail."

FIGHTER OUT TO MAKE PEACE

Virgina Mattthews on the challenges facing the NUJ's new President Lionel Morrison, Guardian, 30 March, 1987

Thirty years ago, *Lionel Morrison* made South African history when, at the age of 21, he became the youngest person ever to be charged for high treason. He was in and out of prison for two years for allegedly plotting the overthrow of a state then presided over by Prime Minister Dr. Verwoerd. *Morrison's* trial and acquittal, along with those of 156 other "traitors", led directly to the Sharpeville massacre.

Next month, *Morrison* makes history of an altogether different sort – by becoming the first black president of the National Union of Journalists. For the former PR adviser to black activist *Michael X,* it will be a relatively quiet life – Wapping notwithstanding, it's barricades of paperwork Morrison will have to guard against – but the battle against racism in the British media remains intense.

Currently principal information officer at the Commission for Racial Equality – a job he'll keep during his year as titular head of the NUJ – *Morrison's* trade union credentials read like a textbook case study. Co-founder of South Africa's first multi-racial journalists union, the NUSAJ, he came to Britain in 1960 to act as a press officer for the Anti-Apartheid Movement here. Stopping long enough to convince the NUJ to donate funds to the nascent NUSAJ, he joined the International Organisation of Journalists who arranged for him to visit the Soviet Union, Bulgaria, Albania and China.

By now banned from returning to South Africa, he moved to Indonesia, helping set up the Afro-Asian Journalists Association. Having already been a reporter for the South African Golden City Post – a job interrupted by his various prison sentences – he launched, and edited, the *Afro-Asian Journalists* newspaper.

"I had to get out of Indonesia when the coup d'etat happened, or I'd have been jailed again, so we moved the Afro Asia Journalists Association to China. When the Cultural *Revolution happened, I was torn between my own support for that movement and the demands of helping run an international organisation whose member countries included supporters of the Soviet Union and its line on China."*

His mistrust of "white experts on black affairs" in contemporary Britain dates back to his experience in China: *"The Americans and British who were working in China at the time of the Cultural Revolution tried to become more Chinese than the Chinese, taking a very macho pro-Revolution stance. They were foreigners but they tried to dictate to the Chinese about how they should feel.*

"The lesson for Britain is that whites must learn to listen to blacks and respect their ambitions, without trying to second-guess them. Perhaps we needs some black experts on white affairs here to redress the balance."

By the late 1960's, *Morrison* was in the throes of British black consciousness, working for *Michael X* at the Black House, co-operative in London's Holloway Road. Of the man later hung in Trinidad for the murder of a former Tory MP's daughter *Morrison* says: *"He's very charismatic, but difficult."*

In 1970, he became treasurer of the NUJ's London Freelance Branch and discovered that British newspapers didn't want to employ black journalists even though they gave jobs to less qualified white South African hacks.

"I was interviewed for a sub-editor's job at a famous liberal newspaper. I hadn't told

them I was black though and when the night sub came down to fetch me, he walked past me three times before asking the receptionist where the interviewee was. She blushed and pointed to the only person in reception – me. Things got better during the interview and I was promised a job starting in two weeks. I never heard from them again and I was certainly too proud to phone and ask what had happened." Although *Morrison* was reluctant to say it, this was an incident involving the *Guardian* in 1970.

Morrison fared better with the *Mirror Group, New Statesman* and ironically, the *Sunday Telegraph,* all of whom he worked for on a freelance basis.

"The assumption then, and it's still true was that black journalists were only useful if there were stones being thrown through windows and flare-ups of racial tension. Black journalists are still pigeon-holed in writing about black issues."

But in spite of the problems, *Morrison* wants to see more black journalists on mainstream newspapers. *"It doesn't matter if the paper is left-wing or right, simply having blacks on the staff punctures the ethno-centricity of the British press. We need more colour in our lily white newsrooms.*

"The 'black muggers' style of tabloid journalism is easy, but it is also socially irresponsible. As NUJ President, I'll be asking all journalists to simply think about the effect that their reporting can have on racial divisions and accept the fact that self-censorship is the only way out of racism in the media. Yes, we do have a Code of Conduct that lays down guidelines on the portrayal of blacks, and women, but it's up to each individual journalist to make it work."

With 100 journalists currently facing fines of £1,000 for working at Wapping – all are up for appeal – isn't the NUJ running the risk of already berating its members into a breakaway ?

"We didn't want to fine those people, but when we had exhausted all other avenues of convincing them not to co-operate with Rupert Murdoch, we had no alternative. Many of our grassroots members made it plain that they were very unhappy with these people disobeying a union instruction and getting away with it, so the fines became inevitable.

"It doesn't matter who the journalists are, the fact is that members of our union laid complaints under the NUJ's Rule l8 (discipline clauses) and our job on the National Executive was to uphold that rule."

The NUJ currently has 34,000 members, a figure that Morrison says has grown steadily over the past l0 years, but aside from a "chronic" financial situation, he believes the union is healthy enough to overcome the split over Wapping.

"With attacks on journalists becoming even more commonplace under this Government, we have to work together to fight the apathy in British journalism. We need to build membership, raise standards and examine once again the feasibility of a single union covering the entire newspaper industry. Wapping was a tragedy but there are even more important things to prepare for with the new media coming onstream. My job is to heal the wounds."

VETERAN OF MANY STRUGGLES

The Voice Interview, 6 October 1992 by Claire Hynes

Campaigning for racial equality is more than just a job for journalist and union leader Lionel Morrison. As Claire Hines hears, the on-going battle for the liberation of Black people is the story of his life.

Lionel Morrison's story spans the continents of Africa, Asia and Europe and reads like a thriller.

As a South African political activist he was imprisoned along with Nelson Mandela and 155 other. He fled a coup in which hundreds of thousands of people were killed in Indonesia, never to see his fiance again. And he was expelled from Zambia before becoming a pioneering Black journalist in Britain.

A softly spoken slightly greying 53-year-old with a pleasant South African accent, he wears the inconspicuous, smart-casual clothes of a quietly assured man.

I first met Lionel when I was just nine years old. His family joined mine on a holiday in Cornwall, and then he seemed just like an ordinary father (whose two little boys were just as troublesome as my two brothers).

His life story, when I heard it, came as quite a surprise to me. *Morrison's* biggest adventure this year may not have put his life on the line, but has certainly thrust him into the full glare of media spotlight.

He has aroused the wrath of his former colleagues at the *Commission for Racial Equality (CRE)* by calling for the race watchdog body to be scrapped.

Lionel admits that the decision to go public with his criticisms of the Commission – after he had been its chief press and public relations officer for l4 years – was a difficult one.

"It was agonising. I thought a lot about it for a whole year after I left the CRE," he says. *"I think that it was an honest decision now. I'm glad that I made it."*

"I did voice various concerns about equal opportunities practises in employment while I was there. Some people might believe people's racism ceases as soon as they join the CRE. I question that. CRE staff themselves should go through anti-racist training."

"The CRE is in its worst state at the moment. It was good for the '70's and the 80's, but we need a different body now, with more clout. For the past few years it has been wobbling along."

Lionel's race relations expertise was hard won. He was brought up by strong, proud parents. His father was the first Black South African to graduate with a BA in social science. He joined the Book keepers Association of South Africa, but was promptly thrown out when association officials found out that he was Black. He is still studying at the age of 83.

His mother, a factory worker, was active in her union and a great anti apartheid activist. The family's defiant 'proud to be Black' stance was all the more surprising since they were officially termed 'coloured' and thus classed as superior to Black and Asian people by the apartheid state.

"I came from a fairly political family. We felt proud to be Black and in South Africa that was quite a thing, coming from a 'coloured' family. 'Amper baas' they used to call us, which means nearly a boss," he recalls with a laugh.

Lionel's parents were insistent that he should not forget his roots. They sent him to an African school in Zululand, where he was the only 'coloured' pupil and where he became involved in student politics. He was finishing his matriculation (the equivalent of 'A' levels) when the ANC began a massive defiance campaign – using services and spaces reserved for Whites only.

Lionel wasn't directly involved in the campaign, but it had a huge impact on him. He won a scholarship and as the only Black person from his township of around 10,000 people to go to university, became a local hero. When he got there he formed an organisation, The Fellowship Society, to campaign against segregation at university. Like the ANC campaign, the Fellowship Society encouraged Black people to use 'Whites-only' facilities. Lionel was then chosen by the ANC to help attract more 'coloured' people to the organisation and helped set up the *South African Coloured People's Congress (SACPO).*

He reveals that it was while at university, when he was only 19, that he experienced his first police raid – and hints that this was a landmark in his political career.

"I'd just spoken at a political meeting", he says. *"Of course Special Branch officers were always around. The raid was very frightening, four or five policemen turned over everything in the house. They took political books by Karl Marx and Engels, and even books like 'Black Beauty'."*

He began his journalistic career in 1954. Under the rather exotic pen of *Sheila Leru,* he was the agony aunt on a new black newspaper called the *Golden City Post* – a job he took very seriously.

"The Post was a popular newspaper, like The Voice," he explains. *"It was a very important job, because you got to know what people were thinking and what was taking place in the community. People bared their heart and soul to you."*

Soon after he started the job he was arrested again. He was part of a Congress group known as the Picasso Gang, which was responsible for putting up political slogans, and he was sentenced to five months in prison. *"I felt proud for being arrested for a political crime,"* he beams.

He was taken to The Fort in Johannesburg and locked up in a 15 x 45 foot cell which held 90 inmates. *"We used to say that if one person turned in their sleep, everyone else would have to turn."*

His bed was two thin, stinking, flea-invested blankets which he says had never been washed, and a tiny mat. "The first night I felt so cold, lying on a cement floor. You either had to keep the blanket on your legs, well away from your face because of the acrid smell, or put it over your head to block out what was going on."

"Sodomy was rife and at nights youngsters were knocked about if they didn't succumb to the sadistic tastes of men"

Morrison spent his 21st birthday in jail and was released soon after. The Congress now regarded him as having served his apprenticeship. He was immediately rewarded with the plum job of becoming a convener of the Union of Domestic Workers and the Brush and Broom Workers Union.

Union meetings were held secretly in the grand houses of the 'masters' and 'mistresses' during their absence.

Months later, on December 6, 1956, Special Branch police raided his house at 5 am with a warrant for his arrest for High Treason. *Lionel* was the youngest of the 156 people arrested on that historic day for high treason - the best known among them was *Nelson Mandela.*

"I felt worried," he admits. "*But also felt good that the campaign that we had unleashed had so rattled the government that they had picked so many of us up for high treason. That meant we were being taken seriously.*"

"The first day I appeared in court, the prosecution got up and asked for the death sentence. That was the first time I was afraid."

The trial took four years, but he was released after two and a half years. During that time he was banned from entering newspaper offices, and having meetings with more than two people. But he had become a local celebrity and people rallied round to support him and other anti apartheid campaigners.

In 1959 came the campaign to burn passes and the Sharpeville massacre. A state of emergency was declared and 3,000 people were detained. Unsurprisingly, *Lionel* was one of them.

He was taken to Central Pretoria Prison, where death row inmates were incarcerated, and spent five months there. On his release he was offered a senior reporter's job at the *Golden City Post.*

He set up the *National Union of South African Journalists,* a non-racial union, because the established *South African Society of Journalists* did not accept Black journalists as members. He was arrested yet again, on suspicion of possessing banned material, and he was again on the run from the security police.

Lionel managed to get out of the country, arriving in Southampton with £1.50 to his name

He became press officer for the *Anti Apartheid Movement* in Britain, but his career changed yet again when he joined a steering group to set up the *International Afro-Asian Journalists Association (AAJA).* He was soon made editor of the *Afro-Asian Journalist* – a mouthpiece for 58 African and Asian countries, which sold one million copies, and helped to train African journalists and forming African journalists unions. From 1963-67 he virtually lived out of a suitcase, travelling through Europe, Africa and Asia. He also worked and contributed to the *Indonesia Herald* and *Warta Bhakhti* newspapers.

While he was working in Indonesia, which was locked in a military coup against *President Sukarno,* his fiance – a trades union activist – was arrested and taken to a concentration prison camp. He never saw her again, and doesn't know whether she was one of the 300,000 people killed during that time. The *AAJA* left Indonesia and its headquarters were then situated in China. After the Cultural Revolution, *Lionel* went to Zambia where he became a sub-editor of the *Zambia Mail.* It was during this period that he was expelled from Zambia for being a member of the Pan-Africanist Congress.

By 1969 he was back in Britain working as a freelance journalist. *Morrison* also helped set up the newspaper *West Indian World* and was the first black person to join the National Union of Journalists (NUJ) executive committee, but also the first ever Black president of the NUJ in 1988. He was one of the first black journalists to work for Fleet Street newspapers – *The People, Sunday Mirror, Sunday Telegraph* and *Evening Standard.*

Being very well versed in racial struggles, he lent his experience to the Black Panther movement in the '70's and helped to run *Michael X's* famous Black House self-help project Harembee in Islington, north London.

He moved on to contributing to more mainstream race work. He was one of the people who put forward ideas for the 1976 Race Relations Act before joining the CRE, as its Principal Press and Publicity Officer, whose formation followed the Act.

By this time he was a happily married man and stayed at the CRE for 14 years before retiring two years ago after suffering a heart attack. But despite that it did not stop him from becoming a Senior Journalism Lecturer at Lambeth College where he trained and helped to set up pioneering journalism courses for black journalism.

Lionel has been married for the past 22 years. His wife, Liz, is a white English social worker and their sons, Sipho, 20 and Dumisa, 18 are both students.

"I feel proud of them. Like other Black youngsters in Britain they have to confront their own difficulties," he said in his understanding manner.

His sons may have been brought up in the tranquil north west London area of Queen's Park, rather than the strife ridden city of Johannesburg, but you can hear the influence of his parents as *Lionel* says, *"I have brought them up to be proud to be Black. That's so important."*

PART IV
Suggestions for further Reading

1. **Race and the Media** – Selected bibliography

2. **Ethical Codes**

3. **Relevant Sites**

'As we stand today in the throes of cataclysmic social change, our young people seem to be seething in a boiling caldron of discontent. Like the youth of every generation they want to know, read and they demand to be heard.'

1. RACE AND THE MEDIA

Selected bibliography

Books

Ethnic Minorities and the Media:Changing cultural boundaries: Cottle Ed. Buckington: Open University Press, 2000.

What is the Minority Media For? Some thoughts about British experience of minority newspapers by John Tullock. Plamen Makariev (Ed) Intercultural Communication and the Civil Society-Scorpion Publicity House, Sofia, 2000

Cultural Diversity – Against Racism. European Media Conference report and published by the European Monitoring Centre on Racism and Xenophobia, Oct 1999. The future of Europe is determined by the cultural, ethnic and religion's diversity of our continent. However, as participants contend, rising levels of xenophobia and racism in several countries are threatening this diversity. What can the media do? - this is the issue participants timely examine.

Welcome or Over Reaction? Refugees and Asylum seekers in the Welsh media. Tammy Speers, pub by the Wales Media Forum, Centre for Journalism Studies, Cardiff University, Cardiff, May 2001.

In April 2000 Wales was set to receive asylum seekers as part of the British government's 'dispersal' programme. As a result, the Welsh media, like the national media based in London, started to report increasingly on this marginalised group. However, by the end of the year, the dispersal programme had not been fully implemented in Wales. **"Welcome or Over-reaction"** examines how the Welsh Media covered issues concerning asylum seekers and refugees during this period of intense scrutiny. Do the Welsh media see this issue differently from the London-based media or are they preparing for a different kind of welcome?

Black and White Media – Ross K. Oxford Policy Press,1996

A Richer Vision – Ed Charles Husband.The Development of ethnic minority media in Western Democracy. Unesco-Published by John Libby, 1994.

Black and Front Journalists and Race Reporting Denis McShane,1978 Pub by the Race Relations Sub Committee of the NUJ UK.
Written for journalists who care about high professional journalistic standards and who stand against the growth of racism in Britain.

Black Journalists – White Media by Beulah Ainley, pub. Trentham Books Based on the experiences of black journalists. One hundred black journalists working in all sections of the media were interviewed by the author.

The Black and White Media Book, Ed: John Twitchin. pub: Trentham Books 1988.
Relevant Contributors: Angela Barry Black Mythologies: The Representation of Black People on British Television, Jim Pines Black Independent Film in Britain; Historical Overview. Gajendra Verma, Attitudes, Race Relations and Television, Zeinab Badawi, Reflections on Recent TV Coverage of Africa, Laura Sparrow Media Studies in Primary School, Brian Thompson Racism and Comics.
Resource book for teachers setting out the why, what and how of deconstructing the effects of TV on children and adults. Tried and tested ways of teaching how television reinforces negative stereotypical thinking about black people.

Black People, Human Rights and The Media, Ed. Lionel Morrison, Conference

Report on the role of Black People, Human Rights and the Media. Pub by Black Rights (UK) and CRE 1989.

A consideration of how Human Rights violations have affected the Black community and the role the media has played in this. Issues explored by community leaders, civil rights groups, lawyers and media leaders.

Black People and the Media Equality in Employment and Training: Policy and Practice. Ed: Joe Harte. Pub: London Borough of Lewisham and CRE with University of Warwick 1988. Papers presented to a Conference on Employment Prospects for Black People in the Media held in May 1988

As They See It: A Race Relations Study of Three Areas from a Black Viewpoint by Lionel Morrison, Pub by the Commission for Racial Equality, 1976 and a reprint in 1982.

The Black Press in Britain by Ionie Benjamin, pub. Trentham Books Examines the growth of the Black Media in Britain.

Daily Racism – The Press and Black People in Britain.
Paul Gordon and David Rosenberg. pub The Runnymede Trust 1989. Describes and analyses press coverage of race issues through he 1980's a period in which many newspapers took an increasingly aggressive position on race.

Immigration and Race British Politics, Paul Foot. Pub Penguin Books, Harmondsworth 1965.

It ain't half racist, mum, Fighting racism in the media. Ed: Phil Cohen and Carl Gardner. pub: Comedia Publishing Group 1982.
Takes on the press, radio and television. Twenty-one media workers contribute experience and observations of the way black people are dealt with in the media. Includes international coverage.

Media, Society and Race Relations. Lionel Morrison. Conference Report - The Media Race and the Community. Pub Enfield Community Relations Council and CRE June 1985 The role of the local media in the field of race and community relations.

The Mass Media and Power in Modern Britain. John Eldridge, Jenny Kitzinger and Kevin Williams pub Oxford
In this thorough introduction to the role of the mass media in modern Britain, the authors examine the development, issues of ownership and roots of media power in the public and political spheres. They also consider the prospect of a global media.

More Bad News, Glasgow University Media Group. Vol 2 of Bad News, Pub by Routledge & Kegan Paul, 1980.
Contrary to the claims, conventions and culture of television journalism, the news is not a neutral product. For television news is a cultural artifact; it is a sequence of socially manufactured messages, which carry many of the culturally dominant assumptions of our society.

News Analysis: Case Studies of International and National News in the Press. Teun A. Van Dijk pub Amazon 1987 www.amazon.com.

The News Media: Racism's First Line of Defence, William Sales. Pub Black World, March 1971 Johnson Pub Co New York.

Public Awareness and The Media: A Study of Reporting on Race, Barry Troyna Pub CRE 1981.

The research project shows a clear relationship between attitudes adopted by the reading public to various race related issues and the way these issues are presented by the national and local Press and radio.

Press Ethics: Regulation and Editorial Practice funded by the International Press Federation. After an extensive analysis of the issue of responsibility in the context of television, the Institute thought it worthwhile to investigate the situation in the printed press. This publication, is the final report of research project which looked at three factors which form the main influence on ethics and editorial standards in the printed press: legislation, voluntary regulation, and the market. It is particularly concerned with the professional and cultural traditions which shape editorial policies in European press media.

The study was not limited to an impressionistic approach but rather offers an analysis of the legal framework, a presentation of a large number of case studies, and a discussion of the professional and public debate on press ethics in the countries studied namely France, Germany, Italy, Great Britain and Sweden. The cultural, economic and legal differences between these countries are great – as are their traditions in journalism.

However, by clearly highlighting the obvious and hidden reasons why some systems seem to work better than others we can provoke a debate on the options available and the ways to achieve a printed press that is more aware of its responsibility towards the public. By Gustaf von Dewall. Duesseldorf 1997. 270 pages. A4. ISBN 3-929673-22-3. DM 50,-.

Racism and the Mass Media, Paul Hartman and Charles Husband. Pub: Davis-Poynter 1974. An interdisciplinary approach used to examine the role of the mass media in the formation of white beliefs and attitudes regarding black people in Britain. Evidence to show the importance of the news media in influencing white Briton's understanding of race relations.

Racism and the Press in Thatcher's Britain, Nancy Murray and Chris Searle Pub by Institute of Race Relations 1989. (Reproduction of Race & Class Vol XXIX no 1 1987) Two articles analysing trends and tendencies and showing how the press and the press barons set the ideological agenda and predicate political power.

Race and the Press pub by Runnymede Trust London 1971. Clement Jones – Immigrants and the Newspaper, Peter Harland – Reporting Race: some problems, Hugo Young – The Treatment of Race in the British Press, Harold Evans – A Positive Policy.

Four essays by journalists looking at various issues on reporting race and the treatment of race in the British Press.

Race as News: A Study of the handling of race in the British national press from 1963 to 1970. Paul Hartmann, Charles Husband, Jean Clark. Pub UNESCO Press, Paris 1974. Studies on newspapers in a multi-ethnic society.

The Manufacture of News, Cohen and Young, London; Constable 1973.

The Political Impact of Mass Media, Seymour-Ure, London Constable,1974.

Race as News. Introduction by James Halloran, Pub by The Unesco Press, Paris 1974.

Two general studies on attitude change by Otto Kilineberg and Colette Guillaumin. Study of the British national Press, by Paul Hartman, Charles Husband and Jean Clark. The first in a series of studies on newspapers in a multi-ethnic society.

Racism and the Press. Teun A Van Dijk Pub Amazon 1999 http://www.amazon.com. Critical studies in racism and migration.

Radio for Ethnic and Linguistic Minorities, Prospects in the 1990s. A Conference Report Pub by CRE 1990. - Introduction by Lionel Morrison and Simon Patridge.

The conference highlighted the importance to community and incremental radio stations; good race relations and equality of opportunity in Britain depend on the creation of understanding between ethnic minorities and the majority community; and what is of importance is the extent to which ethnic minorities are given opportunity to obtain information, entertainment and cultural satisfaction.

Selective Bibliography on Ethnic Minorities, Racism and the Mass Media. Teun A. van Dijk unpub 1998 www.let.uva.nl/~teun.

Silver Linings Ed. by G Bridges and R. Blunt. Pub Lawrence and Wishart 1981

Staying Power, Peter Fryer, Pluto Press,1984, This is the first comprehensive history of black people in Britain. It reveals how Africans, Asians and their descendants, previously hidden from history, have profoundly influenced and shaped events in this country.

Television & the Riots, Howard Tumber. Pub by BFI 1982 First detailed research on television coverage of the riots of the summer 1981.

Television in a Multi-Racial Society, Muhammad Anwar and Anthony Shang, A Research Report pub by CRE 1982.

Research concluded that opportunities for and presentation of ethnic minority actors are still limited and restrictive.

White Media and Black Britain. Ed: Charles Husband. Pub: Arrow Books 1975. Relevant Contributions: Lionel Morrison A -Black Journalist's Experience of British Journalism, Wilfred Wood Black Voices in the Media: an interview. Derek Humphrey Reporting Race Relations.

This provocative book has been written by activists, journalists and academics both black and white – who have direct experience of the media and its effects at grassroots level. They examine in detail the coverage of racial issues – its extent, content and underlying assumptions. They are agreed on one point: for all their liberal pretensions, the British media still represents an essentially white view of the world.

Who Tunes in to What? A Report on Ethnic Minority Broadcasting. Muhammed Anwar Pub 1978, second ed. 1983.

The research project reported in this booklet was the first to be conducted by the Commission for Racial Equality in the audience participation of ethnic minority communities in Britain and deserves to be widely read by those who directly determine policy in this area.

The Media Machine, John Downing, Pluto Press,1980, Chapters 3,4.

'The Mass Media and Racism' in **Media, Politics and Culture** ed. C.Gardner, Macmillan,1979.

Television and Riots, Tumber H, London, British Film Institute,1982.

'News Media, Language and Race Relations: Charles Husband in A Case Study in Identity Maintenance' in **Language, Ethnicity and Inter-group Behaviour,** ed H. Giles, Academic Press,1979.

Let's talk to the media
By Danny Firth ,The Refugee Media Group in Wales
2005

A practical media guide for refugee community organisations and practitioners. Refugee and asylum issues are too often portrayed negatively by certain UK media.

And this is not simply a problem confined to the tabloids. Aims to provide refugee community organisations with some practical tips to deal with the media directly, including:

* building and maintaining constructive relationships with the media;
* writing press releases and undertaking media interviews;
* conducting media monitoring.

The booklet also has some useful 'what worked for us' sections and guidance on interviewing refugee women. Importantly, it provides guidelines to help journalists challenge some of the common myths that can be found in the media.

A copy of ***Let's Talk to the Media*** can be obtained from, email: bucolliv@cardiff.ac.uk.

Policing the Crisis, Stuart Hall, C. Critcher et al, Macmillan,1978.

The Politics of the Media, Whale J, London; Fontana, 1977.

Settlers in Britain, 1555-1958, File and Power, London; Heinemann,1981.

Articles, Reports, Research

Unacceptable faces of the British News Media. Simon Cottle - A paper prepared for the symposium in ethnic minorities on the press. 1999. Organised by the Netherlands Press Fund.

Racism and the Press in Britain's Britain. pub by Carf 48-Feb/March,1998 article-how a local newspaper in Dover (The Dover Express) instigated a campaign of racist resentment towards the Balkan refugees which was then picked up by the national press.

pub by Carf – 48 (Feb/March,1998) http://www.carf.demon.co.uk/feat22.html.

More Colour in the Media; Ethnic minorities and the audiovisual industry by Jamil Ouaj, Researcher at the EIM, The Bulletin Vol.15,No.3.

Within the More Colour in the Media network, the European Institute for the media has been analysing the question of ethnic minorities' access in the European broadcasting industry for some time...the study is a comparative investigation which explores the state and conditions of access to jobs and career progress in European countries.

http://www.eim.org/sep-98-1.htm

'What Could the BBC Do About the NF', Tracy and Troyna, in Broadcast, April 30,1970.

What's wrong with Media and Cultural Studies? Research Report Glasgow Media Group, Glasgow.

Extended report on current state of Media and Culture studies, concluding that much of the work is pointless and has lost the ability to comment critically on society.

'Race' and the Public Face of Television Research. Media Group, Glasgow.

Study of television presenters, looking at ethnic background. Of 25 areas of TV, l5 presented exclusively by white people.

Black Mythologies: Representations of Black People on British Television. Article by A. Bar, in The Black and White Media Book Ed by Twitchin 1988 Pub Trentham Books.

The Newham Recorder in Multi Racial East London. P Cartwright Pub Newham CRC 1977.

The Whites of their Eyes: Racial Ideologies and the Media. S. Hall in **Silver Linings** ed by G. Bridges and R. Blunt Pub. Lawrence and Wishart 1981.

Ethnic Minorities in Television Advertising. Research report.
A major study of TV advertising, examining over 3,000 ads. Glasgow Media Group, Glasgow. Examines numerical representation of ethnic minorities and ways in which they appear. It answers questioned posed by Naomi Campbell and others.

Non Whites in British Television BBC Audience Research Dept 1972.

Race, Migration & Media Research report Glasgow Media Group, Glasgow Study analyses news coverage of isses such as immigration and asylum. It includes detailed examination of news language and highlights apparent 'threat' posed by ethnic minorities.

Media Society and Race Relations. Lionel Morrison Conference Report The Media, Race and Community. Pub Enfield CRC and CRE June 1985.
The role of the local media in the field of race and community relations.

Black Power and the Media. L. Kushnick Race Today Dec 1970.

New(s) Racism, A discourse analytical approach. Teun A van Dijk Second (short) draft of paper for a book Race, Racism and the Mass Media ed by Simon Cottle OU Press 1999 in press. Pub. Lawrence and Wishart 1981.

Race, Migration & Media. Research report from the Glasgow Media Group This study analyses news coverage of issues as immigration and asylum. It includes a detailed examination of news language, and shows how news angles were developed by journalists.. it highlights the apparent "threat" posed by immigration and ethnic minorities.

Reporting the National Front: British Values Observed, Barry Troyna in *Race in Britain: Continuity and Change,* ed C. Husband, Open University/Hutchinson,1981.

2. Ethical Codes

(I) CODE OF CONDUCT

Adopted by British National Union of Journalists

1. A journalist has a duty to maintain the highest professional and ethical standards.

2. A journalist shall at all times defend the principle of the freedom of the press and other media in relation to the collection of information and the expression of comment and criticism. He/she shall strive to eliminate distortion, news suppression and censorship.

3. A journalist shall strive to ensure that the information he/ she disseminates is fair and accurate, avoid the expression of comment and conjecture as established fact and falsification by distortion, selection or misrepresentation.

4. A journalist shall rectify promptly any harmful inaccuracies, ensure that correction and apologies receive due prominence and afford the right of reply to persons criticised when the issue is of sufficient importance.

5. A journalist shall obtain information, photographs and illustrations only by straightforward means. The use of other means can be justified only by over-riding considerations of the public interest. The journalist is entitled to exercise a personal conscientious objection to the use of such means.

6. Subject to the justification by over-riding considerations of the public interest, a journalist shall do nothing which entails intrusion into private grief and distress.

7. A journalist shall protect confidential sources of information.

8. A journalist shall not accept bribes nor shall he/she allow other inducements to influence the performance of his/ her professional duties.

9. A journalist shall not lend himself/herself to the distortion or suppression of the truth because of advertising or other considerations.

10. A journalist shall only mention a person's age, race, colour, creed, illegitimacy, disability, marital status (or lack of it), gender or sexual orientation if this information is strictly relevant. A journalist shall neither originate nor process material which encourages discrimination, ridicule, prejudice or hatred on any of the above-mentioned grounds.

11. A journalist shall not take private advantage of information gained in the course of his/ her duties, before the information is public knowledge.

12. A journalist shall not by way of statement, voice or appearance endorse by advertisement any commercial product or service save for the promotion of his/her own work or of the medium by which he/she is employed.

Guidelines On Race Reporting

NUJ's BLACK MEMBERS COUNCIL (BMC)

NUJ Code of Conduct Clause 10:

A journalist shall only mention a person's age, race, colour, creed, illegitimacy, disability, marital status (or lack of it), gender or sexual orientation if this information is strictly relevant. A journalist shall neither originate nor process material which encourages discrimination, ridicule, prejudice or hatred on any of the above-mentioned grounds.

The NUJ has ratified guidelines for all its members to follow when dealing with race relations subjects.

GUIDELINES:

* Only mention someone's race if it is strictly relevant. Check to make sure you have it right. Would you mention race if the person was white?

* Do not sensationalise race relations issues. It harms Black people and it could harm you.

* Think carefully about the words you use. Words which were once in common usage are now considered offensive, e.g. half-caste and coloured. Use mixed-race and Black instead. Black can cover people of Arab, Asian, Chinese and African origin. Ask people how they define themselves.

* Immigrant is often used as a term of abuse. Do not use it unless the person really is an immigrant. Most Black people in Britain were born here and most immigrants are white.

* Do not make assumptions about a person's cultural background – whether it is their name or religious detail. Ask them, or where this is not possible check with the local race equality council.

* Investigate the treatment of Black people in education, health, employment and housing. Do not forget travellers and gypsies. Cover their lives and concerns. Seek their views of their representatives.

* Remember that Black communities are culturally diverse. Get a full and correct view from representative organisations.

* Press for equal opportunities for employment of Black staff.

* Be wary of disinformation. Just because a source is traditional does not mean it is accurate.

REPORTING RACIST ORGANISATIONS

* When interviewing representatives of racist organisations or reporting meetings or statements or claims, journalists should carefully check all reports for accuracy and seek rebutting or opposing comments. The anti-social nature of such views should be exposed.

* Do not sensationalise by reports, photographs, film or presentation the activities of racist organisations.

* Seek to publish or broadcast material exposing the myths and lies of racist organisations and their anti-social behaviour.

* Do not allow the letters column or 'phone-in' programmes to be used to spread racial hatred in whatever guise.

GUIDELINES ON TRAVELLERS

* Only mention the word gypsy or traveller if strictly relevant or accurate.

* Give balanced reports seeking travellers' views as well as those of others, consulting the local travellers where possible.

* Resist the temptation to sensationalise issues involving travellers ,especially in their relations with settled communities over issues such as housing and settlement programmes and schooling.

* Try to give wider coverage to travellers' lives and the problems they face.
* Strive to promote the realisation that the travellers' community is comprised of full citizens of Great Britain and Ireland whose civil rights are seldom adequately vindicated, who often suffer much hurt and damage through misuse by the media and who have a right to have their special contributions to Irish and British life, especially in music and craftwork and other cultural activities, properly acknowledged and reported.

STATEMENT ON RACE REPORTING

1. The NUJ believes that the development of racist attitudes and the growth of fascist parties pose a threat to democracy, the rights of trade union organisations, a free press and the development of social harmony and well-being.
2. The NUJ believes that its members cannot avoid a measure of responsibility in fighting the evil of racism as expressed through the mass media.
3. The NUJ reaffirms its total opposition to censorship but equally reaffirms the belief that press freedom must be conditioned by responsibility and an acknowledgement by all media workers of the need not to allow press freedom to be abused to slander a section of the community or to promote the evil of racism.
4. The NUJ believes that the methods and the lies of the racists should be publicly and vigorously exposed.
5. The NUJ believes that newspapers and magazines should not originate material which encourages discrimination on grounds of race or colour as expressed in the NUJ's Rule Book and Code of Conduct.
6. The NUJ recognises the right of members to withhold their labour on grounds of conscience where employers are providing a platform for racist propaganda.
7. The NUJ believes that editors should ensure that coverage of race stories be placed in a balanced context.
8. The NUJ will continue to monitor the development of media coverage in this area and give support to members seeking to enforce the above aims.

STATEMENT ON REPORTING IMMIGRATION AND ASYLUM

Reporting which panders to stereotypes can cause much hurt. By repeating stereotypes the media can encourage language and attitudes which, in other circumstances, would be seen as totally unacceptable.

The NUJ believes that immigration and asylum, which are two separate issues, have been used by some politicians and sections of the media to promote racism and xenophobia through their unquestioning acceptance of the belief that asylum seekers constitute a threat to our social fabric, social services, housing, health, security, and of course, good race relations.

The NUJ believes that it is wrong to promote prejudice and fear, over immigration and asylum because this diverts attention from the real causes of social and economic problems. We condemn attempts by politicians and policy makers to win public support and votes by blaming 'others' for their failures and shortcomings.

The NUJ believes that the attitude of our newspapers and broadcasting stations is crucial in race relations and the formation of opinion on asylum seekers. Immigration and colour prejudice can be materially affected by the media.

To perpetuate racism and xenophobia through our media is anti-social and grossly irresponsible.

These guidelines are not intended to make the media shy away from covering issues and stories about asylum seekers and immigration. We want the media to provide a coverage that is fair, balanced and accurate.

Immigration

The NUJ believes that the emigration from Britain and the immigration to the United Kingdom of other nationals is part of a global phenomenon.

Most migrants are skilled workers and professionals who contribute to the economy and diversity of the United Kingdom and Ireland. Immigrants, for instance, constitute a significant percentage of nurses, doctors and pharmacists and have been recruited to make up for shortages in the UK.

Asylum

The NUJ believes that victims of conflict and persecution have a right to seek a safe haven without further victimisation and stigmatisation as guaranteed by international law to which the United Kingdom and Ireland are signatories.

International Law obliges the UK and Irish authorities and citizens to respect the human and other rights of refugees and further obliges the authorities to treat refugee cases quickly and humanely to enable people to resettle, earn a living and contribute to the economy and society.

GUIDELINES ON REPORTING IMMIGRATION AND ASYLUM

"Asylum seeker" is often used as an abusive term against victims of social and political persecution, war and conflict from other countries. Many refugees and asylum seekers are educated professionals or skilled workers and do not wish to flee their homes, jobs and security for uncertainty. Reports on asylum seekers should reflect this.

Journalists should steer clear of exploiting prejudice and avoid reports that portray asylum seekers as causes of problems rather than victims.

When reporting immigration and asylum, journalists should be careful not to

- Promote negative stereotypes based on misconceptions.
- Quote politicians or public figures without cross checking if statements are factual. Go to the experts who can help to set the context, and make sure that wherever possible you check the details with a relevant source and don't just rely on expressions of local or popular prejudice. Offensive stereotypes (for example "bogus asylum seeker", "scroungers", "dole dodgers") should not be used.
- Exaggerate or use phrases or terms that promote prejudice or fear, e.g. "floods of immigrants". Many allegations are made about asylum seekers, but can those making these allegations actually substantiate them?

(II). CODE OF PRACTICE

Ratified by the British Press Complaints Commission

All members of the press have a duty to maintain the highest professional and ethical standards. This code sets the benchmarks for those standards. It both protects the rights of the individual and upholds the public's right to know.

The code is the cornerstone of the system of self-regulation to which the industry has made a binding commitment. Editors and publishers must ensure that the code is observed rigorously not only by their staff but also by anyone who contributes to their publications.

It is essential to the workings of an agreed code that it be honoured not only to the letter but in the full spirit. The code should not be interpreted so narrowly as to compromise its commitment to respect the rights of the individual, nor so broadly that it prevents publication in the public interest.

It is the responsibility of editors to co-operate with the PCC as swiftly as possible in the resolution of complaints.

Any publication which is criticised by the PCC under one of the following clauses must print the adjudication which follows in full and with due prominence

The public interest

There may be exceptions to the clauses marked * where they can be demonstrated to be in the public interest.

1. The public interest includes:

i) Detecting or exposing crime or a serious misdemeanour.

ii) Protecting public health and safety.

iii) Preventing the public from being misled by some statement or action of an individual or organisation.

2. In any case where the public interest is invoked, the Press Complaints Commission will require a full explanation by the editor demonstrating how the public interest was served.

3. In cases involving children, editors must demonstrate an exceptional public interest to over-ride the normally paramount interests of the child.

1. Accuracy

i) Newspapers and periodicals should take care not to publish inaccurate, misleading or distorted material including pictures.

ii) Whenever it is recognised that a significant inaccuracy, misleading statement or distorted report has been published, it should be corrected promptly and with due prominence.

iii) An apology must be published whenever appropriate.

iv) Newspapers, whilst free to be partisan, must distinguish clearly between comment, conjecture and fact v) A newspaper or periodical must report fairly and accurately the outcome of an action for defamation to which it has been a party.

2. Opportunity to reply

A fair opportunity for reply to inaccuracies must be given to individuals or organisations when reasonably called for.

3. Privacy

i) Everyone is entitled to respect for his or her private and family life, home, health and correspondence. A publication will be expected to justify intrusions into any individual's private life without consent.

ii) The use of long lens photography to take pictures of people in private places without their consent is unacceptable.

Note – Private places are public or private property where there is a reasonable expectation of privacy.

4. Harassment

i) Journalists and photographers must neither obtain nor seek to obtain information or pictures through intimidation, harassment or persistent pursuit.

ii) They must not photograph individuals in private places (as defined by the note to clause 3) without their consent; must not persist in telephoning, questioning, pursuing or photographing individuals after having been asked to desist; must not remain on their property after having been asked to leave and must not follow them.

iii) Editors must ensure that those working for them comply with these requirements and must not publish material from other sources which does not meet these requirements.

5. Intrusion into grief or shock

In cases involving personal grief or shock, enquiries should be carried out and approaches made with sympathy and discretion. Publication must be handled sensitively at such times but this should not be interpreted as restricting the right to report judicial proceedings.

6. Children

i) Young people should be free to complete their time at school without unnecessary intrusion.

ii) Journalists must not interview or photograph a child under the age of 16 on subjects involving the welfare of the child or any other child in the absence of or without the consent of a parent or other adult who is responsible for the children.

iii) Pupils must not be approached or photographed while at school without the permission of the school authorities.

iv) There must be no payment to minors for material involving the welfare of children nor payments to parents or guardians for material about their children or wards unless it is demonstrably in the child's interest.

v) Where material about the private life of a child is published, there must be justification for publication other than the fame, notoriety or position of his or her parents or guardian.

7. Children in sex cases

1. The press must not, even where the law does not prohibit it, identify children under the age of 16 who are involved in cases concerning sexual offences, whether as victims or as witnesses.

2. In any press report of a case involving a sexual offence against a child -
i) The child must not be identified.
ii) the adult may be identified.
iii) The word "incest" must not be used where a child victim might be identified.
iv) Care must be taken that nothing in the report implies the relationship between the accused and the child.

8. Listening Devices

Journalists must not obtain or publish material obtained by using clandestine listening devices or by intercepting private telephone conversations.

9. Hospitals

i) Journalists or photographers making enquiries at hospitals or similar institutions should identify themselves to a responsible executive and obtain permission before entering nonpublic areas.

ii) The restrictions on intruding into privacy are particularly relevant to enquiries about individuals in hospitals or similar institutions.

10. Innocent relatives and friends

The press must avoid identifying relatives or friends of persons convicted or accused of crime without their consent.

11. Misrepresentation

i) Journalists must not generally obtain or seek to obtain information or pictures through misrepresentation or subterfuge.

ii) Documents or photographs should be removed only with the consent of the owner.

iii) Subterfuge can be justified only in the public interest and only when material cannot be obtained by any other means.

12. Victims of sexual assault

The press must not identify victims of sexual assault or publish material likely to contribute to such identification unless there is adequate justification and, by law, they are free to do so.

13. Discrimination

i) The press must avoid prejudicial or pejorative reference to a person's race, colour, religion, sex or sexual orientation or to any physical or mental illness or disability.

ii) It must avoid publishing details of a person's race, colour, religion, sexual orientation, physical or mental illness or disability unless these are directly relevant to the story.

14. Financial journalism

i) Even where the law does not prohibit it, journalists must not use for their own profit financial information they receive in advance of its general publication, nor should they pass such information to others.

ii) They must not write about shares or securities in whose performance they know that they or their close families have a significant financial interest without disclosing the interest to the editor or financial editor.

iii) They must not buy or sell, either directly or through nominees or agents, shares or securities about which they have written recently or about which they intend to write in the near future.

15. Confidential sources

Journalists have a moral obligation to protect confidential sources of information.

16. Payment for articles

i) Payment or offers of payment for stories or information must not be made directly or through agents to witnesses or potential witnesses in current criminal proceedings except where the material concerned ought to be published in the public interest and there is an overriding need to make or promise to make a payment for this to be done. Journalists must take every possible step to ensure that no financial dealings have influence on the evidence that those witnesses may give.

(An editor authorising such a payment must be prepared to demonstrate that there is a legitimate public interest at stake involving matters that the public has a right to know. The payment or, where accepted, the offer of payment to any witness who is actually cited to give evidence should be disclosed to the prosecution and the defence and the witness should be advised of this).

ii) Payment or offers of payment for stories, pictures or information, must not be made directly or through agents to convicted or confessed criminals or to their associates – who may include family, friends and colleagues – except where the material concerned ought to be published in the public interest and payment is necessary for this to be done.

(III). GUIDANCE FOR JOURNALISTS

Commission for Racial Equality

Complaints about the media
Travellers, Gypsies
and the media

A good practice guide

Coverage of race and ethnic issues across the media has significantly improved over the past 20 years. There has been a wider and more constructive exploration of many questions and a reduction in the use of language that is offensive to members of different ethnic groups. However many problems remain.

These recommendations are designed to help in dealing with one of them: the way parts of the media report on Traveller and/or Gypsy issues.

Poor quality reporting which exploits or panders to stereotypes can cause much hurt to those about whom the stories are written. By repeating false and negative stereotypes the media can encourage bad practice on the part of those with whom Travellers and Gypsies deal and can validate the expression of language and attitudes which in any other circumstances would be seen as totally unacceptable.

The Commission for Racial Equality has handled cases under the Race Relations Act for Travellers and Gypsies for over 20 years. The number of such cases continues to run at several dozen each year. The majority of these cases involve clear breaches of the Act.

These guidelines are not intended to make the media shy away from covering issues and stories to do with Travellers and Gypsies. Quite the contrary. The CRE and those organisations representing Travellers and Gypsies want to see more coverage in the media but are keen to help the media develop a coverage that is honest and fair, open and inclusive.

Steer clear of exploiting prejudice.

The public wants a media that is campaigning, but those campaigns should be built on matters of genuine public concern, not simply prejudices against particular groups.

Check the facts

Go to the experts who can help to set the context. With these recommendations we include a list of contacts of individuals and organisations which can help you with various aspects of your story. Make sure that wherever possible you check the details with a relevant source and don't just rely on expressions of local or popular prejudice. Many allegations are made about Travellers, Gypsies and now Roma asylum seekers from Eastern Europe, but can those making the allegations actually substantiate them?

Don't let your news agenda only be driven by the way others are handling the issue.

Certain story lines easily dominate media discussion of Travellers or Gypsies while issues of great importance to the communities involved are downplayed or ignored altogether.

Don't write about Travellers and Gypsies only in the context of disputes over stopping places, look also at the problems Travellers face.

Look behind the story line.

Don't assume there is only one point of view. Always seek the views of Traveller and Gypsy organisations to see whether or not there is an alternative interpretation or a different and more significant story line to be presented.

Listen to the people you are writing about.

This is particularly important when it comes to the terms and language you use. Terms like 'tinker', 'itinerant' or 'gypo' are all highly offensive to those about whom they are used and should be avoided. The terms Traveller(s), Gypsy or Irish Traveller should be used with initial capital letters. Offensive stereotypes (for example 'scroungers', 'dole dodgers', 'bogus asylum seeker') should only be used when they are accurate descriptions of particular individuals and should not be employed to negatively stereotype whole groups.

Don't label people if it is not relevant.

Reference to the fact than an individual is a Traveller, Gypsy or Irish Traveller should only be made when it is relevant and appropriate.

(IV) RECOMMENDATIONS FOR BROADCASTERS ON FAIR PORTRAYAL OF ETHNIC MINORITIES

Why a Set of Recommendations for Broadcasters ?

These recommendations are formulated to provide broadcasters, with some starting points and tools for considering the fair portrayal of our multicultural societies. Programme makers, editors and managers have to consider the impact of their output on the development of stable and harmonious multicultural societies. Is their programming a fair and accurate reflection of a diverse society or are they unconsciously giving the impression of a monocultural, monolingual reality? Are they inadvertently reinforcing racism, prejudice and xenophobia through the content of their programmes? These issues are not about special treatment for ethnic minorities but about the professional practice of public service broadcasters – their duty to serve a diverse public and reflect it as accurately and as fairly as possible.

These recommendations do not pretend to be comprehensive and recognise that the context will differ from country to country. However, it is important to note that these recommendations are distilled from similar codes developed by broadcasters and journalists in, Belgium, the Netherlands, Germany, the UK and other European Countries.

Towards a Fairer Portrayal of a Multicultural Europe in the Broadcast Media

The majority of European countries are moving towards becoming multicultural/multiracial societies, in which it will be vital to guarantee all citizens peaceful co-existence, freedom of expression and the ability to exercise civic rights of one of the obstacles to this guarantee is the rise of racism and xenophobia across the continent of Europe from East to West.

It is clear that broadcasting does not create racism and xenophobia but it can choose to ignore or challenge it. Research in many European countries has revealed that whereas programme makers may have wished to adopt a neutral stance the output far too often confirms the perceptions and attitudes of racists and xenophobes in the audience in a variety of ways.

One of the major ways it can do this is through a process of marginalisation of black and ethnic minority communities by their omission from broadcast reality. If white Europeans do not see black and ethnic minority people reflected in everyday programming this serves to confirm the view of them as outsiders. To compound this general lack of presence these groups may often feature in news, current affairs and documentaries as being part of the problem or being the problem. Whether directly in commentaries or by the use of images or indeed the way images are juxtaposed, associations are being made between minority groups and crime, drugs, terrorism, social problems, violence, crisis in society because of the other absences this appears as their only contribution to European societies.

Many countries have some form of 'ethnic' broadcasting on local radio or often at unsociable times on national radio and television. This service, whilst being essential is not a substitute for a multicultural approach to programming, although it is often presented as such. Well meaning attempts to make 'exotic' programmes about the 'strangers within our midst' and programmes made about countries in the south (or Third World) can create a further distance between 'them and us'. Broadcasters need to avoid a form of programming that makes people that may well be residents, or indeed European by birth, appear to be foreign and exotic in a way that encourages exclusion.

Also, the lack of fair representation and positive portrayal by European public broadcasters with the development of satellite services mainly originating from the Southern hemisphere, can serve to drive audiences from ethnic minority backgrounds away from the national public broadcasters.

Acts of discrimination and racism create exclusion and produce feelings of alienation amongst minority groups. This is compounded by disproportionate lack of education, training and employment opportunities. Although we cannot transform economic inequality, the media can help to create an atmosphere in which racism and xenophobia can be successfully challenged. By making cultural diversity part of the reality of television and radio, multicultural programming, aims to shift the focus of the audience away from the conflict model of us and them. This shifting of the reality reflected by television and radio towards a multicultural perspective would have a profound effect on the perceptions and attitudes of the viewing and listening public.

Multicultural Programming

Against the backdrop of a rapidly changing media environment in which black and ethnic minority people are invisible and given the situation in which xenophobia and racism are growing creating further marginalisation and alienation amongst these groups, public broadcasters have a special obligation to adopt a multicultural programming policy.

By making cultural diversity part of the reality of television and radio, multicultural programming, aims to shift the focus of the audience away from the conflict model of us and them. This shifting of the reality reflected by television and radio towards a multicultural perspective would have a profound effect on the perceptions and attitudes of the viewing and listening public.

The main elements of such a multicultural programming policy should be:

* to assure a balanced and diverse programming, permeating all programme areas and ensuring fair portrayal, ensuring black and ethnic communities to be part of broadcast reality; * incorporate an equal opportunities policy that ensures a diverse workforce to produce programmes that include a range of perspectives and cultures produce and commission programmes that challenge racism and xenophobia directly;

* where necessary to include specific niche programming to serve minority communities;

* to promote an awareness of these issues amongst sections of the general public and amongst governmental and non-governmental bodies and organisations in Europe in the field of human rights, broadcasting regulation, independent production, education and training, etc.

Recommendations

The following recommendations are in line with the EBU Television Programme Committee's declaration of intent adopted on 26th October 1994. They are also a response to the plan of action contained in the October 1993 Vienna declaration

NUJ delegation visiting occupied territories under the auspices of the Palestinian Trade Union Federation and the Arab Journalists Association, together with Scarlet McGwire, Vice President and Gen Secretary Harry Conroy.

Accused no.: 89	MORRISON, Lionel E.	
	Born in:	1935.
In 1956:	Made a living as:	Clerk and journalist.
	Political activities:	National Executive, S.A.C.P.O.
After 1956:	Trial outcome:	Charges withdrawn, 1957.
	After the Trial	Joined P.A.C. in exile.

Accused Number 89 – Treason Trial Case in South Africa (1956).

In Johannesburg as a reporter on the Golden City Post (1955)

President Kwame Nkrumah of Ghana during a AAJA visit to various African journalists unions and journalists (1963).

Addressing the Printers Trade Union the National Graphical Association (1987). Copyright: John Smith

Wearing a black armband in memory of the victims of judicial execution whilst moving the motion on the death penalty at the NUJ's ADM (1988). Copyright: Martin Jenkinson

2 JOURNALIST April 198

ADM... PRESIDENT'S ADDRESS... PRESIDENT'S ADDRESS... PRESIDENT'S ADDRESS

THE WAY FORWARD

THE UNION is about to embark on a new year — its 82nd — one in which it will cope with the effects of challenge and confrontation of closures and cutbacks, of gross government interference and attacks, all of which has been the bannerol of a hectic 81st term.

It has been a most complicated, vocal and challenging year for the Union.

In looking back, I have also tried to look forward, and at the end of this week, with a fresh set of targets firmly and determinedly mapped out, the NUJ ought to be allowed some room for optimism, if only on the basis that after a year as frustrating and as challenging as 1987, the next 12 months can only get better.

Whether it will, depends entirely on ourselves.

Clearly this is a time for frank and serious discussion, particulary for honest and searching examination of our relations with other media unions and our own members, our methods of work and obviously some of our policies.

But it is not a time for defeatism or division in our ranks or for deserting our basic principles as trade unionists.

Promote

Calls to examine various facets

But what is even more disturbing is the lack of outcry by the trade union movement generally against this concerted attack. This Bill must be taken seriously by all in the Trade Union and labour movement — its aim is nothing less than the destruction of union effectiveness and hence eventually of the need for unions.

The NUJ must play an important role in this fight. We have attempted to but must alert our members even more of the evils of this Bill. We must step up our campaign. We must not give the green light to employers and allow this government to decimate our union.

But that is only one example of what Tory rule over the past nine years has meant.

A few years ago we could still speak of the increasing encroachment by government on press and broadcasting freedom. Today the pace and the extent of that encroachment has reached alarming proportions.

Both the police and the courts have demonstrated their willingness to be the handmaiden of this government.

Alarming

Our member Jeremy Warner, a business news writer on the *Independent*, was fined £20,000 for refusing to name his sources for two stories on company takeovers.

● NUJ president Lionel Morrison addressing ADM.

But the function of the NUJ is not only to be protective. We seek to be positive; to play our full part in adaptation to change and to eradicate any Luddites, to press for equal opportunities, to combat racism; to secure a better and healthier working environment, and in every way to strengthen our members in their workplaces.

The industry itself has changed. Newspaper managements have expanded their interests. The days when a successful newspaper used to be the sole property of a media organisation are long gone. Maxwell and Murdoch preside over a conglomerate of media interests — newspapers, cable, satellite, books.

Interests

Along with these new media interests, managements are moving towards treating the communications industry as one. In the broadcasting sector, casualisation is increasing and more freelance-based as traditional areas break down.

In this atmosphere of electronic advancement and a multi-facet media industry, the NUJ with only 32,000 members will soon find it difficult to continue to exist effectively as a union.

As the recent TV AM experience shows, the contradictory nature of inter-union relations has become clearer. The tough line of TV AM's management reveals the

media, particularly in the tabl press, has sunk to an all-time lo

Fabrication, gross distorti and sensationalisation of news h increased, to a point where ev the Press Council has ackno ledged that voluntary "restrai has broken down.

Media attacks on black peop lesbians and gay men have creased. And what is worse is t when government plans for bro casting are allowed to go ahe then we will see how TV co panies will be forced to comp with the tabloids for a niche in gutter.

Our members have been for to write lies and an atmosph has been created where journa tic ethics are low on the agen

Standards have dropped badly and inaccuracy is so wi spread, that we desperately nee law like Anne Clwyd's ill-fa Right of Reply Bill to enfo consumer rights on editors w deliberately misinform th readers.

What it comes down to is try to reconcile the endless and av cious pursuit of profit with pursuit of truth.

Object

But, despite this terrible a lanche of bad reporting, I cont that it is not the NUJ's main to clean up British journalism. can try, but the primary objec the Union is to get better pay

Presidential address – NUJ ADM (1988)

Receiving an award at a Hansib Community Award Ceremony from Arif Ali (1984)

During a presidential visit to Scottish NUj branches (1987).

With Alex Pascall, former Black Londoners presenter, at the BMC's AGM.

Holding the OBE medal, with my son Sipho and my wife Liz at Buckingham Palace.

1976. Aubrey Baines, founder and Editor of the black British National Newspaper, 'The West-Indian World' Newspaper.

Claudia Jones, Editor of the West Indian Gazette.

Beverley Anderson made her first television appearance as presenter of 'Black on Black', a London Weekend Television production for Channel 4.

C. B. Patel, Editor, New Life and Gujarat Samachar, Vick Nair, Journalist, Ramniklal Solanki, Editor, Garavi Gujarat, Arif Ali of Asian Times.

Yvonne Guy and Glenton Wright, presenters of Black Roots, an Afro-Caribbean magazine programme on Radio Derby.

Aaron Haynes, founder and former Editor of New Independent.

Shyama Perera, of ITV's Six-O'Clock show and LWT's Eastern Eye fame.

Juliette Alexander and Vince Herbert - Black Londoners pressenters.

L-R: Leon Mitchell (Weekly Gleaner), Val McCALLA (Voice), Neil Kenlock (Root Magazine) and Arif Ali (CaribbeanTimes).

Greg Edwards, disc jockey - presents Capital Radio programme.

made by the Heads of State and Government of the Council of Europe. They have been worked out in close co-operation between experts of the EBU, the Council of Europe and PBME (Public Broadcasting for a Multicultural Europe).

These recommendations are issued with the following objectives:

* to inform and sustain the continuing debate in public broadcasting (nationally and in the European Broadcasting Union) about standards in broadcasting in relationship to the public perceptions and expectations in European democratic societies;
* to propose guidance for programme and policy makers in broadcasting;
* to stimulate measures for both the creation and development of multicultural broadcasting and equal employment initiatives for ethnic minorities.

Recommendations for all Areas of Broadcasting

Broadcasters should:

* Ensure that programmes include nothing which offends the equal rights and dignity of all human beings and which is likely to incite racism, xenophobia and destructive nationalism. Similar considerations apply to the treatment of minority religious faiths or language groups.
* Avoid using terminology to describe minorities that gives offence to minority communities. Descriptions such as "immigrant" can create negative associations of "otherness". This term is particularly inappropriate when describing members of minority communities born in the broadcaster's country.
* Recognise that terminology that seeks to belittle, denigrate or abuse individuals on grounds of their ethnicity, race or religion. This has no place on television or radio. Those contributors using such terms in live broadcasts should have made clear to them that the company does not support their views or language. There should be public statements to that effect where necessary.
* Develop creative ways of challenging racism and xenophobia.
* Avoid reinforcing stereotypes of minorities by unnecessarily emphasising race or ethnicity. Ethnic origin or colour should only be mentioned when it is relevant to the story.
* Avoid unfounded or thoughtless associations between minorities and social problems.
* Address the under representation on the air of people from minority communities in the full range of output.
* Beware of depicting a fictional reality which may reproduce and perpetuate prejudice.
* Seek out experts, commentators, game show contestants from the widest variety of backgrounds, It is important to show minorities in a variety of roles in society rather than confirm fixed views of their roles.
* Challenge unsubstantiated racist and xenophobic statements when interviewing representatives of racist organisations or reporting their meetings, statements or claims.

They should also carefully check all reports for accuracy and seek rebutting or opposing comments. The anti-social nature of such views should be exposed.

* Take care with statistical information and its presentation to ensure that it does not create unnecessary alarm by exaggerating or sensationalising issues.
* Avoid making resident and naturalised groups into exotic exhibits for the television

audience. All residents and nationalised citizens need to be treated a such and not identified as outsiders on the basis of linguistic, ethnic, religious or cultural difference.

Particular vigilance needs to be given to programmes about countries of the South and films about particular groups, their cultures and religions.

* Portray an accurate picture of the diversity within minority communities;
* Equip audiences to interpret racist and xenophobic constructions;
* Avoid making assumptions about a person's cultural background based on their name or religious details.

Recommendations for Specific Programme Genres
News and Factual Programmes

Broadcasters in this area have a duty as part of their public service remit to give audiences access to accurate information about the causes of social, economic and political crisis. In this regard news gathering, editing and presentation should seek to:

* avoid sensationalising race relation issues;
* investigate the treatment of black, migrant, refugee, gypsy and other ethnic or linguistic minority groups, as well as enable programme makers to cover their lives and concerns by reflecting the views of their representatives;
* explore the diverse views, opinions, tastes and interests within these communities;
* include "experts" and commentators from a wide variety of backgrounds when compiling news or documentary pieces;
* be wary of intentional and unintentional misinformation which exposes audiences to negative myths and distortions of reality and which foster racist or xenophobic views;
* avoid promotion of points of view that exploit people's anxieties or fears, or that play on the susceptibilities of viewers.
* avoid portrayal of racists and xenophobes which glamorise such groups.

Sports and Events

Sports reporting especially of competitions between nations, can indulge in national stereotyping of visiting teams. Reporters need to make an effort to be non-xenophobic in describing the actions of visiting teams and supporters both on and off the field.

* Efforts need to be made to correctly pronounce the unfamiliar names of players from other nations.
* Increasingly ethnic minorities are present in significant members in European sport, especially in athletics and football. They need to be given recognition for their skills and not merely remarked on for their difference.
* Commentators and reporters need to beware and avoid ethnic stereotypes when describing events involving black and ethnic minority players.
* When asking for analysis or comments on events broadcasters should include sports men and women from a variety of backgrounds.
* Where there are racist and xenophobic reactions towards ethnic minority participants in events, commentators should acknowledge this and comment on its antisocial impact.

Drama & Light Entertainment

Light entertainment attracts the biggest audiences in television and can potentially influence popular perceptions. Broadcasters and programme makers in this area should:

* Strive to increase the participation, casting and representation of ethnically/culturally diverse participants/entertainers in hosted chat shows, comedy, entertainment and game shows.
* Make attempts to show a diverse society in soap opera's rather than a monocultural one. Care needs to be taken in avoiding stereotyped black and migrant characterisations in such programmes.
* Avoid humour that depends on stereotypes, or which derives from racial bias and xenophobia.
* Make efforts to adopt new ideas and programme treatments by programme makers from different backgrounds. This will help to generate comedy that does not depend on making fun of minorities.
* Ensure that casting of drama enables minorities to play a part in classical or modern pieces and not only participate when there is a foreigner written into the part.

Educational Broadcasting

Educational broadcasters have the opportunity to provide additional non-broadcast materials that help to educate and inform children and adults to acquire attitudes/behaviour conductive to the development of a multicultural Europe.

Educational broadcasters need to ensure that all their output is set in a multicultural context. In particular they should seek to initiate programmes aimed at eliminating bias and prejudice in the following curriculum areas by:

* the teaching of history which emphasises the positive and mutual influence between countries, religions and ideas in the historical environment of Europe;
* in the area of geography, programmes similarly need to be fair and unbiased in their construction, Programmes that emphasise passivity, dependence, poverty and famine without examining the nature of the economic and social history of North-South relationships, can serve to confirm negative views of the South;
* in other areas of human knowledge for example, science and mathematics, the contributions to these disciplines of the world community should be sought out and included. At the moment much of these contributions are hidden and unacknowledged.

Education broadcasts in general should avoid condemning and moralising in a simplistic way when challenging racism and xenophobia. This can serve to entrench views rather than change them.

* Acts of racism and xenophobia should not merely be exposed but the underlying forces explained and positive actions suggested.
* All educational broadcasting output should encourage positive inter community relations, cross cultural understanding and equality of opportunity.

Religious Broadcasting

Programme makers should avoid any abusive treatment of the religious views and beliefs of those belonging to a particular religion or religious denomination. In addition programme makers:

* should explore the variety of faiths, beliefs and practices within society.

Science Programmes

The practice of Science is a global human activity and programming ought to reflect the scientific contribution of human communities around the world where appropriate:

* the contribution, originality and credibility of scientific and technological innovation by third world countries should be acknowledged and promoted;

* wherever possible programme makers should include experts and scientists from a variety of backgrounds.

Music and Arts

Music and Arts is one of the most vibrant areas of development in our multicultural societies.

* Programming should reflect the wide variety of tastes and cultural expressions present in the society.

* Assumptions should not be made about the musical tastes/artistic expressions of ethnic minority groups.

* Wherever appropriate the music and arts of resident minorities must be presented as part of the society not outside it.

* Cross – cultural change, particularly in popular culture, ought to be reflected in programming.

* Programme makers should make efforts to find artists, performers, critics and experts from a variety of cultural back grounds when renewing/analysing or commenting on performance.

* Avoid creating a hierarchy of cultural expressions.

Children and Young People

It is particularly important in Children and Young Peoples Programming to increase understanding of and respect for diversity in European societies. This generation are the key to a more tolerant future.

Children and Young People, in particular, form a captive audience for television. There are as many outlets for disseminating positive images of multicultural diversity in programmes for Children and Young People as in the mainstream schedules. These programmes are a microcosm for the wider schedules, reflecting drama, factual, light entertainment, comedy and news.

Apart from what has been mentioned above programme makers should:

* aim to enable young viewers to unpick unreliable and distorted information that underpins racism and xenophobia;

* provide opportunities for young people to understand and empathise with people who face racist and xenophobic treatment.

Conclusions

These measures will not by themselves eradicate racism and xenophobia. However, they can provide part of the climate in which political and social actions can begin to build a more tolerant, harmonious and culturally diverse Europe of the future. The recruitment of a culturally diverse workforce can also assist broadcasters in implementing the above recommendations, as well as, contribute to the creation of a dynamic and innovative public broadcasting service relevant to the needs of the 21st century.

3 Relevant Sites

National Union of Journalist (UK) of Britain and Ireland
Headland House, 308-312 Gray's Inn Road,
London WCIX 8DP
www.nuj.org.uk

George Viner Memorial Fund Trust
Headland House, 308-312 Gray's Inn Road,
London WC1X 8DP
www.georgeviner.org.uk

Press Complaints Commission
Halton House, 20/23 Holborn,
London EC1N 2JD
www.pcc.org.uk

International Federation of Journalists
IPC-Residence Palace, Bloc C,
Rue de la Loi 155
B-1040 Brussels, Belgium
www.ifj.org

Institute of Race Relations
2-6 Leeke Street, London WC1X 9HS
www.irr.org.uk

Commission for Racial Equality
St Dunstan's House, 201-211 Borough High Street,
London SE1 1GZ
www.cre.gov.uk

The 1990 Trust
Suite 12 Winchester House,
9 Cranmer Road, London SW9 6EJ
www.blink.org.uk

PART V

Commentary

In Defence of Minority Rights

"The mounting campaign against multiculturalism by politicians, pundits and the press, in Britain and across Europe, is neither innocent nor innocuous. It is a prelude to a policy that deems there is one dominant culture, one unique set of values, one nativist loyalty- a policy of assimilation. And yet it is passed off as a virtuous attempt at integration, thereby deliberately and dishonestly conflating the two terms. To use 'integration' and 'assimilation' as synonyms is not just to misuse language and confuse concepts, but to dissimulate practice. Integration provides for coexistence of minority cultures with the majority culture; assimilation requires the absorption of minority cultures into the majority culture. The aim of assimilation is a monocultural, even a monofaith society; the aim of integration is a multicultural, pluralist society."

- A.Sivanandan ,director of the Institute of Race Relations speaking on multiculturalism *at an IRR conference on Racism. Liberty and the War on Terror, London, Sept, 2006.*

In Defence of Minority Rights

I have always believed that the litmus test of liberty and the rule of law is the defence of minority rights. And if the social contract which we have all entered into as members of the larger state means anything at all, it must surely mean the inviolability of the individual and his or her rights to express their views, their interests and their belief. These in turn assume the reality of a humane life of full citizenship for all, the right of movement, and abode, the accessibility to decent housing, employment and other accepted life chances, the protection of the law, the right to be treated fairly and equally before the courts and be treated fairly by the media.

Ethnic minorities in Europe, whether they are citizens in Britain or in other European countries must, like everybody else, have a guaranteed right to have a life of full citizenship. These are the inviolable rights which bind us together in our struggle against these inequalities whether they are in Europe or in their former home countries.

Unfortunately, however, the majority do not in practice enjoy these rights, in fact many of them do not enjoy such a humane life of full citizenship and all that it entails. Whether in Britain or in other European countries the law and legal processes are stacked against them. It is so many times more difficult for ethnic minority youngsters to get a job than it is for their white peers. When they are lucky enough to get a job, various discriminatory hurdles are placed in their path to promotion and advancement.

They are subjected to racial harassment and assaults in schools, housing estates and by the judiciary system, the police and courts. Racism and poverty persist as the major obstacles isolating thousands of ethnic minorities road-blocked on the way to enjoying the same rights and advantages as their white peers. And in the final analysis most stories and reports in the media are the projections of white society about their own worries, fears and pathological practices.

Reflecting upon the bus boycott in Montgomerry, Alabama, that launched the direct action phase of the contemporary Civil Rights Movement in America, the late Martin Luther King Jnr, said that racial discrimination *"scars the soul and degrades the personality";* it creates within some white people a false sense of superiority and among black people a false sense of inferiority. There is no doubt that these false beliefs encourage the dominance of one group over another.

Ethnic minorities in Europe are generally corralled into being sub dominant in the community power structure where the white community per se controls the nation's resources. The result is that the customs and conventions of whites are considered normative for the total society. Ethnic minorities – as black European citizens, Muslims or asylum seekers – are assigned the role of the scapegoat in contemporary Europe, the manifestation of that which is evil and threatening in the society at large and in our contemporary communities the black community bears the blame of theirs as scapegoats, through the irrational hostility and guilt of many whites.

We know of course, that the practice of scapegoating can be devastatingly effective but is also unethical. Most major newspapers and some television broadcasting stations in Britain and in other European countries are guilty of such scapegoating when reporting issues which affect or are about the ethnic minorities. Their reports in the final analysis are the projections of whites about their own worries, fears and pathological practices.

Some of the 'white' press is able to sustain a discreet and sugar-coated racism through a constant appeal to European norms and habits, and more traditionally minded newspapers still enjoy almost daily appeal to 'white' virtues and assimilation which requires the absorption of minority cultures into the majority culture.

Racial inequality in economic life is still with us and is also very extensive. More disturbing is the fact that the evidence suggests that society has not been making any measurable progress in the last few years to ameliorate the high rates of poverty, low incomes, low levels of wealth, limited business ownership, and disadvantaged labour market positions that continue to characterise the economic status of the ethnic minority population in Europe.

It is also true that in various fields, a measurable percentage of black Britons have moved up the ladder in the last decades. Their success can be measured from two points of view the comparative and the proportional. When one compares the present status of people of colour with what went before, an optimistic picture emerges (more black faces on TV, newsmen and women, lawyers, doctors, businessmen and women, MPs, Peers, and local councillors), but when one compares achievement in statistical terms as a proportion of the population, the picture is rather dismal.

Now in the early years of the 21st Century, black people in this country, find their civil, political, social and economic rights intruded upon in unprecedented ways.

The selections of 50 years of my writing and reports about Media, Racism and Diversity, show that racism, poverty and now Islamophobia persists as major obstacles. Inequities in education and job opportunities contribute to a pervasive sense of despair and helplessness among the black community and the media pre-formulates prejudice and racism.

They have to deal with the effects of racist and discriminatory practices and the mounting attacks on multiculturalism to strip it of its anti-racist roots. This sometimes finds expression and redress in various extremes. It demonstrates both the magnitude, the complexity and the entrenchment of some of the problems facing Britain's and Europe's black communities.

To state problems is not to succumb to them, however. There are, hopefully, in the collection of articles, comments and reports a constant theme and belief of hope, of motivation, of counting on the collective British conscience to commit to the eradication of obstacles to equality.

We must continue to sound the call that Britain ignores at its peril: of translating good intentions into realities; of four-squarely meeting reasonable demands which accelerate change and challenge the ugly face of racism and of restoring more than a modicum of faith in the law, the courts and the system.

This collection is, hopefully, a kaleidoscopic vision of a Britain where people are not scapegoated, insulted, degraded in the media because their skin happens to be black or because they are an asylum seeker or is a Muslim; a Britain which glories in diversity and respects the unique contributions and traditions of all of its people, both black and white; a Britain where basic human and civil rights of every citizen are protected and defended.

This is a responsibility and challenge which involves all of us. As journalists we must share this responsibility for the uncertainty and which are sometimes hard to discern or lost in the din.

In the words of that great American civil rights leader Whitney Young, *"The Open Society will come about when all decent people, both blacks and whites, are galvanised to change the present society".*